On Mediation

INTEGRATION AND CONFLICT STUDIES

Published in association with the Max Planck Institute for Social Anthropology, Halle/Saale

The objective of the Max Planck Institute for Social Anthropology is to advance anthropological fieldwork and enhance theory building. 'Integration' and 'conflict', the central themes of this series, are major concerns of the contemporary social sciences and of significant interest to the general public. They have also been among the main research areas of the institute since its foundation. Bringing together international experts, *Integration and Conflict Studies* includes both monographs and edited volumes, and offers a forum for studies that contribute to a better understanding of processes of identification and inter-group relations.

Recent volumes:

Volume 22
On Mediation: Historical, Legal, Anthropological and International Perspectives
Edited by Karl Härter, Carolin Hillemanns and Günther Schlee

Volume 21
Space, Place and Identity: Wodaaɓe of Niger in the 21st Century
Florian Köhler

Volume 20
Mobile Urbanity: Somali Presence in Urban East Africa
Edited by Neil Carrier and Tabea Scharrer

Volume 19
Playing the Marginality Game: Identity Politics in West Africa
Anita Schroven

Volume 18
The Wheel of Autonomy: Rhetoric and Ethnicity in the Omo Valley
Felix Girke

Volume 17
Bishkek Boys: Neighbourhood Youth and Urban Change in Kyrgyzstan's Capital
Philipp Schröder

Volume 16
Difference and Sameness as Modes of Integration: Anthropological Perspectives on Ethnicity and Religion
Edited by Günther Schlee and Alexander Horstmann

Volume 15
On Retaliation: Towards an Interdisciplinary Understanding of a Basic Human Condition
Edited by Bertram Turner and Günther Schlee

Volume 14
'City of the Future': Built Space, Modernity and Urban Change in Astana
Mateusz Laszczkowski

Volume 13
Staying at Home: Identities, Memories and Social Networks of Kazakhstani Germans
Rita Sanders

For a full volume listing, please see the series page on our website: http://www.berghahnbooks.com/series/integration-and-conflict-studies

On Mediation

Historical, Legal, Anthropological and International Perspectives

Edited by Karl Härter, Carolin Hillemanns
and Günther Schlee

berghahn
NEW YORK • OXFORD
www.berghahnbooks.com

First published in 2020 by
Berghahn Books
www.berghahnbooks.com

Library of Congress Cataloging-in-Publication Data

Names: Härter, Karl, 1956- editor. | Hillemanns, Carolin, editor. | Schlee, Günther, editor.
Title: On mediation : historical, legal, anthropological, and international perspectives / edited by Karl Härter, Carolin Hillemanns, and Günther Schlee.
Description: New York : Berghahn Books, 2020. | Series: Integration and confl ict studies; volume 22 | Includes bibliographical references and index.
Identifi ers: LCCN 2020015778 (print) | LCCN 2020015779 (ebook) | ISBN 9781789208696 (hardback) | ISBN 9781789208702 (ebook)
Subjects: LCSH: Mediation, International. | Mediation, International—History.
Classifi cation: LCC KZ6045 .O56 2020 (print) | LCC KZ6045 (ebook) | DDC 341.5/2—dc23
LC record available at https://lccn.loc.gov/2020015778
LC ebook record available at https://lccn.loc.gov /2020015779

British Library Cataloguing in Publication Data

A catalogue record for this book is available from the British Library

EU GPSR Authorized Representative

LOGOS EUROPE, 9 rue Nicolas Poussin, 17000, LA ROCHELLE, France
Email: Contact@logoseurope.eu

ISBN 978-1-78920-869-6 hardback
ISBN 978-1-80758-507-5 epub
ISBN 978-1-78920-870-2 web pdf

https://doi.org/10.3167/9781789208696

This open access edition has been made available with funding from the Max Planck Institute for Social Anthropology.

Contents

Illustrations

Figure

Tables

Introduction

On Mediation

Historical, Legal, Anthropological and International Perspectives on Alternative Modes of Conflict Regulation

Karl Härter, Carolin Hillemanns and Günther Schlee

Following the basic design of the International Max Planck Research School on Retaliation, Mediation and Punishment (REMEP),[1] the approach of this volume is to explore concepts and modes of mediation and related practices of conflict regulation such as arbitration in current, historical and international settings, with particular emphasis on the interdependence of judicial procedures, punishment and retaliation.[2] Current developments and research in the disciplines of the humanities, and especially law, testify to a growing interest in mediation.[3] Mediation is commonly defined as a non-violent, cost-saving mode of negotiating, regulating or settling conflicts and disputes between two or more actors using the help of a third party as mediator who, in contrast to an adjudicator, has no authority to pass final judgement.[4] Studies on mediation have been numerous and focused on practices and techniques of mediation, their efficiency, the training and qualification of mediators, questions of costs, challenges and shortcomings.[5] However, conventional normative and social theories often conceptualize mediation as a mode of extrajudicial alternative dispute resolution.[6] As a result, they undervalue its complex relationship with retaliation and punishment, which are interrelated and complementary concepts and logics that also seek to establish, negotiate, maintain and regain social order, peace and (human) security at different levels and in various settings.[7] This volume strives to fill this gap and to shed light on these complex relationships through an interdisciplinary approach that includes historical, legal, anthropological and international perspectives.

Mediation and related practices of third party conflict regulation are used in a variety of conflict-related scenarios, including social and economic disputes, in the context of diverging normative orders, violence and crime or in international conflicts.[8] Thus, they are often embedded in plural normative orders and judicial hybridity, approached in this volume on different levels from historical, legal, anthropological and international angles.[9] Especially in these constellations, mediation and related practices of conflict regulation can influence or even challenge retaliation, punishment or formal legal procedures, and vice versa.[10] From the early modern period up to the present, authorities or legal systems have therefore attempted to regulate mediation and arbitration procedures by law or other control instruments. Since (private) parties do not only resort to mediation, but can also use negotiation, arbitration or the legal system to regulate conflicts, they are able to manoeuvre within or among these repertoires, especially in plural normative settings or conditions of legal hybridity or cultural diversity.[11]

The settings in which mediation and other forms of conflict regulation take place range from central political/judicial authorities, states, global governance institutions and transnational organizations to non-governmental, regional actors, ethnic or religious communities, kinship groups and local, diaspora, expatriate or migrant groups.[12] Within this broad field, a specific aim is to analyse the role and function of mediation with regard to the interdependences, overlaps, tensions and collisions between local societies characterized by the absence of a central political authority or areas of limited governance on the one hand – in particular studied from an anthropological perspective in the case studies of the second section of this volume – and, on the other hand, states and other central authorities which are manifested at local, regional and national as well as trans- and international levels, as presented in the third section. In combining historical, legal, anthropological and international perspectives, the volume shows that mediation and arbitration on local, national and transnational levels are undergoing a reconfiguration and challenging traditional concepts of conflict regulation as well as the respective normative orders and legal systems. Such current developments are also routed in specific historical settings, studied in the chapters by Karl Härter, Pia Letto-Vanamo and Jakob Zollmann. The modern state did not only abolish modes of 'private' mediation and arbitration, but also regulated or partly integrated them into the various legal systems. In this respect, the legal systems of modern states still produce hybridity, collisions or complementarities, as the anthropological case studies in Section II and the chapter by Hubert Rottleuthner on the privatization of the criminal justice system also demonstrate. This concerns large-scale conflicts and international security, studied in the section on mediation and arbitration in international arenas, as well as exchanges of violence or conflicts related to cultural diversity.

As a consequence, the chapters in this volume explore mediation in the context of institutional and normative hybridity as well as plural normative configurations, often conceptualized or manifest as state-based or non-state normative orders and modes of conflict regulation.[13] Local or customary law, religious law, private or criminal law or supranational norms are reference points, as are diplomacy and political considerations. Although traditionally considered as 'alternative' private dispute resolution, mediation, analysed in the context of normative hybridity, verifies (as a general result of this volume) the interplay, conjunctions, overlaps, collisions or blurred boundaries between extrajudicial and judicial conflict resolution and the ways in which conflicts and disputes are addressed within, beyond, across or even independently from state legal orders and institutions.[14]

This allows the contributors to this volume to explore the variety of actors that have resorted to mediation and arbitration or acted as mediators and arbitrators in different historical, legal, social, political or transnational settings, and to examine and compare the different roles and functions of various 'third parties'. All chapters provide an analysis of how these actors manoeuvre in the complex web of informal and formal procedures, practices of mediation and other modes of conflict regulation. They illuminate forms of communication, languages employed, logics and techniques of mediation and conflict regulation as well as analyse questions of access, the social construction (or labelling) of conflict parties, and the strategies for inclusion and exclusion in situations of conflict.

A relevant example constitutes the interrelation between private, non-governmental mediators/arbitrators and formal legal systems/institutions, studied in particular in the chapters of the first and second sections by analysing historical and current developments as well as through anthropological case studies. These examples also demonstrate the ambiguous function of mediation within formal/legal procedure, manifested, for instance, in victim–offender mediation, out-of-court settlements, various attempts to legally regulate mediation, and transitional or restorative justice and related reconciliation processes. Hence, the chapters in this volume examine the complex interplay between mediation and other modes or institutions of conflict regulation, notably with regard to their function and capability to regulate, solve or reconcile disputes (particularly in settings of cultural diversity) and to provide actors with different options to manage conflicts.

This is related to the problem – also addressed in several chapters of this volume – of whether and how mediation and other practices establish or construct 'the truth' and an adequate sense of justice, and whether and how they produce acceptable, viable and sustainable results concerning the regulation of conflicts, the resolution of disputes and reconciliation after violence, or whether they induce other modes and logics of conflict regulation. This leads back to a comparison of the capacity of mediation to establish social order, peace and security with the interrelated and complementary concepts of retaliation and punishment. Hence, in this collected volume, external experts from different disciplines as well as members of the International Max Planck Research School on Retaliation, Mediation and Punishment present basic theoretical and empirical approaches, recent research and case studies in current as well as in historical, in local as well as in international settings, with a focus on the interdependences and interrelations to other judicial and extrajudicial practices of conflict regulation. Reflecting on the variety of disciplines and approaches, the chapters are organized in three sections.

Mediation, Arbitration and the Criminal Justice System: Historical and Current Developments

Current studies usually conceptualize mediation as the prime mode of alternative dispute resolution, clearly separated from other practices (such as arbitration) and the judiciary of the state. However, as the chapters in the first section demonstrate, historical perspectives on the development of the criminal justice system in Europe reveal a different picture. Not only were mediation, arbitration and other modes of conflict regulation closely intertwined with formal procedures, but current criminal justice systems are still characterized by the participation of private actors and practices of mediation and arbitration.

In the first chapter on 'Infrajudicial Modes of Conflict Regulation through Negotiation, Mediation and Arbitration in Early Modern European Criminal Justice', Karl Härter gives a historical overview of the various modes of conflict regulation related to deviant behaviour and crime, such as arbitration, mediation, negotiation, supplicating, intercession, petitioning, pardon and criminal asylum, which were closely intertwined with the criminal justice system in early modern (continental) Europe. These internal and external practices are conceptualized as 'infrajudicial' modes of conflict regulation, since the pre-modern state had not yet established a monopoly on the use of force and justice. They were used by different actors and 'infrajudicial agents' to negotiate and mediate compensation, agreements, reconciliation, support, grace and pardon. In this regard, 'infrajudicial' conflict regulation provided alternatives to formal criminal procedure and adjudication, substituted to some extent lacking legal remedies, made possible the flexibilization of public punishment and served to prevent retaliatory violence as well as to mediate compensation. However, this was not independent from the criminal justice system that gradually incorporated and controlled negotiation, mediation and arbitration, which, as a result, obtained 'public' purposes and helped to maintain social control and social order. It could therefore be concluded that, on the one hand, these early modern practices of infrajudicial conflict regulation offered similar functions to 'mediation' and related practices in modern societies. On the other hand, the historical analysis shows comparable limits and ambivalences, also mapped out in other chapters of this volume: negotiation, mediation and arbitration could fail to produce a permanent resolution of conflicts or to establish the 'truth' of a crime, and, to some extent, they were characterized by arbitrariness, legal uncertainty and social inequalities.

The chapter on adjudication and forms of mediation in the history of conflict resolution in the Nordic countries consolidates and exemplifies the general historical developments observed in the first chapter. In her case study on 'Mediation as Non-modern Element in Conflict Resolution in the Nordic Countries', Pia Letto-Vanamo demonstrates that modern alternative conflict resolution is rooted in long-lasting historical settings that reach back to the late Middle Ages. The pre-modern legal system of Sweden and Finland was characterized by a hybrid mixture of local communities and the state, of 'old' consensual, negotiated law and 'new' authoritative law. Hence, the actual practices and procedures in the local assemblies as the main arenas of conflict regulation in various matters (land, violence, manslaughter) were characterized by formal modes, but also by the participation of 'private' parties and representatives of the *ting* community. They were elected by the community and/or proposed by the parties and performed different functions as jurors, assayers, oath-helpers, truth-seekers, arbitrators or mediators, who negotiated solutions that could range from economic redress and private compensation to harsh punishment. The participation of such 'third party' actors and private parties in a formal procedure that was based on traditional and authoritative law created a communitarian and consensual nature of conflict resolution and substantiated legitimacy and acceptance. In the long term, these historical experiences shaped the relation between the judiciary and a 'mediation system' in the Nordic countries that is still considered as complementary, rather than as antagonistic competition. Hence, it should be stressed as a general result of this chapter that mediation and other modes of 'infrajudicial' conflict regulation, which are based on the participation of parties and non-state actors, not only complement formal procedures but could be integrated into the judiciary.

As Hubert Rottleuthner in his study on 'Mediation, Extrajudicial Conflict Regulation and the Privatization of the Criminal Justice System' demonstrates, recent developments in Germany seem to partially confirm the conclusions of the former chapter. However, the German mediation law does not extend to criminal justice, although 'private agents' are participating in various roles in proceedings, of which some could be characterized as rudimentary forms of 'mediation', in particular 'victim–offender mediation' and the regulation through arbitrators. Beyond that, the chapter presents various practices of 'private' actors dealing with criminal issues and related conflicts, often in order to avoid criminal justice: churches, companies, sports arbitration courts, 'honour courts' of the military, craftsmen and other professions as well as recently the so-called Muslim 'parallel justice' are negotiating, mediating and arbitrating religious, cultural, social and honour conflicts and deviant behaviour. In particular, cultural diversity and honour conflict not only seem to intensify extrajudicial 'private' dispute resolution but they also influence the criminal justice system, for instance through the acceptance of religious norms and cultural defence. Rottleuthner concludes that the various modes of extra- and infrajudicial conflict regulation, on the one hand, provide advantages of private, mutually agreed settlements of criminal conflicts and help to maintain social order, but, on the other hand, can be interpreted as a privatization of criminal justice. The latter threatens the state monopoly of power and the rule of law, since mediation and other 'secret' practices of extrajudicial conflict regulation are violating the principles of publicity and legality.

As the chapters in this section have already shown, the historical development and the current situation can be characterized as an ongoing struggle to establish a balanced relation between mediation, arbitration and other modes of extrajudicial conflict regulation and the criminal justice system, through autonomy, complementarity, integration and juridification. Moreover, these current developments are not only deeply rooted in the history of mediation, arbitration and other modes of conflict regulation, but they also show structural similarities to agents, procedures and fundamental issues analysed in the chapters in the following sections.

Mediation: Anthropological Perspectives and Case Studies

The expectation that anthropologists might only deal with the small scale and the local is not confirmed by the four contributions in this section. They all have a global dimension, be it a comparison across continents or the interaction of institutions and forms of human interaction connecting different scales from the local to the national, the transnational and the global.

In the chapter 'What Is Mediation? Definitions and Anthropological Discomforts', Andrea Nicolas analyses concepts and models of mediation, a field increasingly systematized, professionalized and dogmatized. She contests the universal claims with which European and North American models come along and contrasts these with her own ethnographic experience from Ethiopia, which does not fit these models and concepts. She also digs deep into another regional example, the Ifugao of the Philippines. Here she shows how the misfit between Ifugao forms of conflict regulation and scholarly models is explained away by temporalizing the anthropological findings. They are said to represent an earlier and less differentiated form of mediation and therefore do not diminish the validity of the models claimed to be universal.

Stefanie Bognitz in her chapter on 'Mediation in Circumstances of the Existential: Dispute and Justice in Rwanda' shows how tightly mediation is interwoven with the state and state-administered adjudication in Rwanda. She pursues this close interconnection both in the symbolic dimension (like the role of the national colours in the clothing worn by mediators) as well as in the analysis of procedure. As mediation has become an obligatory step before access to state courts is granted, proactively written documentation, rules of evidence inspired by what can be observed in court, and state law in general are taken into account in forms of mediation that derive parts of their legitimacy from the claim to 'tradition'. Her account links a case history described in rich detail with a complex account of such institutional extensions and interconnections.

Günther Schlee, in his discussion of 'Mediation and Truth', explores the logic of mediation in different settings, from plea bargaining in the administration of penal law in Western countries to African politics. Contrary to the idea of 'Truth and Reconciliation', the economy of negotiation (effort in relation to outcome) often seems to favour short-lived successes in making peace at the expense of the recognition of historical facts. Moreover, deals are elite driven and also at the expense of ordinary people, including the victims of earlier elite-driven mass violence. Like the other contributions to this section, this one bridges the gap between micro and macro, involving not only local but also global actors such as the International Criminal Court at The Hague.

In her chapter 'Crossing the Boundaries of Mediation', with a focus on Indonesia and West Sumatra (Minangkabau) in particular, Keebet von Benda-Beckmann describes mediation and statehood in interaction. This interaction may take the form of state personnel with the implicit threat of use of state power silencing claims against state justice in mediation processes, or, taking us further through Indonesian political history, people with experience in administration using improvements in communication to participate as mediators in local settings and to strengthen local institutions. She also describes miscommunication and the failure of imported models ('US mediation'). Needless to say, in its focus on the relationship between state, state personnel and 'tradition', this chapter resonates with the one by Bognitz, and the critique of imported models resonates with Nicolas' critique of universalist claims.

Mediation and Arbitration in International Arenas

This section offers three contributions, which analyse mediation and arbitration practices in different historical periods and on different scales, making it apparent that the boundaries between these interrelated conflict resolution modes are blurred and less clear-cut than one might expect.

In his chapter 'Interstate Mediation and Arbitration: Concepts, Cases, and Actors of Third Party Dispute Resolution (Seventeenth to Nineteenth Century)', Jakob Zollmann sketches the practice of third party dispute resolution between states during the seventeenth and nineteenth centuries with a focus on what was at the time interchangeably called arbitration and mediation. Zollmann observes that even though the modes of both conflict regulation practices were historically connected and blurred, noteworthy differences became increasingly visible. Mediation was rather perceived as diplomatic manoeuvring. In contrast, arbitration – that is, the issuing of a binding arbitral award by a third party to which the disputing states had previously submitted their conflict – he claims, was hailed as the progressive means to achieving sustainable peace between civilized nations; the peace movement had successfully pushed for an increasing juridification of the conflict settlement process. He then identifies conditions under which states tended to resort to arbitration rather than to negotiation, mediation or military force. In so doing, he addresses one of the core questions of international relations, as do Nathan Danneman and Kyle Beardsley. In their chapter, 'International Mediation and the Problem of Insincere Bargaining', the authors look at intrastate conflict resolution processes and observe that parties to such a conflict often use negotiation as a stalling tactic in order to improve, for instance, their armed conflict capabilities and/or to resolve it. They argue that mediators can use leverage – threats or uses of retaliation and punishment – to enhance the possibility that the conflict parties negotiate in good faith. Evidence supportive of this hypothesis is explored empirically using cross-national data on intrastate disputes, including civil wars, from 1944 to 1999. Danneman and Beardsley claim that third parties who are geographically proximate and major powers – characteristics of third parties that are both willing and capable to enforce good faith bargaining – greatly improve the likelihood that a mediation initiative will achieve an agreement. This finding is consistent with Zollmann's observation, according to which primarily those states with a direct political interest in the dispute undertook mediation of interstate disputes during the eighteenth and nineteenth centuries.

Pierre d'Argent provides the third and last chapter of this section with a contribution on 'The International Court of Justice and Mediation'. He focuses on the International Court of Justice (ICJ), the principal judicial organ of the United Nations. D'Argent discerns some mediating effects of the court in international relations even though he contends that neither the contentious jurisdiction of the court nor its advisory jurisdiction has much to do with the institution of mediation as traditionally understood in international relations and law. He makes out an appeasing and conciliatory effect of the judicial procedure he sketches, despite being by nature contentious and adversarial. The author shows that choosing adjudication from the menu of available peaceful means for the settlement of international disputes never entirely excludes mediation from a substantive point of view; the separation between adjudication and mediation is even nowadays less clear-cut and more blurred than those categories suggest when they are idealized as distinct processes, and separately envisaged.

The volume ends with a brief conclusion that addresses the different scales involved in our topic, the different logics of action and the interaction between different modes of conflict regulation. Readers who want more guidance can read our conclusions before proceeding to the single chapters, while those who want to come to their own conclusions are invited to read the chapters first and then to compare their conclusions with ours.

Karl Härter is Professor, Research Group Leader and Senior Research Scientist at the Max Planck Institute for European Legal History in Frankfurt/Main. He is a member of the International Max Planck Research School on Retaliation, Mediation and Punishment, the Association for Constitutional History, the Commission for Hessian History and other academic and historical institutions.

Carolin Hillemanns is scientific coordinator at the Max Planck Institute for the Study of Crime, Security and Law (formerly Max Planck Institute for Foreign and International Criminal Law). She is a trained mediator. She has given presentations and conducted research in the fields of corporate social responsibility, international criminal law and policy, transitional justice, international human and victims' rights law, institutional law of the European Communities, democracy and federalism, globalization, and German constitutional law.

Günther Schlee is one of the Founding Directors of the Max Planck Institute for Social Anthropology in Halle, Germany. His main publications include *Identities on the Move: Clanship and Pastoralism in Northern Kenya* (Manchester University Press, 1989) and *How Enemies Are Made: Towards a Theory of Ethnic and Religious Conflict* (Berghahn Books, 2008).

Notes

1. We thank the Max Planck Society for the generous funding of the REMEP programme over a period of twelve years and the Fritz Thyssen Foundation for generously supporting the project that resulted in this publication.
2. See Schlee and Turner (2008), Turner and Schlee (2017).
3. For an overview of the research on mediation, cf. Kressel and Pruitt (1989), Busch and Mayer (2012), Menkel-Meadow, Love and Kupfer Schneider ([2006] 2013).
4. For a comprehensive definition and an overview of the ongoing debate on how to define mediation, see Menkel-Meadow, Love and Kupfer Schneider ([2006] 2013), Hopt and Steffek (2013).
5. As an example, cf. Boulle (2011), Ade and Alexander (2017), Friedman and Himmelstein (2008), Menkel-Meadow ([2001] 2018).
6. See Goldberg et al. ([1985] 2012).
7. This refers to the basic concept of REMEP as outlined in Kohlhagen and IMPRS REMEP (2015).
8. For a comprehensive overview of the wide variety of disputes in which mediation and other forms of alternative dispute settlement are used, cf. Kressel and Pruitt (1989), Baruch Bush and Folger (2004), Goldberg et al. ([1985] 2012).
9. For a basic outline of these concepts, cf. Benda-Beckmann and Benda-Beckmann (2006), Schiff Berman (2012), Kötter et al. (2015), Duve (2017); on the various modes of dispute resolution and 'hybrid dispute resolution processes', see Goldberg et al. ([1985] 2012: 1–4).
10. On the complex relation of mediation and law/justice, see, for example, Zenk (2008), Goldberg et al. ([1985] 2012: 505–10).
11. On the concept of 'diversity and law' and the importance of mediation, arbitration and alternative modes of conflict regulation, see Foblets, Gaudreault-DesBiens and Renteln (2010), Ertl and Kruijtzer (2017); various examples and cases can be found in Goldberg et al. ([1985] 2012).

12. On the various actors in mediation processes and conflict regulation, cf. Menkel-Meadow, Love and Kupfer Schneider ([2006] 2013), Hopt and Steffek (2013), Kötter et al. (2015).
13. For this approach and the basic concepts, see, for example, Benda-Beckmann and Benda-Beckmann (2006), Benda-Beckmann (2009), Kötter et al. (2015), Duve (2017).
14. The various settings are exemplarily explored by Zekoll, Bälz and Amelung (2014), Wolfrum and Gätzschmann (2013), Goldberg et al. ([1985] 2012), Kötter et al. (2015), Wright and Galaway (1989), Rössner (2006).

References

Ade, J., and N. Alexander. 2017. *Mediation und Recht: Eine praxisnahe Darstellung der Mediation und ihrer rechtlichen Grundlagen*, 3rd edn. Frankfurt am Main: Wolfgang Metzner Verlag.

Baruch Bush, R.A., and J.P. Folger. 2004. *The Promise of Mediation: The Transformative Approach to Conflict*, 2nd ed. San Francisco: Jossey-Bass Publishers.

Benda-Beckmann, F. von. 2009. 'Gefangen im Rechtspluralismus: Zum Umgang mit Normkollisionen in rechtlich pluralen sozialen Räumen', in M. Kötter and G.F. Schuppert (eds), *Normative Pluralität ordnen: Rechtsbegriffe, Normenkollisionen und Rule of Law in Kontexten dies- und jenseits des Staates*. Baden-Baden: Nomos, pp. 169–89.

Benda-Beckmann, F. von, and K. von Benda-Beckmann (eds). 2006. 'Dynamics of Plural Legal Orders', *Journal of Legal Pluralism and Unofficial Law 53/54 (Special issue).*

Boulle, L. 2011. *Mediation: Principles, Processes, Practice*, 3rd edn. Chatswood, NSW: LexisNexis Butterworths.

Busch, D., and C.H. Mayer (eds). 2012. *Mediation erforschen: Fragen – Forschungsmethoden – Ziele*. Wiesbaden: VS Verl. für Sozialwiss.

Duve, T. 2017. 'Was ist "Multinormativität"? Einführende Bemerkungen', *Rechtsgeschichte – Legal History* 25: 88–101.

Ertl, T., and G. Kruijtzer (eds). 2017. *Law Addressing Diversity: Pre-Modern Europe and India in Comparison (12th to 18th Centuries)*. Berlin: De Gruyter Oldenbourg.

Foblets, M.-C., J.-F. Gaudreault-DesBiens and A.D. Renteln (eds). 2010. *Cultural Diversity and the Law: State Responses from around the World*. Brussels: Bruylant.

Friedman, G., and J. Himmelstein. 2008. *Challenging Conflict: Mediation through Understanding*. Chicago: ABA Publishing.

Goldberg, S.B., F.E.A. Sander, N.H. Rogers and S.R. Cole. [1985] 2012. *Dispute Resolution: Negotiation, Mediation, Arbitration, and Other Processes*, 6th edn. New York: Wolters Kluwer Law & Business.

Hopt, K.J., and F. Steffek (eds). 2013. *Mediation: Principles and Regulation in Comparative Perspective*. Oxford: Oxford University Press.

Kohlhagen, D., and IMPRS REMEP (eds). 2015. *REMEP – Retaliation, Mediation and Punishment: Research Agenda and Projects*. Halle (Saale): Max Planck Institute for Social Anthropology.

Kötter, M., T.J. Röder, G.F. Schuppert and R. Wolfrum (eds). 2015. *Non-State Justice Institutions and the Law: Decision-Making at the Interface of Tradition, Religion and the State*. Basingstoke: Palgrave Macmillan.

Kressel, K., and D.G. Pruitt (eds). 1989. *Mediation Research: The Process and Effectiveness of Third-Party Intervention*. San Francisco: Jossey-Bass.

Menkel-Meadow, C. (ed.). [2001] 2018. *Mediation. Theory, Policy and Practice*. London: Routledge.

Menkel-Meadow, C., L.P. Love and A. Kupfer Schneider (eds). [2006] 2013. *Mediation: Practice, Policy, and Ethics*, 2nd edn. New York: Wolters Kluwer Law & Business.

Rössner, D. 2006. 'Konfliktregelung im Strafrecht', in J. Hengstl and U. Sick (eds), *Recht gestern und heute: Festschrift zum 85. Geburtstag von Richard Haase*. Wiesbaden: Harrassowitz, pp. 319–31.

Schiff Berman, P. 2012. *Global Legal Pluralism: A Jurisprudence of Law beyond Borders*. Cambridge: Cambridge University Press.

Schlee, G., and B. Turner (eds). 2008. *Vergeltung: Eine interdisziplinäre Betrachtung der Rechtfertigung und Regulation von Gewalt*. Frankfurt am Main: Campus.

Turner, B., and G. Schlee (eds). 2017. *On Retaliation: Towards an Interdisciplinary Understanding of a Basic Human Condition*. New York: Berghahn Books.

Wolfrum, R., and I. Gätzschmann (eds). 2013. *International Dispute Settlement: Room for Innovations?* Berlin: Springer.

Wright, M., and B. Galaway (eds). 1989. *Mediation and Criminal Justice: Victims, Offenders and Community*. London: Sage.

Zekoll, J., M. Bälz and I. Amelung. 2014. *Formalisation and Flexibilisation in Dispute Resolution*. Leiden: Brill.

Zenk, K. 2008. *Mediation im Rahmen des Rechts: Eine Herausforderung für die Justiz*. Baden-Baden: Nomos.

Part I

Mediation, Arbitration and the Criminal Justice System

Historical and Current Developments

Chapter 1

Infrajudicial Modes of Conflict Regulation through Negotiation, Mediation and Arbitration in Early Modern European Criminal Justice

Karl Härter

Introduction: Mediation and Arbitration in Historical Perspective

In modern Western societies, mediation is conceptualized as an extrajudicial form of alternative dispute resolution to settle a variety of conflicts related to family, juveniles, business, workplace, religion, intercultural and international settings. Mediation appears to be the better alternative to the formal, adjudicative treatment of conflicts because it is regarded as a non-violent, peaceful, non-compulsive, preventive, cost-saving mode to solve disputes (Horn 2006; Menkel-Meadow, Love and Kupfer Schneider 2006; Busch and Mayer 2012). However, with regard to crime and criminal justice, the function of mediation is still controversially disputed. Although 'victim–offender mediation' or 'plea bargaining' constitute 'alternatives' to formal sentencing and punishment, they are closely intertwined with formal criminal procedure and hardly apply to a strict definition of private mediation.[1]

From a historical perspective, it seems to be even more difficult to study mediation and arbitration by using an ideal type concept of private alternative dispute resolution which is characterized by conflicting parties that voluntarily choose an impartial third party which should negotiate a settlement but had no authority to pass a judgement. First of all, it is difficult to conceptualize mediation only as a mode of alternative dispute resolution opposite to adjudicative dispute resolution managed by state institutions and courts. Prior to the formation of the modern state with a monopoly of power in the nineteenth century, the various justice systems in pre-modern Europe cannot be regarded as solely 'public' or state based. Although in early modern Europe a public criminal justice system developed – characterized by inquisitorial procedure, professional jurists and courts, and the learned law – its final establishment only happened in the nineteenth century with the implementation of new criminal codes such as the French *Code d'instruction criminelle* (1808) and the *Code pénal* (1810) and a public judiciary that was only based on the sovereign state with a monopoly on the use of force and justice.[2]

In pre-modern Europe, the society and the state were not yet separated into 'private' and 'public' spheres, and as a hybrid or plural legal system, criminal justice still comprised to some extent traditional, local, popular, social or other norms, procedures, communities and actors.[3] Thus, we cannot classify conflict parties as 'private individuals', who possessed the liberty to use alternative dispute resolution and mediation autonomously from the authorities or their respective estate, order, corporation and community, nor can we identify completely independent private 'mediators'. Third parties involved in extrajudicial conflict regulation were most often related to or held a semi-public function or position and can be characterized as 'infrajudicial agents'. In the pre-modern society of orders, all kinds of disputes as well as deviant behaviour could be regarded as a 'public' or 'social' conflict that could affect the concerned group, the common weal, the good order, the common peace and the legal order.[4] Hence, dispute resolution cannot be clearly separated from a public criminal justice system as an alternative and private means to settle conflicts.

Furthermore, extrajudicial alternative dispute resolution in which third parties acted as 'mediators' or 'arbitrators' hardly produced (written) sources and at best left a few traces in public and judicial documents (Ruff 2008: 44). An empirically based survey is most often only possible in cases where semi-public actors or the legal system were to some extent involved or intertwined with practices of alternative dispute resolution. As a result, the (legal) history of extrajudicial dispute resolution is still at its very beginning, in particular regarding the variety of arbitration and mediation practices.[5] Only a few studies in the history of crime and criminal justice have focused on extra- or infrajudicial practices that involved third party conflict regulation, arbitration and mediation.[6]

Focus and Structure of the Chapter

Considering the state of research, this chapter can only give an overview of conceptual issues and problems of the legal history of mediation, arbitration and related modes of alternative dispute resolution in the field of deviant behaviour, crime and criminal justice in early modern Europe, with a spatial focus on France, Italy, Spain and the Holy Roman Empire of the German Nation. As open, hybrid systems, early modern criminal justice in most European states was characterized by several internal and external practices of infrajudicial conflict regulation, such as arbitration, mediation, negotiation, supplicating, intercession, petitioning, pardon and criminal asylum, which were more or less intertwined with formal judicial procedures, in particular concerning the inquisitorial criminal process in continental Europe. These practices functioned as alternatives and supplements to formal adjudication and sentencing, and can therefore be characterized as infrajudicial, hybrid modes of mediation and arbitration. They were used by different actors and 'infrajudicial agents' to negotiate and mediate compensation, agreements, reconciliation, support, grace and pardon as well as social control and sanctions, which, therefore, constituted alternative options to punishment and retaliation to establish and maintain social order and peace.[7]

This concerned a broad variety of conflicts related to wrongdoing, deviant behaviour and crime that were not regarded as a matter of 'private individuals', but concerned families, communities and the social order of the early modern society as a whole. Since in the early modern period no separation of society and state or crime and private conflicts existed, wrongdoing and crime not only affected 'private' individuals or parties, but constituted a social as well as public conflict that could be regulated through public criminal justice or extrajudicial means such as negotiation, mediation or arbitration. This concerned violence, notably homicide, physical injuries, assault and battery; verbal insults, swearing and cursing, blasphemy and various religious wrongdoings; marital conflicts and deviant or criminal sexual behaviour such as fornication and adultery; as well as property crimes or wrongdoings in the economic sphere.[8]

Since it is difficult to clearly distinguish mediation and arbitration from other practices of extrajudicial dispute resolution, just as it is impossible to separate a sphere of private alternative dispute resolution from the public criminal justice system, I use the concept of 'infrajustice' to analyse the mentioned internal and external judicial practices of conflict regulation. Infrajustice emphasizes the complex relations between the judicial and extrajudicial spheres and the various hybrid modes of conflict regulation, which, nevertheless, were related to some extent to the sphere of public criminal law and justice. Infrajustice refers to plural legal configurations and includes alternatives to authoritarian jurisdiction and court justice, and interactions between social and judicial practices of conflict regulation, as well as all non-formal extrajudicial practices related to or used within the legal systems that functioned as alternatives to prevent or mitigate retaliation and punishment and aimed to maintain the social (and legal) order as well. These practices are characterized by *harmonie, jugement en équité, médiation, réparation et non la répression* to regulate or settle conflicts and crimes via and with the help of various third parties and 'infrajudicial agents', but often in interaction with judicial or legal institutions.[9]

Building on this basic consideration and using the concept of infrajustice, the following issues and questions will be analysed:

- mediation, arbitration and conflict regulation by third parties/'infrajudicial agents' in pre-modern judicial discourses;
- actors, parties and agents of infrajudicial practices of mediation and arbitration;
- supplicating, intercession, petitioning, pardon and criminal asylum as infrajudicial practices of negotiation, mediation and arbitration intertwined with formal criminal procedure;
- the types of conflicts related to crimes and deviant behaviour and the respective functions of arbitration and mediation to regulate these conflicts.

The Emergence of Mediation and Arbitration in the Legal Sphere

In late medieval Europe, 'infrajudicial agents' of arbitration and mediation emerged in various conflicts related to the legal sphere, which were designated in the sources as *Vermittler*, *freundlicher*, *guter Mittler*, *Minneteidinger*, *Mittelsmann*, *Mitter*, *Mittmann*, *Moderator*, *schidmann*, *intercessor*, *interpres*, *arbiter*, *mediator*, *pacator*, *conciliator*, *interventor*, *disceptator* and *amicabilis compositor*. They were considered as a third party that negotiated, arbitrated and mediated settlements, compensation or agreements in various types of conflicts, ranging from manslaughter and homicide over feuds to political disputes and armed conflicts.[10]

However, despite the frequent use of such modes of conflict regulation, the legal discourse did not establish a distinguished concept of mediation in and of itself, and rather subsumed conflict regulation by third parties under the concept of arbitration. Hence, mediation and mediators were (more or less) discussed as a specific form of arbitration without sharply distinguishing between the two.[11] Instead, arbitration, mediation and negotiation by 'infrajudicial agents' were generally accepted as a kind of legally based mode besides ordinary formal procedure, following the dichotomy of courtly love or adjudication (*Minne oder Recht / per amorem vel per iusticiam/iustitiam*).[12] It was not strictly based on the law but on the principle of *aequitas* and resulted not in a legally binding decision but in an amicable composition (*amicabilis compositio*), an equitable/reasonable arbitrament (*Schiedsspruch ex aequo et bono*), an arbitration agreement (*Schiedsvertrag*) or an agreement of atonement (*Sühnevertrag*), for instance concerning the settlement of a feud or compensation for manslaughter, homicide or other types of wrongdoing, injury and damage.[13]

This corresponded to a variety of third parties and 'infrajudicial agents', which legal theory systematically described by their function as:

- the *arbiter* who decided or adjudicated a dispute via equitable/reasonable discretion not strictly based on the law and formal procedure;
- the *arbitrator* (*Schiedsmann / vir bonus*) chosen and authorized by both parties to determine via equitable discretion (*billiges Ermessen*) a proposal, an obligation, a composition or compensation;

- the *amicabilis compositor* legitimated through personal authority who acted as mediator, negotiated a settlement and encouraged the parties to settle a dispute via an amicable agreement (*amicabilis compositio*) without any binding decision and with the prime purpose to re-establish the peace between the parties as well as the common one.[14]

However, in many cases, we find a conglomeration of these ideal types of third party actors that mediated and arbitrated outside or inside the legal system, and neither legal theory nor practice clearly separated mediation and arbitration: 'no one excluded mediation when they spoke of arbitration. It was an integral part of the process' (Roebuck 2013: xvi).

Since the Late Middle Ages, courts of arbitration (*Schiedsgerichte*) that arbitrated, mediated and negotiated various types of conflicts and wrongdoings according to the principles of *aequitas* and an amicable agreement were gradually established. Although denoted as courts by contemporaries, they were not considered regular institutions of the judiciary, since they were composed of laypeople and members of the social peer group or estate, for instance noblemen in the case of the *Austrägalgerichte* (courts of arbitration). The regulation of conflicts between rulers and states through various arbitrators and mediators developed into a widespread practice in early modern Europe, although on the interstate level an international arbitration court was only established at the beginning of the nineteenth century.[15]

Furthermore, local lay courts served as forums of arbitration and mediation. Discussions and negotiations took place in the court or with the help of judges and jurors, but these mostly informal infrajudicial proceedings did not result in a formal sentence and conflicts were finally settled outside the court or through other means than punishment. In many early modern criminal justice systems, judicial institutions served as a forum to propose and negotiate acceptable solutions, and officials acted as mediators and arbitrators to negotiate a dispute instead of to adjudicate and decide. Since the Late Middle Ages and with the gradual establishment of inquisitorial criminal procedure in early modern continental Europe, local institutions and actors even gained in importance as third parties and agents in the infrajudicial regulation of crime and conflicts.[16]

Criminal Procedure and Infrajudicial Practices of Mediation and Arbitration

In conceptualizing mediation and arbitration as infrajudicial modes of regulating conflicts related to deviant behaviour, crime and criminal justice, research should focus on practices, communication and functions: the intervention of third parties and 'infrajudicial agents' to negotiate, settle or reconcile a conflict or crime besides the strict law, ordinary criminal procedure, formal verdicts and formal ordinary punishment. Although the latter limited arbitration and mediation in criminal cases that qualified to inquisitorial procedure and ordinary punishment through the rule that they should not prohibit the public prosecution of crimes, it also partly retained or integrated infrajudicial elements of conflict regulation. The predominance of inquisitorial procedure in continental Europe since the Late Middle Ages resulted in the state-based, public prosecution of crimes following the principles that the authorities should investigate the substantive facts and the objective truth of a crime as well as prosecute every crime that could be detected and punish every perpetrator. Inquisitorial criminal procedure was ideal-typically separated into investigative proceedings, often carried out by local courts, officials and actors and the decision-making by more or less professional, judicial dicasteries which adjudicated on the basis of written documents, followed by the enforcement of verdicts and punishments on the local level (Roeck 1993; Härter 2000; Alessi 2001). This was paralleled by infrajudicial forms of negotiation such as supplicating, petitioning and pardoning, which could involve local and central actors or institutions. As a result, criminal proceedings were not restricted to the public, state-based criminal justice system, but extended to social communities and were characterized by specific forms of interaction between various actors at different stages. Some of these actors could also take the role of a 'third party' that did not adjudicate or punish but was involved in subsequent infrajudicial practices.

During the early modern period, infrajudicial modes of conflict regulation such as supplicating, petitioning, intercession or pardoning developed into a common practice in criminal proceedings. To some extent, this provided opportunities for the resident subjects of a jurisdiction to negotiate punishment and pardon with the help of 'infrajudicial agents' that could be involved as mediators, arbitrators, intercessors and supporters. Infrajudicial practices were used at nearly all stages of criminal procedure: to start proceedings, to avoid torture, to negotiate compensation and punishments or to receive pardon. This was possible because every subject obtained the customary right to submit a complaint, supplication, *lettre de cachet*, petition or *lettre de grâce* to judicial and governmental authorities and to the ruler as the holder of the judicial power. Although jurisprudence considered them as extrajudicial modes that did not constitute a formal element of criminal procedure, judicial institutions and rulers in many European countries integrated petitions, supplications and pardons into decision-making, even after a criminal judgement had been passed and the execution of punishment had been started. Many of these practices were rooted in traditional law and customs.[17]

In the first place, arbitration and atonement proceedings (*Schiedsverfahren*, *Sühneverfahren*) were widespread in medieval Europe and still in use in the early modern period to regulate conflicts and cases of wrongdoing – often acts of violence, manslaughter and homicide. Various 'infrajudicial agents', ranging from courts, officials and arbitrators to mediators, negotiated a compensation or a 'man price' (*Sühne*, *Wergeld*) between wrongdoer and victim or the related conflicting parties, which resulted in an atonement agreement (*Sühnevertrag*) as well as in various practices such as an expiatory sacrifice, the erection of an atonement cross or public penitence. Besides the material compensation between the two parties, such public practices should demonstrate reconciliation and therefore establish peace. Although these procedures cannot be considered merely 'private', they were not a formal part of the criminal process and constituted an alternative to public punishment as well as to blood feud and retaliation. The proceedings and the role of 'infrajudicial agents', most often chosen or accepted voluntarily by the parties, could vary considerably, from the conception and mediation of an agreement that parties could accept or not to more or less binding arbitration awards.[18]

Even after public inquisitorial procedure began to dominate in early modern Europe, various practices of such infrajudicial victim–offender mediation were still in use. In cases of serious violent crimes, perpetrators and victims could negotiate an extrajudicial settlement or compensation with the help of various semi-official 'mediators' (notaries, lay jurors, local officials, clerics) and send the agreement (or even the offer of such a mediation) via a petition or supplication to the adjudicating court. In many cases, this resulted in the mitigation of punishment or in homicide pardons, although many European jurisdictions had criminalized manslaughter as a serious crime and threatened the death penalty.[19]

Petitioning and supplicating to a ruler and to a judicial or administrative authority was considered a customary right in pre-modern Europe and was frequently used as an infrajudicial mode to negotiate various conflicts related to crime and deviant behaviour.[20] Third parties and 'infrajudicial agents' could be involved at various stages and in different functions, as authors, conceptionists, writers, notaries, supporters and intercessors. In particular, the intercession by an authority, official or notable acting as a third party and 'mediator' between a perpetrator and a court developed as a specific mode of infrajudicial conflict regulation through a supplication or petition.[21]

In verbal, violent or marital conflicts and the respective crimes, victims, family members or local notables could file or support a petition to start criminal proceedings and use this as a form of pressure to discipline a deviant member of the community or to negotiate compensation. In conflicts concerning alimony and support payments for illegitimate children, women could use such means to put pressure on recalcitrant fathers, who, as a result, were prosecuted as fornicators. Unwed mothers with illegitimate children often failed to receive child support payment from the father and had fewer chances to litigate their cause via a private law suit. However, illegitimacy, fornication and adultery constituted crimes that affected the social order, and without a settlement the women could became welfare cases. Thus, local authorities or clerics negotiated a settlement (marriage or alimony/child support payment) or the case was reported to the authorities (even through self-denunciation) to initiate criminal procedure and to prosecute the fornicator and father of the child. An infrajudicial settlement could lead to the mitigation of punishment, and even criminal courts informally negotiated the payment of alimony/child support or marriage and mitigated punishment if a settlement was achieved.[22]

Conversely, during an inquisitorial procedure in which a perpetrator was held in pre-trial detention, family members and other supporters could file a supplication, petition or intercession for better prison conditions, early release or to present arguments in favour of the perpetrator and to obtain a more lenient punishment. Defendants or their supporters also used supplications to communicate an agreement on compensation with victims of violent attacks, the forgiveness of a spouse in cases of adultery, an arrangement for the payment of alimony or child support in cases of fornication, and other forms of reconciliation such as the French *transaction* or the remission of a party, which, for example, was a common form in Naples or France.[23]

Agreements, arrangements, statements of forgiveness, transaction or remission were often negotiated or mediated by notaries or other officials who prepared a formal document or a supplication. Particularly in cases of violent crimes, injuries, insult, fornication and adultery, courts took mediated compensation and 'forgiveness' into consideration and mitigated penalties, waived the punishment or granted pardon in favour of compensation and reconciliation.[24]

In cases of sexual crimes – in particular adultery that was often threatened with capital punishment – and related marital conflicts, infrajudicial agents sometimes negotiated a settlement between the spouses. Criminal courts could take them into account and mitigate or waive serious punishments if formal forgiveness of an insulted partner, a promise to continue the marriage, child support payments for illegitimate children, a family arrangement and material compensation (concerning, for instance, debts or inheritance) was achieved and the perpetrator made atonement, for instance through a public church penance.[25]

Particularly in regard to violent conflicts and the related crimes of assault and battery, manslaughter and homicide, infrajudicial agreements and compensation achieved with the help of a mediator or arbitrator were common throughout the early modern period. Even in the eighteenth century, French courts recognized the settlements that mediators negotiated in violent interpersonal conflicts, and such 'infrajudicial resolution of disputes not only survived but became institutionalised' (Ruff 2008: 45–46) in French criminal justice. Local lay courts and judges frequently dispensed sentencing and public punishment, and arbitrated or mediated crime and conflict through compensation. Through petitions and supplications, which were often negotiated or supported by local authorities, perpetrators offered compensation to victims or introduced a settlement, and if an agreement was achieved, the criminal court mitigated or waived public punishment, particularly in cases of manslaughter and homicide. Sometimes criminal courts even proposed negotiating or mediating an agreement and indicated the amount of compensatory payment. Reconciliation, peace and good order as well as avoiding fiscal and social costs predominated over harsh public punishment prescribed by penal law in cases of violent crimes and conflicts. Until the nineteenth century, criminal courts of various European jurisdictions accepted supplications, petitions and other forms of mediated compensation, and as a result mitigated penalties or pardoned perpetrators if they compensated victims or if an infrajudicial settlement was achieved.[26] In this regard, 'victim–offender mediation' was intertwined with criminal procedure and the courts or local officials partly acted as institutionalized infrajudicial agents, mediators or arbitrators. Although victims and offenders could negotiate compensation on their own, this kind of 'victim–offender mediation' was clearly mandatory, because refusing compensation could result in harsher punishments. In the case that victims and offenders did not agree on a settlement or the crime had seriously infringed public order and security (for instance in cases of robber gangs), criminal courts adjudicated on the basis of strict penal law and meted out retributive capital punishment.

Furthermore, pardon and the remission of crimes were often the result of infrajudicial practices and involved third parties, which, however, were closely intertwined with criminal justice. Since the Late Middle Ages, pardon constituted an element of arbitration and mediation procedures and was considered as negotiated 'courtly love' (*Minne*) or as judging according to grace (*Richten nach Gnade*).[27] After many European authorities had enacted criminal codes that threatened harsh punishments, and inquisitorial procedure had been widely established in the early modern period, pardon constituted an alternative mode to regulate crime and related conflicts after a court had sentenced a perpetrator, most often in cases of homicide and violent crimes. The convicted or his relatives could file a petition for pardon to the ruler, based on the customary right that a ruler should grant every subject access, hearing and justice. Being the highest holder of criminal jurisdiction, the ruler obtained the right to grant mercy and pardon without considering the law.[28]

As a result, pardoning constituted an infrajudicial procedure in which the ruler acted as an 'infrajudicial agent' between the criminal court, the convicted and other involved parties (victims, families, communities). Moreover, other actors and third parties such as family members, local authorities, officials, clerics, advocates and notaries took part by authoring, conceiving or supporting a petition or filing a concomitant intercession and providing arguments, information and 'social capital' that should convince the ruler to abandon or substantially mitigate punishment. Besides compensation and reconciliation, petitions or intercessions for pardon often substantiated utilitarian and social arguments – the conduct of a perpetrator, his status and grade of integration, his usefulness for a family or community – as well as ensuring that the pardoned would behave in a disciplined and law-abiding manner in the future. In some cases, even the adjudicating judges or local judicial officials recommended petitioning and pardon after they had formally convicted a perpetrator in accordance with the harsh law. The infrajudicial practice of pardon involved a variety of third parties and 'infrajudicial agents' that helped to negotiate and even mediate the regulation of crime and conflict through mercy, reconciliation and social control as alternative modes to formal (and often capital) punishment – and was widely used in Europe until the nineteenth century.[29]

However, only delinquents with adequate material and social resources could use petitioning, supplicating and pardon to negotiate with the authorities, and the inquisitorial criminal procedure with its pre-trial detention limited the infrajudicial options as a whole. As a result, some perpetrators preferred to run from the law and seek refuge in churches, monasteries, towns or other places of legal immunity that obtained the privilege to grant asylum, particularly in cases of manslaughter. These sanctuaries not only offered protection from prosecution (and sometimes charged a fee), but could also help to negotiate safe conduct (*salvus conductus*) and the mitigation of capital punishment. Clerics in particular acted as mediators and negotiated agreements with prosecuting authorities who renounced capital punishment, while in return perpetrators surrendered and were extradited to a court. On the other hand, pre-modern criminal asylum generated numerous jurisdictional conflicts and most early modern states achieved the substantial limitation and finally the complete abolishment of the various forms of asylum and sanctuary by the end of the eighteenth century.[30]

Agents and Actors

The outlined infrajudicial practices included a great variety of 'infrajudicial agents' that negotiated, arbitrated, mediated or were otherwise involved as a third party in the complex triangle of perpetrator, victim and court. This concerned family members, social communities, corporations and guilds to which defendants and victims belonged, as well as notables and office holders ranging from advocates, councillors, advisors, solicitors, notaries, jurors, local officials or clerics to judges or rulers. Their key role was not to act in a formal function within criminal procedure, but to perform an extrajudicial role as negotiator, arbitrator, mediator, intercessor, ombudsman, supplicant, supporter or communicator interacting with parties (perpetrator and/or victim) and the criminal justice system. Many of these infrajudicial agents charged a fee or were somehow reimbursed for expenses, and infrajudicial regulation of conflict and crime developed into a profitable business, particularly concerning supplicating, petitioning and pardon, which could incur considerable costs for the concerned parties and actors.[31]

In principle, parties and actors could voluntarily choose an arbitrator, mediator or infrajudicial agent. However, during the early modern period, for certain types of conflict regulation and crimes – in particular violence and homicide – the function of a mediator or arbitrator was gradually formalized and a certain procedure was obligatory. For instance, in the case of criminal asylum, bishops or abbots acted as 'infrajudicial agents'; in matrimonial conflicts, church courts and clerics arbitrated and mediated; regarding conflicts and wrongdoing in the economic field, semi-officials, visitators, wardens, commerce and guild courts used arbitration and summary procedures. In some cases, corporations, guilds, neighbourhoods and local and village assemblies formed 'alternative' judicial institutions and arbitration or settlement courts that substituted formal criminal procedure and sentencing and operated on the principle of 'love in place of law' to achieve an amicable settlement and reconciliation.[32]

Such functions were also performed by individual members of judicial institutions (often local rural or municipal courts) as jurymen/jurors, lay assessors and aldermen, justices of the peace, clerks, notaries and advocates, as well as by ecclesiastical institutions (church courts, vicariates) and clerics.[33] They regulated conflicts outside the court, but used their authority, position and institution as a vehicle or leverage to negotiate and propose an acceptable settlement. This underlines the infrajudicial nature of officials who acted as 'infrajudicial agents': they could change roles and functions and act as mediator, arbitrator, negotiator, advisor, councillor or advocate, and could even shift to a mandatory proposal or a more or less binding decision. Even a court could act as an 'infrajudicial agent' and negotiate and mediate an infrajudicial settlement without formal adjudication and sentencing. Several case studies on various jurisdictions in early modern Europe have verified that municipal, local lay courts and even criminal high courts aimed to settle violent conflicts in families or neighbourhoods by imposing an agreement and monetary compensation and refrained from sentencing and harsh punishment.[34] Hence, 'plea bargaining' constituted a frequent practice in early modern courts (although not strictly comparable with the modern practice in a substantially different judicial setting). Although most of these infrajudicial actors and agents cannot be characterized as 'mediators' according to a strict modern definition, they nevertheless provided crucial functions of a third party to negotiate infrajudicial regulation of crime and conflict as an alternative to adjudication, sentencing and punishment on the basis of strict penal law.

Proceedings and Techniques

The proceedings and techniques of infrajudicial conflict regulation were numerous, and ranged from a binding decision over an arbitrament (*Schiedsspruch ex aequo et bono*) to an amicable settlement, composition or voluntary agreement. The negotiated, mediated or arbitrated results manifested in arbitration agreements (*Schiedsvertrag*) to be signed by both parties, a proposal of compensation, a transaction, a remission of offended parties, letters of pardon and various other agreements, sometimes signed or acknowledged by the 'infrajudicial agent' who had participated in the proceedings. To ensure an agreement and to enforce monetary as well as social compensation, a contractual penalty or other social sanctions were sometimes threatened, or parties had to acknowledge a settlement and compensation through an oath. Furthermore, traditional practices and rituals could confirm the regulation of a conflict, as, for example, a perpetrator had to make atonement, to formally apologize to a victim in public, to revoke an assault or injury, or to give a public statement of honour. Sometimes this was coupled with atonement pay/indulgence, the ritual of handshaking or the swearing of an oath to not offend (*Urfehdeschwur*). These rituals should prevent future retaliatory violence against victims or other parties.[35]

However, in historical research it is often difficult to determine clearly whether a settlement was the result of mediation and arbitration or of other judicial procedures, as adjudication and infrajudicial practices were often closely intertwined and 'infrajudicial agents' could change role and proceedings and the concerned parties could use different options, ranging from a mediated private agreement to criminal procedure, punishment or pardon. As a result, infrajudicial conflict regulation was strongly related to the uses of and access to criminal justice, the social status or construction of conflict parties and the respective strategies for inclusion or exclusion. Whereas social minorities and marginal groups such as vagrants or the poor had fewer or no opportunities, resident subjects with a certain social capital (status, honour, income), who were integrated into their respective social order or local community and possessed sufficient legal knowledge, could make use of the various modes of infrajudicial conflict regulation. They could, for instance, negotiate a settlement, compensation and the mitigation of punishment or pardon, by putting forward social, economic and utilitarian arguments that were in line with the 'good order' of the early modern society and the interests of the early modern state, arguing with their utility (*Nützlichkeit*), industriousness, social reputation and prospective disciplined behaviour.[36]

Functions and Purposes

Although the public criminal justice systems in early modern Europe claimed to prosecute and punish crimes according to strict penal law, they still approved or tolerated the infrajudicial regulation of crime and conflict, as it served various purposes, ranging from the prevention of retaliatory violence, appropriate material and social compensation for a wrongdoing (and therefore easing the burden of social welfare costs) and reconciliation to maintenance of the 'common peace' and 'social order'.[37] Furthermore, infrajudicial procedures provided to some extent defence and legal remedies that the inquisitorial criminal procedure lacked. On the other hand, it enabled the flexibilization of harsh public punishment. The principles of equity and amicable composition allowed the strict penal law to be adjusted to the 'circumstances' of offenders, victims, families and communities, and met the fiscal interests of the state too, since the mitigation of penalties or even pardoning reduced the costs of public punishment and generated additional financial sources (fines, fees for petitions, supplications etc.). However, many infrajudicial practices comprised various forms of material and social sanctions and punitive damages – sometimes referred to as private penalties (*Privatstrafe*, *peine privée*) – and could have comparable effects and aimed at social control. As a consequence, infrajudicial conflict regulation through negotiation, mediation and arbitration served to incorporate means of informal social control into criminal justice.[38]

Infrajudicial practices, however, also enabled and justified exemplary harsh punishment regarding wrongdoers who could not make use of such means and belonged to marginal groups and minorities, and were considered or labelled as incorrigible and a threat to the order and security of the early modern society. As a result, the penal practice of criminal justice in early modern Europe showed considerable differences between the harsher punishment of 'non-integrated' perpetrators who lacked infrajudicial opportunities and 'integrated' resident subjects who could use infrajudicial modes of conflict regulation. This finally points to the limits of the infrajudicial regulation of crime and conflict through negotiation, mediation and arbitration, as pointed out by Cummins and Kounine: 'Resolution of conflict is far from always a positive and consensual act. Instead it is often a product of domination and the reinforcement of inequality' (Cummins and Kounine 2016b: 6). In many cases, these methods did not produce acceptable, viable and sustainable results or a permanent resolution of conflicts, and failed to establish the 'truth' of a conflict/crime or 'justice'. Therefore, they could turn out to be a pre-stage to formal criminal procedure and induce other logics of conflict regulation, ranging from punishment to retaliation.

Thus, the hybrid structure of early modern criminal justice with its infrajudicial modes also implied ambivalences, arbitrariness, legal uncertainty, social/legal inequalities and increasing social control. This was heavily criticized by the Enlightenment and stimulated (or legitimized) the juridification and finally the abolishment of infrajudicial modes of conflict regulation from the eighteenth century onwards. After the French Revolution, with the codification of criminal law and the establishment of a state-based monopoly of power, the modern criminal justice systems in Europe formally abolished extrajudicial practices. However, some infrajudicial modes were partially transferred and incorporated in modified forms, such as arbitration and private compensation in cases of verbal and minor injuries. With regard to the social bias of current adjudication, plea bargaining, forum shopping, victim–offender mediation and the various efforts to expand mediation and arbitration, the complex interdependencies of infrajudicial conflict regulation and state-based criminal justice still challenge the modern state and legal history.

Karl Härter is Professor, Research Group Leader and Senior Research Scientist at the Max Planck Institute for European Legal History in Frankfurt/Main. He is a member of the International Max Planck Research School on Retaliation, Mediation and Punishment, the Association for Constitutional History, the Commission for Hessian History and other academic and historical institutions.

Notes

1. Felstiner and Williams (1980), Wright and Galaway (1989), Feltes (1993), Rössner (2006).
2. Rousseaux and Lévy (1997), Chauvaud (2002), Petit (2002), Carbasse (2006), Härter (2008, 2009), Tedoldi (2008).
3. Bossy (1983), Dunn (1996), Österberg and Sogner (2000), Chiffoleau, Gauvard and Zorzi (2007), Dauchy et al. (2008), Farcy (2008), McMahon (2008), Allinne, Gauvard and Jean (2014).
4. Schedensack (1997, 2007), Eriksson and Krug-Richter (2003), Hoareau-Dodinau (2003), Krug-Richter and Mohrmann (2004), Haack (2008), Grüne (2011), Collard and Cottret (2012).
5. Insufficient and unhistorical: Barrett and Barrett (2004); recent state of legal history: Roebuck (2002, 2006, 2010, 2013), Lück (2012), Zekol, Bälz and Amelung (2014), Cordes (2015a). On the social history of mediation, see Chabot, Gal and Tournu (2006).
6. For an overview see Bossy (1983), Blauert and Schwerhoff (2000), Garnot (2000b), Bellabarba, Schwerhoff and Zorzi (2001), Mantecón (2003, 2004), Broggio and Paoli (2011), Schwerhoff (2011), Fikentscher and Kolb (2012), Cummins and Kounine (2016a).
7. Castan (1983), Härter (1999, 2000, 2005), Bellabarba (2001), Rudolph (2001a), Zorzi (2001), Schwerhoff (2011).
8. For a general overview, see Garnot (1998, 2000a, 2000b), Blauert and Schwerhoff (2000), Bellabarba, Schwerhoff and Zorzi (2001), Carroll (2006, 2007), Mantecón (2007), Musin, Rousseaux and Vesentini (2008), Body-Gendrot and Spierenburg (2009), Schwerhoff (2011).
9. On the concept in general, see Garnot (1996, 2000c), Loetz (2000), Härter (2012).
10. Kamp (2001), Esders (2007), Auge et al. (2008), Althoff (2011), Broggio and Paoli (2011), Andersen et al. (2013), Cordes (2015b).
11. Bader (1984a, 1984b), Godfrey (2002, 2004), Roebuck (2006, 2013), Sigurdsson (2013).
12. Gaisser (1955), Hattenhauer (1963), Kim-Wawrzinek (1974), Clanchy (1983), Cordes (2015b).
13. Fourgous (1906), Bader (1960), Kornblum (1976), Coing (1984), Mayenburg (2016).
14. Grolman (1689), Bader (1960), Martone (1984), Lück (1999, 2012), Deutsch (2005), Lefebvre-Teillar (2008).
15. Frey (1928), Krause (1930), Kobler (1967, 1975), Kampmann (2001, 2010), Meyerhuber (2004); see also the contribution by Zollmann in this volume.
16. Mantecón (2004), Arlinghaus et al. (2006), Lück (2012), Godfrey (2015).
17. Castan (1983), Schaffstein (1987), Willoweit (1996, 2002), Lück (1999), Härter (2000, 2005), Mantecón (2003, 2004), Krug-Richter (2004), Bulst (2006), Wenzel (2008), Edigati (2011), Abreu-Ferreira (2015).
18. Kornblum (1976), Rousseaux (1999), Deutsch (2005), Lück (2012: 87–93), Mayenburg (2016).

19. Castan (1983), Schaffstein (1987), Chaulet (1997, 2007), Ruff (2001), Marcarelli (2004), Mantecón (2007), Bergère (2008), Musin, Rousseaux and Vesentini (2008), Nassiet (2011), Rose (2012), Cummins (2016), Härter (2017).
20. Ebeling (1992), Würgler (1999), Härter (2002), Nubola and Würgler (2002), Ludwig (2008), Rehse (2008), Bercé (2014), Haug-Moritz and Ullmann (2015).
21. Schuster (2000: 293–95), Rudolph (2001a: 265–327), Moeglin (2004), Blickle (2005), Ludwig (2008: 151–271).
22. Farr (1995: 118–23), Härter (2001a, 2001b), Klammer (2004: 225–51). See also Castan (1983), Winkelbauer (1992), Piant (1998), Dalla Corte (2005), Lutz (2006), Walch (2009), Korpiola (2011), Abreu-Ferreira (2015), Heijden (2016: 35–37, 113–18).
23. Martinage (2008), Taylor (2009: 194–225), Nassiet (2011: 25–58), Cummins (2016).
24. Muchembled (1989), Bulst (1999a, 1999b), Thauer (2001: 226–30), Brachtendorf (2003: 245–46), Cesco (2004), Klammer (2004: 225–51), Marcarelli (2004), Eibach (2005, 2008), Mantecón (2007), Follain et al. (2008), Ludwig (2008: 219–38), Ruff (2008), Cristellon and Seidel Menchi (2011), Dunn (2011), Nassiet (2011), Abreu-Ferreira (2015), Heijden (2016: 35–37).
25. Cesco (2004), Härter (2005: 635–39, 874–916), Schmidt (2009), Taylor (2009: 194–225), Korpiola (2011, 2015), Abreu-Ferreira (2015).
26. Rudolph (2001a, 2001b), Ruff (2001: 83–87), Marcarelli (2004), Härter (2005), Ambroise-Rendu (2006), Carroll (2006), Mantecón (2007), Caron et al. (2008), Chaulet (2008), Eibach (2008), Piant (2008), Nassiet (2011), Franke (2013: 168–72), Abreu-Ferreira (2015), Godfrey (2015).
27. Schuster (2000: 273–85), Willoweit (2002), Arlinghaus (2004), Bulst (2006), Mayenburg (2014).
28. Davis (1987), Bauer (1996), Hoareau-Dodinau, Rousseaux and Texier (1999), Härter and Nubola (2011), Mayenburg (2016: 11–13).
29. Davis (1987), Bauer (1996), Hoareau-Dodinau, Rousseaux and Texier (1999), Schuster (2000: 285–311), Deutsch (2005: 147–49), Härter (2005), Chaulet (2007), Kotkas (2007), Niccoli (2007), Ludwig (2008: 151–271), Rehse (2008), Abad (2011), Härter (2011), Dauven and Rousseaux (2012), Kesper-Biermann (2012), Abreu-Ferreira (2015), Cummins (2016).
30. Latini (2002), Härter (2003a, 2007), Turner (2005), Shoemaker (2011).
31. Castan (1983), Garnot (1996), Mantecón (2002), Dalla Corte (2005), Edigati (2011), Lück (2012), Mayenburg (2016).
32. Kobler (1967), Castan (1983), Winkelbauer (1992), Willoweit (1996), Krug-Richter (1997), Schuster (2000: 166–80), Thauer (2001), Brachtendorf (2003: 71–77, 87–88, 114–17, 245–46), Mantecón (2003, 2004), Marcarelli (2004), Meyerhuber (2004), Piant (2006), Roebuck (2010: 400–403).
33. Landau (1984), Wettmann (1987), Garnot (1997a, 1997b), Misericordia (2001), Dartmann (2003), Petit (2003), Farcy (2008), Schmidt (2009), Franke (2013: 168–72), Korpiola (2015).
34. Chaulet (1997, 2008), Blok (2001), Rudolph (2001a: 227–61), Thauer (2001), Brachtendorf (2003: 71–77, 87–88, 114–17, 140–42), Mantecón (2003, 2004), Behrisch (2005: 134–76), Härter (2005), Carroll (2006), Caron et al. (2008), Eibach (2008: 65–67), Ludwig (2008), Musin, Rousseaux and Vesentini (2008), Rose (2012), Godfrey (2015).
35. Schaffstein (1987), Blauert (2000, 2004), Thauer (2001: 226–30), Brachtendorf (2003: 245–46), Deutsch (2005), Piant (2006), Bernaudeau (2008), Bors (2011), Franke (2013: 168–72), Mayenburg (2016).

36. Hoareau-Dodinau, Rousseaux and Texier (1999), Härter (2002, 2003b, 2005: 930–1122), Mantecón (2003), Rehse (2008), Abad (2011), Härter and Nubola (2011), Dauven and Rousseaux (2012), Rose (2012), Bercé (2014).
37. Rudolph (2001b), Sbriccoli (2001), Zorzi (2001), Mantecón (2003), Eibach (2004), Krug-Richter (2004), Wenzel (2008), Edigati (2011).
38. Schaffstein (1987), Härter (1999), Dinges (2000, 2001), Hoffmann (2000), Sälter (2000), Montazel (2001), Zorzi (2001), Mantecón (2004), Behrisch (2005), Wenzel (2008), Edigati (2011).

References

Abad, R. 2011. *La Grâce du roi: Les lettres de clémence de Grande Chancellerie au* XVIIIe *siècle.* Paris: Presses de l'Universitaires Paris-Sorbonne.

Abreu-Ferreira, D. 2015. *Women, Crime, and Forgiveness in Early Modern Portugal.* Burlington, VA: Ashgate.

Alessi, G. 2001. *Il Processo Penale: Profilo storico.* Rome: Laterza.

Allinne, J.-P., C. Gauvard and J.-P. Jean (eds). 2014. *Le peuple en justice.* Paris: La Documentation Française.

Althoff, G. 2011. *Frieden stiften: Vermittlung und Konfliktlösung vom Mittelalter bis heute.* Darmstadt: Wissenschaftliche Buchgesellschaft.

Ambroise-Rendu, A.-C. 2006. *Crimes et délits: Une histoire de la violence de la Belle Époque à nos jours.* Paris: Nouveau Monde Édition.

Andersen, P., et al. 2013. 'Law and Disputing in the Middle Ages', in *Proceedings of the Ninth Carlsberg Academy Conference on Medieval Legal History 2012.* Copenhagen: DJØF Publishing.

Arlinghaus, F.-J. 2004. 'Gnade und Verfahren: Kommunikationsmodi in spätmittelalterlichen Stadtgerichten', in R. Schlögl (ed.), *Interaktion und Herrschaft: Die Politik der frühneuzeitlichen Stadt.* Konstanz: UVK-Verl., pp. 137–62.

Arlinghaus, F.-J., et al. 2006. *Praxis der Gerichtsbarkeit in europäischen Städten des Spätmittelalters.* Frankfurt am Main: Klostermann.

Auge, O., et al. 2008. *Bereit zum Konflikt: Strategien und Medien der Konflikterzeugung und Konfliktbewältigung im europäischen Mittelalter.* Ostfildern: Thorbecke.

Bader, K. 1960. 'Arbiter, arbitrator seu amicabilis compositor', *Zeitschrift der Savigny-Stiftung für Rechtsgeschichte / Kanonistische Abteilung* 77: 239–76.

———. 1984a. 'Das Schiedsverfahren in Schwaben vom 12. bis zum ausgehenden 16. Jahrhundert', in K.S. Bader, *Schriften zur Rechtsgeschichte*, ed. C. Schott. Sigmaringen: Jan Thorbecke, pp. 157–225.

———. 1984b. 'Die Entwicklung und Verbreitung der mittelalterlichen Schiedsidee in Südwestdeutschland und in der Schweiz', in K.S. Bader, *Schriften zur Rechtsgeschichte*, ed. C. Schott. Sigmaringen: Jan Thorbecke, pp. 226–51.

Barrett, J.T., and J.P. Barrett. 2004. *A History of Alternative Dispute Resolution: The Story of a Political, Cultural, and Social Movement.* San Francisco: Jossey Bass.

Bauer, A. 1996. *Das Gnadenbitten in der Strafrechtspflege des 15. und 16. Jahrhunderts.* Frankfurt am Main: Lang.

Behrisch, L. 2005. *Städtische Obrigkeit und Soziale Kontrolle:* Görlitz 1450–1600. Epfendorf: Bibliotheca-Academica-Verl.

Bellabarba, M. 2001. 'Pace pubblica e pace privata: linguaggi e istituzioni processuali nell'Italia moderna', in M. Bellabarba, G. Schwerhoff and A. Zorzi (eds), *Criminalità e giustizia in*

Germania e in Italia: Pratiche giudiziarie e linguaggi giuridici tra tardo Medioevo ed età moderna / Kriminalität und Justiz in Deutschland und Italien: Rechtspraktiken und gerichtliche Diskurse in Spätmittelalter und Früher Neuzeit. Bologna and Berlin: Duncker & Humblot, pp. 189–213.

Bellabarba, M., G. Schwerhoff and A. Zorzi (eds). 2001. *Criminalità e giustizia in Germania e in Italia: Pratiche giudiziarie e linguaggi giuridici tra tardo Medioevo ed età moderna / Kriminalität und Justiz in Deutschland und Italien: Rechtspraktiken und gerichtliche Diskurse in Spätmittelalter und Früher Neuzeit.* Bologna and Berlin: Duncker & Humblot.

Bercé, Y.-M. 2014. *La dernière chance: Histoire des suppliques du Moyen Âge à nos jours.* Paris: Perrin.

Bergère, M. 2008. 'Pratiques et régulations des violences intracommunautaires dans la société française en épuration', in A. Follain et al. (eds), *La violence et le judiciaire du Moyen Age à nos jours: Discours, perceptions, pratiques.* Rennes: Presses Universitaires de Rennes, pp. 323–31.

Bernaudeau, V. 2008. 'Invectives, injures et diffamations: les violences verbales et leur réparation devant les justices de paix au XIXe siècle', in A. Follain et al. (eds), *La violence et le judiciaire du Moyen Age à nos jours: Discours, perception, pratiques.* Rennes: Presses Universitaires de Rennes, pp. 161–72.

Blauert, A. 2000. *Das Urfehdewesen im deutschen Südwesten im Spätmittelalter und in der Frühen Neuzeit.* Tübingen: Bibliotheca-Acad.-Verl.

———. 2004. 'Sühnen und Strafen im sächsischen Freiberg vom 15. bis 17. Jahrhundert', in R. Schlögl (ed.), *Interaktion und Herrschaft: Die Politik der frühneuzeitlichen Stadt.* Konstanz: UVK-Verl., pp. 163–80.

Blauert, A., and G. Schwerhoff (eds). 2000. *Kriminalitätsgeschichte: Beiträge zur Sozial- und Kulturgeschichte der Vormoderne.* Konstanz: UVK-Verl.

Blickle, R. 2005. 'Interzession: Die Fürbitte auf Erden und im Himmel als Element der Herrschaftsbeziehungen', in C. Nubola (ed.), *Bittschriften und Gravamina: Politik, Verwaltung und Justiz in Europa (14.–18. Jahrhundert).* Berlin: Duncker & Humblot, pp. 293–322.

Blok, A. 2001. *Honour and Violence.* Cambridge: Polity Press.

Body-Gendrot, S., and P. Spierenburg (eds). 2009. *Violence in Europe: Historical and Contemporary Perspectives.* New York: Springer.

Bors, M. 2011. 'Abbitte, Widerruf und Ehrenerklärung: Zur Geschichte der Privatgenugtuung im Ehrverletzungsrecht des 19. Jahrhunderts', in S. Kesper-Biermann, U. Ludwig and A. Ortmann (eds), *Ehre und Recht: Ehrkonzepte, Ehrverletzungen und Ehrverteidigungen vom späten Mittelalter bis zur Moderne.* Magdeburg: Meine, pp. 133–42.

Bossy, J. (ed.). 1983. *Disputes and Settlements: Law and Human Relations in the West.* Cambridge: Cambridge University Press.

Brachtendorf, R. 2003. *Konflikte, Devianz, Kriminalität: Justiznutzung und Strafpraxis in Kurtrier im 18. Jahrhundert am Beispiel des Amts Cochem.* Marburg: Tectum-Verl.

Broggio, P., and M.P. Paoli. 2011. *Stringere la pace: Teorie e pratiche della conciliazione nell'Europa moderna (secoli XV–XVIII).* Rome: Viella.

Bulst, N. 1999a. 'Kriterien der Rechtsprechung zur Gewalt: Zum Problem strafrechtlicher Normen im Übergang vom Mittelalter zur Neuzeit', *ZIF Mitteilungen* 1: 9–18.

———. 1999b. 'Wirkungen von Normen zur Regulierung von Gewaltverhalten im Übergang vom Mittelalter zur Frühen Neuzeit', in H. Hof and G. Lübbe-Wolff (eds), *Wirkungsforschung zum Recht I: Wirkungen und Erfolgsbedingungen von Gesetzen.* Baden-Baden: Nomos, pp. 279–88.

———. 2006. 'Richten nach Gnade oder nach Recht: Zum Problem spätmittelalterlicher Rechtsprechung', in F.-J. Arlinghaus et al. (eds), *Praxis der Gerichtsbarkeit in europäischen Städten des Spätmittelalters*. Frankfurt am Main: Klostermann, pp. 465–90.

Busch, D., and C.-H. Mayer (eds). 2012. *Mediation erforschen: Fragen – Forschungsmethoden – Ziele*. Wiesbaden: Springer.

Carbasse, J.-M. 2006. *Histoire du droit pénal et de la justice criminelle*, 2nd édn, refondue. Paris: Presses Universitaires de France.

Caron, J.-C., F. Chauvaud, E. Fureix and J.-N. Luc (eds). 2008. *Entre violence et conciliation: La résolution des conflits sociopolitiques en Europe au XIXe siècle*. Rennes: Presses Universitaires de Rennes.

Carroll, S. 2006. *Blood and Violence in Early Modern France*. Oxford: Oxford University Press.

——— (ed.). 2007. *Cultures of Violence: Interpersonal Violence in Historical Perspective*. Basingstoke: Palgrave Macmillan.

Castan, N. 1983. 'Arbitration of Disputes under the Ancien Regime', in J. Bossy (ed.), *Disputes and Settlements: Law and Human Relations in the West*. Cambridge: Cambridge University Press, pp. 219–60.

Cesco, V. 2004. 'Il *rapimento* a fine di matrimonio: Una pratica sociale in età moderna tra retorica e cultura', in G. Chiodi and C. Povolo (eds), *L'amministrazione della giustizia penale nella Repubblica di Venezia (secoli XVI–XVIII)*, vol. 2. Verona: Cierre, pp. 349–95.

Chabot, J.L., S. Gal and C. Tournu. 2006. *Figures de la médiation et lien social*. Paris: L'Harmattan.

Chaulet, R. 1997. 'La violence en Castille au XVIIe siècle à travers les Indultos de Viernes Santo (1623–1699)', *Crime, Histoire & Sociétés / Crime, History & Societies* 1(2), online 3 April 2009. http://chs.revues.org/1007.

———. 2007. *Crimes, rixes et bruits d'épées: Homicides pardonnés en Castille au siècle d'or*. Montpellier: Presses Universitaires de la Méditerranée.

———. 2008. 'Royal Justice, Popular Culture and Violence: Homicide in Sixteenth- and Seventeenth-Century Castile', in R. McMahon (ed.), *Crime, Law and Popular Culture in Europe, 1500–1900*. Cullompton: Willan, pp. 74–95.

Chauvaud, F. 2002. 'La Justice en France, 1789–1939: Un modèle à l'épreuve'. *Crime, Histoire & Sociétés / Crime, History & Societies* 6: 105–25. http://chs.revues.org/index240.html.

Chiffoleau, J., C. Gauvard and A. Zorzi. 2007. *Pratiques sociales et politiques judiciaires dans les villes de l'Occident à la fin du Moyen Âge*. Rome: École Française de Rome.

Clanchy, M. 1983. 'Law and Love in the Middle Ages', in J. Bossy (ed.), *Disputes and Settlements: Law and Human Relations in the West*. Cambridge: Cambridge University Press, pp. 47–67.

Coing, H. 1984. 'Zur Entwicklung des Schiedsvertrages im Ius Commune: Die amicabilis compositio und der Schiedsspruch ex aequo et bono', in H.J. Becker and G. Baumgärtel (eds), *Festschrift für Heinz Hübner zum 70. Geburtstag am 7. November 1984*. Berlin: De Gruyter, pp. 35–46.

Collard, F., and M. Cottret. 2012. *Conciliation, réconciliation aux temps médiévaux et modernes*. Paris: Presses Universitaires de Paris Ouest.

Cordes, A. 2015a. *Mit Freundschaft oder mit Recht? Inner- und außergerichtliche Alternativen zur kontroversen Streitentscheidung im 15.–19. Jahrhundert*. Cologne: Böhlau.

———. 2015b. '"Mit Freundschaft oder mit Recht": Quellentermini und wissenschaftliche Ordnungsbegriffe', in A. Cordes (ed.), *Mit Freundschaft oder mit Recht? Inner- und außergerichtliche Alternativen zur kontroversen Streitentscheidung im 15.–19. Jahrhundert*. Cologne: Böhlau, pp. 9–18.

Cristellon, C., and S.S. Menchi. 2011. 'Rituals before Tribunals in Renaissance Italy: Continuity and Change, 1400–1600', in M. Korpiola (ed.), *Regional Variations in Matrimonial Law and Custom in Europe, 1150–1600*. Leiden: Brill, pp. 275–87.

Cummins, S. 2016. 'Forgiving Crimes in Early Modern Naples', in S. Cummins and L. Kounine (eds), *Cultures of Conflict Resolution in Early Modern Europe*. Aldershot: Ashgate, pp. 255–79.

Cummins, S., and L. Kounine. 2016a. *Cultures of Conflict Resolution in Early Modern Europe*. Aldershot: Ashgate.

———. 2016b. 'Introduction: Confronting Conflict in Early Modern Europe', in S. Cummins and L. Kounine (eds), *Cultures of Conflict Resolution in Early Modern Europe*. Aldershot: Ashgate, pp. 1–14.

Dalla Corte, G. 2005. 'L'art et la manière: Infrajustice des médiateurs familiaux et des "arbitres qui arbitrent" en Catalogne au XVIIIe siècle', in M. Bertrand (ed.), *Pouvoirs des familles, familles de pouvoir*. Toulouse: CNRS, pp. 509–24.

Dartmann, C. 2003. 'Schiedsgerichtsbarkeit und die gütliche Beilegung von Konflikten in Westfalen: Das Beispiel der Abtei Liesborn', *Westfälische Forschungen. Zeitschrift des Westfälischen Instituts für Regionalgeschichte des Landschaftsverbandes Westfalen-Lippe* 53: 241–72.

Dauchy, S., et al. 2008. *La résolution des conflits. Justice publique et justice privée: Une frontière mouvante*. Lille: Centre d'histoire judiciaire.

Dauven, B., and X. Rousseaux (eds). 2012. 'Préférant miséricorde à rigueur de justice: Pratiques de la grâce (XIIIe–XVIIe siècles)', *Actes de la journée d'études de Louvain-la-Neuve*, 15 octobre 2007. Louvain-la-Neuve: UCL, Presses Universitaires de Louvain.

Davis, N.Z. 1987. *Fiction in the Archives: Pardon Tales and Their Tellers in Sixteenth-Century France*. Stanford: Stanford University Press.

Deutsch, A. 2005. 'Späte Sühne: Zur praktischen und rechtlichen Einordnung der Totschlagsühneverträge in Spätmittelalter und früher Neuzeit', *Zeitschrift der Savigny-Stiftung für Rechtsgeschichte. Germanistische Abteilung* 122: 113–49.

Dinges, M. 2000. 'Justiznutzungen als soziale Kontrolle', in A. Blauert and G. Schwerhoff (eds), *Kriminalitätsgeschichte: Beiträge zur Sozial- und Kulturgeschichte der Vormoderne*. Konstanz: UVK-Verl., pp. 503–44.

———. 2001. 'Usi della giustizia come elemento di controllo sociale nella prima età moderna', in M. Bellabarba, G. Schwerhoff and A. Zorzi (eds), *Criminalità e giustizia in Germania e in Italia: Pratiche giudiziarie e linguaggi giuridici tra tardo Medioevo ed età moderna / Kriminalität und Justiz in Deutschland und Italien: Rechtspraktiken und gerichtliche Diskurse in Spätmittelalter und Früher Neuzeit*. Bologna and Berlin: Duncker & Humblot, pp. 285–324.

Dunn, C. 2011. 'Forfeiting the Marriage Portion: Punishing Female Adultery in the Secular Courts of England and Italy', in M. Korpiola (ed.), *Regional Variations in Matrimonial Law and Custom in Europe, 1150–1600*. Leiden: Brill, pp. 161–87.

Dunn, D.E.S. (ed.). 1996. *Courts, Counties and the Capital in the Later Middle Ages*. New York: St. Martin's Press.

Ebeling, H.-H. 1992. '"Appellieren, Supplizieren und Brotbetteln steht jedermann frei": Reichskammergerichts-Prozesse aus dem westlichen Niedersachsen – Untersuchungen zu Streitgegenstand, Prozeßverlauf und Urteilsdurchsetzung', *Niedersächsisches Jahrbuch für Landesgeschichte* 64: 89–129.

Edigati, D. 2011. 'Pace e transazione nella storia del processo criminale: il caso toscano nell'età moderna', in P. Broggio and M.P. Paoli (eds), *Stringere la pace: Teorie e pratiche della conciliazione nell'Europa moderna (secoli XV–XVIII)*. Rome: Viella, pp. 369–410.

Eibach, J. 2004. 'Städtische Strafjustiz als konsensuale Praxis: Frankfurt a.M. im 17. und 18. Jahrhundert', in R. Schlögl (ed.), *Interaktion und Herrschaft: Die Politik der frühneuzeitlichen Stadt.* Konstanz: UVK-Verl., pp. 181–216.

———. 2005. 'Institutionalisierte Gewalt im urbanen Raum: "Stadtfrieden" in Deutschland und der Schweiz zwischen bürgerlicher und obrigkeitlicher Regelung (15.–18. Jahrhundert)', in C. Ulbrich, C. Jarzebowski and M. Hohkamp (eds), *Gewalt in der Frühen Neuzeit: Beiträge zur 5. Tagung der Arbeitsgemeinschaft Frühe Neuzeit im VHD.* Berlin: Duncker & Humblot, pp. 189–205.

———. 2008. 'The Containment of Violence in Central European Cities, 1500–1800', in R. McMahon (ed.), *Crime, Law and Popular Culture in Europe, 1500–1900.* Cullompton: Willan, pp. 52–73.

Eriksson, M., and B. Krug-Richter (eds). 2003. *Streitkulturen: Gewalt, Konflikt und Kommunikation in der ländlichen Gesellschaft der frühen Neuzeit.* Cologne: Böhlau.

Esders, S. 2007. *Rechtsverständnis und Konfliktbewältigung: Gerichtliche und außergerichtliche Strategien im Mittelalter.* Cologne: Böhlau.

Farcy, J.C. 2008. 'Justice privée et Justice publique: Approches de l'historiographie (France, XVIIIe–XXe siècles)', in S. Dauchy et al., *La résolution des conflits. Justice publique et justice privée: Une frontière mouvante.* Lille: Centre d'histoire judiciaire, pp. 23–32.

Farr, J.R. 1995. *Authority and Sexuality in Early Modern Burgundy (1550–1730).* Oxford: Oxford University Press.

Felstiner, W., and L. Williams. 1980. 'Mediation as an Alternative to Criminal Prosecution: Ideology and Limitations', in E. Blankenburg et al. (eds), *Alternative Rechtsformen und Alternativen zum Recht.* Opladen: Westdeutscher Verlag, pp. 195–214.

Feltes, T. 1993. 'Die außergerichtliche Erledigung von Konflikten: Historische Aspekte und aktuelle Bezüge', in H. Mohnhaupt and D. Simon (eds), *Vorträge zur Justizforschung: Geschichte und Theorie*, vol. 2. Frankfurt am Main: Klostermann, pp. 581–97.

Fikentscher, R., and A. Kolb (eds). 2012. *Schlichtungskulturen in Europa.* Halle (Saale): mdv.

Follain, A., B. Lemesle, M. Nassiet, É. Pierre and P. Quincy-Lefebvre (eds). 2008. *La violence et le judiciaire du Moyen Age à nos jours: Discours, perception, pratiques.* Rennes: Presses Universitaires de Rennes.

Fourgous, J. 1906. *L'arbitrage dans le droit français aux XIIIe et XIVe siècles.* Paris: Fontemoing.

Franke, E. 2013. *Von Schelmen, Schlägern, Schimpf und Schande: Kriminalität in einer frühneuzeitlichen Kleinstadt – Strasburg in der Uckermark.* Cologne: Böhlau.

Frey, S. 1928. *Das öffentlich-rechtliche Schiedsgericht in Oberitalien im XII. und XIII. Jahrhundert.* Lucerne: Keller.

Gaisser, E. 1955. *Minne und Recht in den Schöffensprüchen des Mittelalters.* Tübingen: Universitätsverlag.

Garnot, B. 1996. 'L'infrajudiciaire du Moyen Âge à l'époque contemporaine', in *Actes du colloque de Dijon, 5–6 octobre 1995.* Dijon: Éditions Universitaires de Dijon.

———. (ed.) 1997a. *Juges, notaires et policiers délinquants: XIV.–XX. Siècle.* Dijon: Éditions Universitaires de Dijon.

———. 1997b. 'Le bon magistrat et les mauvais juges à la fin du XVIIe siècle', in B. Garnot (ed.), *Juges, notaires et policiers délinquants.* Dijon: Éditions Universitaires de Dijon, pp. 17–25.

———. 1998. 'La petite délinquance du Moyen Age à l'époque contemporaine', in *Actes du colloque de Dijon 9 & 10 octobre 1997.* Dijon: Éditions Universitaires de Dijon.

———. 2000a. *Crime et justice aux XVIIe et XVIIIe siècles.* Paris: Imago.

———. 2000b. *Justice et société en France au XVIe, XVIIe et XVIIIe siècles.* Paris: Ophrys.

———. 2000c. 'Justice, infrajustice, parajustice et extra justice dans la France d'Ancien Régime', *Crime, Histoire & Sociétés / Crime, History & Societies* 4. http:// chs.revues.org/index855.html.

Godfrey, M. 2002. 'Arbitration and Dispute Resolution in Sixteenth Century Scotland', *Tijdschrift voor Rechtsgeschiedenis* 70: 109–36.

———. 2004. 'Arbitration in the Ius Commune and Scots Law', *Roman Legal Tradition* 2: 122–35.

———. 2015. 'Alternative Dispute Resolution within Law Courts in 16th-Century Scotland', in A. Cordes (ed.), *Mit Freundschaft oder mit Recht? Inner- und außergerichtliche Alternativen zur kontroversen Streitentscheidung im 15.–19. Jahrhundert*. Cologne: Böhlau, pp. 149–58.

Grolmann, M.D. 1689. *De officio et potestate arbitratorum*. Marburg: Stockius.

Grüne, N. 2011. *Dorfgesellschaft – Konflikterfahrung – Partizipationskultur: Sozialer Wandel und politische Kommunikation in Landgemeinden der badischen Rheinpfalz (1720–1850)*. Stuttgart: Lucius&Lucius.

Haack, J. 2008. *Der vergällte Alltag: Zur Streitkultur im 18. Jahrhundert*. Cologne: Böhlau.

Härter, K. 1999. 'Social Control and the Enforcement of Police-Ordinances in Early Modern Criminal Procedure', in H. Schilling (ed.), *Institutions, Instruments and Agents of Social Control and Discipline in Early Modern Europe*. Frankfurt am Main: Klostermann, pp. 39–63.

———. 2000. 'Strafverfahren im frühneuzeitlichen Territorialstaat: Inquisition, Entscheidungsfindung, Supplikation', in A. Blauert and G. Schwerhoff (eds), *Kriminalitätsgeschichte: Beiträge zur Sozial- und Kulturgeschichte der Vormoderne*. Konstanz: Universitätsverlag Konstanz, pp. 459–80.

———. 2001a. 'Erfahrungen in der frühneuzeitlichen Strafjustiz', in P. Münch (ed.), *'Erfahrung' als Kategorie der Frühneuzeitgeschichte*. Munich: Oldenbourg, pp. 377–88.

———. 2001b. 'Kriminalität und Praxis der Strafjustiz im geistlichen Territorialstaat des Alten Reiches: Sexuelle Delinquenz und Justiznutzung im frühneuzeitlichen Kurmainz', in M. Bellabarba, G. Schwerhoff and A. Zorzi (eds), *Criminalità e giustizia in Germania e in Italia: Pratiche giudiziarie e linguaggi giuridici tra tardo Medioevo ed età moderna / Kriminalität und Justiz in Deutschland und Italien: Rechtspraktiken und gerichtliche Diskurse in Spätmittelalter und Früher Neuzeit*. Bologna and Berlin: Duncker & Humblot, pp. 101–34.

———. 2002. 'Negoziare sanzioni e norme: la funzione e il significato delle suppliche nella giustizia penale della prima età moderna', in C. Nubola and A. Würgler (eds), *Suppliche e 'gravamina': Politica, amministrazione, giustizia in Europa (secoli XV–XVIII)*. Bologna: Il Mulino, pp. 263–305.

———. 2003a. 'Vom Kirchenasyl zum politischen Asyl: Asylrecht und Asylpolitik im frühneuzeitlichen Alten Reich', in M. Dreher (ed.), *Das antike Asyl: Kultische Grundlagen, rechtliche Ausgestaltung und politische Funktion*. Cologne: Böhlau, pp. 301–36.

———. 2003b. 'Zum Verhältnis von "Rechtsquellen" und territorialen Rahmenbedingungen in der Strafgerichtsbarkeit des 18. Jahrhunderts: Vagabondage und Diebstahl in der Entscheidungspraxis der Kurmainzer Landesregierung', in H. Rudolph and H. Schnabel-Schüle (eds), *Justiz = Justice = Justicia? Rahmenbedingungen von Strafjustiz im frühneuzeitlichen Europa*. Trier: Kliomedia, pp. 433–65.

———. 2005. *Policey und Strafjustiz in Kurmainz: Gesetzgebung, Normdurchsetzung und Sozialkontrolle im frühneuzeitlichen Territorialstaat*. Frankfurt am Main: Klostermann.

———. 2007. 'Frühneuzeitliche Asylkonflikte vor dem Reichshofrat und anderen europäischen Höchstgerichten', in L. Auer, W. Ogris and E. Ortlieb (eds), *Höchstgerichte in Europa: Bausteine frühneuzeitlicher Rechtsordnungen*. Cologne: Böhlau, pp. 139–62.

———. 2008. 'Strafen mit und neben der Zentralgewalt: Pluralität und Verstaatlichung des Strafens in der Frühen Neuzeit', in G. Schlee and B. Turner (eds), *Vergeltung: Eine interdisziplinäre Betrachtung der Rechtfertigung und Regulation von Gewalt*. Frankfurt am Main: Campus, pp. 105–26.

———. 2009. 'Die Entwicklung des Strafrechts in Mitteleuropa 1770–1848: Defensive Modernisierung, Kontinuitäten und Wandel der Rahmenbedingungen', in R. Habermas and G. Schwerhoff (eds), *Verbrechen im Blick: Perspektiven der neuzeitlichen Kriminalitätsgeschichte*. Frankfurt am Main: Campus, pp. 71–107.

———. 2011. 'Grazia ed equità nella dialettica tra sovranità, diritto e giustizia dal tardo medioevo all'età moderna', in K. Härter and C. Nubola (eds), *Grazia e giustizia: Figure della clemenza fra tardo medioevo ed età contemporanea*. Bologna: Il Mulino, pp. 43–70.

———. 2012. 'Konfliktregulierung im Umfeld frühneuzeitlicher Strafgerichte: Das Konzept der Infrajustiz in der historischen Kriminalitätsforschung', *Kritische Vierteljahresschrift für Gesetzgebung und Rechtsprechung* 95: 130–44.

———. 2017. 'Violent Crimes and Retaliation in the European Criminal Justice System between the Seventeenth and Nineteenth Century', in B. Turner and G. Schlee (eds), *On Retaliation: Towards an Interdisciplinary Understanding of a Basic Human Condition*. Oxford: Berghahn Books, pp. 101–21.

Härter, K., and C. Nubola (eds). 2011. *Grazia e giustizia: Figure della clemenza fra tardo medioevo ed età contemporanea*. Bologna: Il Mulino.

Hattenhauer, H. 1963. '"Minne und Recht" als Ordnungsprinzipien des mittelalterlichen Rechts', *Zeitschrift der Savigny-Stiftung für Rechtsgeschichte. Germanistische Abteilung* 80: 325–44.

Haug-Moritz, G., and S. Ullmann (eds). 2015. 'Frühneuzeitliche Supplikationspraxis und monarchische Herrschaft in europäischer Perspektive', *Beiträge zur Rechtsgeschichte Österreichs* 5(2): 178–369.

Heijden, M. van der. 2016. *Women and Crime in Early Modern Holland*. Leiden: Brill.

Hoareau-Dodinau, J. 2003. *Résolution des conflits*. Limoges: PULIM.

Hoareau-Dodinau, J., X. Rousseaux and P. Texier (eds). 1999. *Le pardon*. Limoges: PULIM.

Hoffmann, C.A. 2000. 'Außergerichtliche Einigungen bei Straftaten als vertikale und horizontale soziale Kontrolle im 16. Jahrhundert', in A. Blauert and G. Schwerhoff (eds), *Kriminalitätsgeschichte: Beiträge zur Sozial- und Kulturgeschichte der Vormoderne*. Konstanz: UVK-Verl., pp. 563–79.

Horn, C.H. 2006. 'Einführung in die Mediation', in J. Hengstl and U. Sick (eds), *Recht gestern und heute: Festschrift zum 85. Geburtstag von Richard Haase*. Wiesbaden: Harrassowitz, pp. 267–80.

Kamp, H. 2001. *Friedensstifter und Vermittler im Mittelalter*. Darmstadt: Wissenschaftliche Buchgesellschaft.

Kampmann, C. 2001. *Arbiter und Friedensstiftung: Die Auseinandersetzung um den politischen Schiedsrichter im Europa der frühen Neuzeit*. Paderborn: Schöningh.

———. 2010. 'Schiedsgerichtsbarkeit', in *Enzyklopädie der Neuzeit* 11. Stuttgart: J.B. Metzler, pp. 713–17.

Kesper-Biermann, S. 2012. 'Gerechtigkeit, Politik und Güte: Gnade im Deutschland des 19. Jahrhunderts', *Jahrbuch für Juristische Zeitgeschichte* 13: 21–47.

Kim-Wawrzinek, U. 1974. *Minne und Recht: Untersuchungen zu funktionalen Wortgruppen bei rechtlichen Handlungsverläufen im 12. und 13. Jahrhundert*. Bonn: Universitätsverlag.

Klammer, P. 2004. *In Unehren beschlaffen: Unzucht vor kirchlicher und weltlicher Gerichtsbarkeit im frühneuzeitlichen Salzburger Lungau*. Frankfurt am Main: Lang.

Kobler, M. 1967. *Das Schiedsgerichtswesen nach bayerischen Quellen des Mittelalters*. Munich: C.H. Beck.

———. 1975. 'Zu den Anfängen der Schiedsgerichtsbarkeit in Südtirol', in S. Gagnér, H. Schlosser and W. Wiegand (eds), *Festschrift für Hermann Krause*. Cologne: Böhlau, pp. 94–109.

Kornblum, U. 1976. 'Zum schiedsrichterlichen Verfahren im späten Mittelalter', in H.-J. Becker et al. (eds), *Rechtsgeschichte als Kulturgeschichte: Festschrift für Adalbert Erler zum 70. Geburtstag*. Aalen: Scienti, pp. 289–312.

Korpiola, M. (ed.). 2011. *Regional Variations in Matrimonial Law and Custom in Europe, 1150–1600*. Leiden: Brill.

———. 2015. 'Marriage-Counselling and Reconciliation in Marriage Cases in the Ecclesiastical Courts of Reformation Sweden (16th–17th Centuries)', in A. Cordes (ed.), *Mit Freundschaft oder mit Recht? Inner- und außergerichtliche Alternativen zur kontroversen Streitentscheidung im 15.–19. Jahrhundert*. Cologne: Böhlau, pp. 133–48.

Kotkas, T. 2007. 'Pardoning in Nineteenth-Century Finland', *Rechtsgeschichte* 10: 152–68.

Krause, H. 1930. *Die geschichtliche Entwicklung des Schiedsgerichtswesens in Deutschland*. Berlin: Heymann.

Krug-Richter, B. 1997. 'Konfliktregulierung zwischen dörflicher Sozialkontrolle und patrimonialer Gerichtsbarkeit: Das Rügegericht in der Westfälischen Gerichtsherrschaft Canstein 1718/19', *Historische Anthropologie* 5: 212–28.

———. 2004. 'Peasants on Trial: Village Conflicts between Local Social Control and Manorial Court', in K. Sundberg, T. Germundsson and K. Hansen (eds), *Modernisation and Tradition: European Local and Manorial Societies 1500–1900*. Lund: Nordic Academic Press, pp. 351–73.

Krug-Richter, B., and R.-E. Mohrmann (eds). 2004. *Praktiken des Konfliktaustrags in der Frühen Neuzeit*. Münster: Rhema.

Landau, N. 1984. *The Justices of the Peace, 1679–1760*. Berkeley: University of California Press.

Latini, C. 2002. *Il privilegio dell'immunità: Diritto d'asilo e giurisdizione nell'ordine giuridico dell'età moderna*. Milan: Giuffrè.

Lefebvre-Teillar, A. 2008. 'Arbiter, arbitrator seu amicabilis compositor', *Revue de l'arbitrage* 3: 369–87.

Loetz, F. 2000. 'L'infrajudiciaire: Facetten und Bedeutung eines Konzepts', in A. Blauert and G. Schwerhoff (eds), *Kriminalitätsgeschichte: Beiträge zur Sozial- und Kulturgeschichte der Vormoderne*. Konstanz: UVK-Verl., pp. 545–62.

Lück, H. 1999. 'Sühne und Strafgerichtsbarkeit im Kursachsen des 15. und 16. Jahrhunderts', in H. Schlosser and D. Willoweit (eds), *Neue Wege strafrechtsgeschichtlicher Forschung*. Cologne: Böhlau, pp. 83–99.

———. 2012. 'Von Ombudsleuten, Mediatoren, Schlichtern und Sühneverträgen – Institutionen der Konfliktlösung außerhalb des gerichtlichen Streitverfahrens im Mittelalter', in R. Fikentscher and A. Kolb (eds), *Schlichtungskulturen in Europa*. Halle (Saale): mdv, pp. 85–101.

Ludwig, U. 2008. *Das Herz der Justitia: Gestaltungspotentiale territorialer Herrschaft in der Strafrechts- und Gnadenpraxis am Beispiel Kursachsens 1548–1648*. Konstanz: UVK-Verl.

Lutz, A. 2006. *Ehepaare vor Gericht: Konflikte und Lebenswelten in der Frühen Neuzeit*. Frankfurt am Main: Campus.

Mantecón, T.A. 2002. 'El peso de la infrajudicialidad en el control del crimen durante la Edad Moderna', *Estudis: Revista de historia moderna* 28: 43–75.

———. 2003. 'Popular Culture and Arbitration of Disputes in the Northern Spanish 18th Century', in L.A. Knafla (ed.), *Crimes, Punishment and Reform in Europe*. Westport, CT: Praeger Publishers, pp. 39–55.

———. 2004. 'Social Control from Below: Popular Arbitration of Disputes in Old Regime Spain', in H. Roodenburg and P. Spierenburg (eds), *Social Control in Europe 1, 1500–1800*. Columbus: Ohio State University Press.

———. 2007. 'The Patterns of Violence in Early Modern Spain', *Journal of the Historical Society* 7: 229–64.

Marcarelli, M. 2004. 'Pratiche digiustizia in età moderna: riti di pacificazione e *mediazione nella* Terraferma veneta', in G. Chiodi and C. Povolo (eds), *L'amministrazione della giustizia penale nella Repubblica di Venezia (secoli XVI–XVIII)*, vol. 2. Verona: Cierre Edizioni, pp. 259–309.

Martinage, R. 2008. 'Compromis, transaction, cession de droits en matière pénale', in S. Dauchy et al., *La résolution des conflits: Justice publique et justice privée. Une frontière mouvante.* Lille: Centre d'histoire judiciaire, pp. 64–73.

Martone, L. 1984. *Arbiter – arbitrator: Forme di giustizia privata nell'età del diritto commune.* Naples: Jovene.

Mayenburg, D. v. 2014. 'Begnadigung aus rechtshistorischer Perspektive', in C. Waldhoff (ed.), *Gnade vor Recht – Gnade durch Recht?* Berlin: Duncker & Humblot, pp. 33–74.

———. 2016. 'Streitschlichtung auf dem Lande: Untersuchungen zur südwestdeutschen Schiedsordnung zwischen Spätmittelalter und Bauernkrieg (Conflict Resolution in the Countryside: A Study on the Rules of Arbitration in Southwestern Germany between Late Middle Ages and the Great Peasant War (1525)', *Max Planck Institute for European Legal History Research Paper Series* No. 2016-12. https://ssrn.com/abstract=2866977.

McMahon, R. (ed.). 2008. *Crime, Law and Popular Culture in Europe, 1500–1900.* Cullompton: Willan.

Menkel-Meadow, C., L.P. Love and A. Kupfer Schneider (eds). 2006. *Mediation: Practice, Policy, and Ethics.* New York: Aspen.

Meyerhuber, S. 2004. *Die privilegierte Austragsgerichtsbarkeit der freien Reichsstadt Weißenburg im Nordgau.* Frankfurt am Main: Lang.

Misericordia, M.D. 2001. 'La mediazione giudiziaria dei conflitti sociali alla fine del medioevo: Tribunali ecclesiastici e resistenza comunitaria in Valtellina', in M. Bellabarba, G. Schwerhoff and A. Zorzi (eds), *Criminalità e giustizia in Germania e in Italia: Pratiche giudiziarie e linguaggi giuridici tra tardo Medioevo ed età moderna / Kriminalität und Justiz in Deutschland und Italien: Rechtspraktiken und gerichtliche Diskurse in Spätmittelalter und Früher Neuzeit.* Bologna and Berlin: Duncker & Humblot, pp. 135–71.

Moeglin, J.M. 2004. *L'intercession du Moyen Âge à l'époque moderne: Autour d'une pratique sociale.* Genf: Droz.

Montazel, L. 2001. 'La peine privée en France et Allemagne (XVIème–XIXème siècles): Essai sur une notion doctrinale commune', *Ius commune* 28: 161–202.

Muchembled, R. 1989. *La violence au village: Sociabilité et comportements populaires en Artois du XVe au XVIIe siècle.* Turnhout: Brepols.

Musin, A., X. Rousseaux and F. Vesentini (eds). 2008. *Violence, conciliation et repression: Recherches sur l'histoire du crime, de l'Antiquité au XXIe Siècle.* Louvain-la-Neuve: Presses Universitaires de Louvain.

Nassiet, M. 2011. *La violence, une histoire sociale: France, XVIe–XVIIIe siècles.* Paris: Champ Vallon.

Niccoli, O. 2007. *Perdonare: idee, pratiche, rituali in Italia tra Cinque e Seicento.* Rome: Laterza.

Nubola, C., and A. Würgler (eds). 2002. *Suppliche e 'gravamina': Politica, amministrazione, giustizia in Europa (secoli XV–XVIII)*. Bologna: Il Mulino.

Österberg, E., and S. Sogner (eds). 2000. *People Meet the Law: Control and Conflict-Handling in the Courts. The Nordic Countries in the Post-Reformation and Pre-Industrial Period*. Oslo: Universitetsforlaget.

Petit, J.G. 2002. 'La Justice en France, 1789–1939: Une étatisation modèle?', *Crime, Histoire & Sociétés / Crime, History & Societies* 6: 85–103.

———. 2003. *Une justice de proximité: La justice de paix (1790–1958)*. Paris: Presses Universitaires de France.

Piant, H. 1998. 'La petite délinquance entre infrajudiciaire, procédure civile et répression pénale: L'injure et sa réparation dans la prévôté de Vaucouleurs sous l'Ancien Régime', in B. Garnoit (ed.), *La petite délinquance du Moyen Age à l'époque contemporaine: Actes du colloque de Dijon 9 & 10 octobre 1997*. Dijon: Éditions Universitaires de Dijon, pp. 441–53.

———. 2006. *Une justice ordinaire: Justice civile et criminelle dans la prévôté royale de Vaucouleurs sous l'Ancien Régime*. Rennes: Presses Universitaires de Rennes.

———. 2008. '"Car tels excès ne sont pas permis": l'injure et la résolution judiciaire dans un tribunal de première instance sous l'Ancien Régime', in A. Follain et al. (eds), *La violence et le judiciaire du Moyen Age à nos jours: Discours, perception, pratiques*. Rennes: Presses Universitaires de Rennes, pp. 125–36.

Rehse, B. 2008. *Die Supplikations- und Gnadenpraxis in Brandenburg-Preußen: Eine Untersuchung am Beispiel der Kurmark unter Friedrich Wilhelm II. (1786–1797)*. Berlin: Duncker & Humblot.

Roebuck, D. 2002. *The Charitable Arbitrator: How to Mediate and Arbitrate in Louis XIV's France*. Oxford: Holo Books.

———. 2006. 'The Prehistory of Dispute Resolution in England', *Arbitration* 72: 93–103.

———. 2010. *Disputes and Differences: Comparisons in Law, Language and History*. Oxford: Holo Books.

———. 2013. *Mediation and Arbitration in the Middle Ages: England 1154–1558*. Oxford: Holo Books.

Roeck, B. 1993. 'Criminal Procedure in the Holy Roman Empire in Early Modern Times', *International Association for the History of Crime and Criminal Justice Bulletin* 18: 21–40.

Rose, C. 2012. '"To Be Remedied of Any Vendetta": Petitions and the Avoidance of Violence in Early Modern Parma', *Crime, Histoire & Sociétés* 16: 5–27. http://chs.revues.org/1355.

Rössner, D. 2006. 'Konfliktregelung im Strafrecht', in J. Hengstl and U. Sick (eds), *Recht gestern und heute: Festschrift zum 85. Geburtstag von Richard Haase*. Wiesbaden: Harrassowitz, pp. 319–31.

Rousseaux, X. 1999. 'From Case to Crime: Homicide Regulation in Medieval and Modern Europe', in D. Willoweit (ed.), *Die Entstehung des öffentlichen Strafrechts: Bestandsaufnahme eines europäischen Forschungsproblems*. Cologne: Böhlau, pp. 143–75.

Rousseaux, X., and R. Lévy (eds). 1997. *Le pénal dans tous ses Etats: Justice, Etats et Sociétés en Europe (XIIe–XXe siècles)*. Brussels: Faculté Universitaire Saint-Louis.

Rudolph, H. 2001a. *Eine gelinde Regierungsart: Peinliche Strafjustiz im geistlichen Territorium. Das Hochstift Osnabrück (1716–1803)*. Konstanz: UVK-Verl.

———. 2001b. 'Konfliktregelung als Leitprinzip frühneuzeitlicher Strafjustiz: Die Peinliche Gerichtsbarkeit im Hochstift Osnabrück im 18. Jahrhundert', in M. Bellabarba, G. Schwerhoff and A. Zorzi (eds), *Criminalità e giustizia in Germania e in Italia: Pratiche giudiziarie e linguaggi giuridici tra tardo Medioevo ed età moderna / Kriminalität und Justiz in Deutschland und Italien: Rechtspraktiken und gerichtliche Diskurse in Spätmittelalter und Früher Neuzeit*. Bologna and Berlin: Duncker & Humblot, pp. 65–84.

Ruff, J.R. 2001. *Violence in Early Modern Europe*. Cambridge: Cambridge University Press.
———. 2008. 'Popular Violence and its Prosecution in Seventeenth- and Eighteenth-Century France', in R. McMahon (ed.), *Crime, Law and Popular Culture in Europe, 1500–1900*. Cullompton: Willan, pp. 32–51.
Sälter, G. 2000. 'Lokale Ordnung und soziale Kontrolle in der frühen Neuzeit: Zur außergerichtlichen Konfliktregulierung in einem kultur- und sozialhistorischen Kontext', *Kriminologisches Journal* 32: 19–42.
Sbriccoli, M. 2001. 'Giustizia negoziata, giustizia egemonica: Riflessioni su una nuova fase degli studi di storia della giustizia criminale', in M. Bellabarba, G. Schwerhoff and A. Zorzi (eds), *Criminalità e giustizia in Germania e in Italia: Pratiche giudiziarie e linguaggi giuridici tra tardo Medioevo ed età moderna / Kriminalität und Justiz in Deutschland und Italien: Rechtspraktiken und gerichtliche Diskurse in Spätmittelalter und Früher Neuzeit*. Bologna and Berlin: Duncker & Humblot, pp. 345–64.
Schaffstein, F. 1987. 'Wiedergutmachung und Genugtuung im Strafprozeß vom 16. bis zum Ausgang des 18. Jahrhunderts', in H. Schöch (ed.), *Wiedergutmachung und Strafrecht*. Munich: Fink, pp. 9–27.
Schedensack, C. 1997. 'Formen der außergerichtlichen gütlichen Konfliktbeilegung, Vermittlung und Schlichtung am Beispiel nachbarrechtlicher Konflikte in Münster (1600–1650)', *Westfälische Forschungen* 47: 643–67.
———. 2007. *Nachbarn im Konflikt: Zur Entstehung und Beilegung von Rechtsstreitigkeiten um Haus und Hof im frühneuzeitlichen Münster*. Münster: Aschendorff.
Schmidt, C.D. 2009. *Sühne oder Sanktion? Die öffentliche Kirchenbuße in den Fürstbistümern Münster und Osnabrück während des 17. und 18. Jahrhunderts*. Münster: Aschendorff.
Schuster, P. 2000. *Eine Stadt vor Gericht: Recht und Alltag im spätmittelalterlichen Konstanz*. Paderborn: Schöningh.
Schwerhoff, G. 2011. *Historische Kriminalitätsforschung*. Frankfurt am Main: Campus.
Shoemaker, K. 2011. *Sanctuary and Crime in the Middle Ages, 400–1500*. New York: Fordham University Press.
Sigurdsson, J.V. 2013. 'The Role of Arbitration in the Settlement of Disputes in Iceland c. 1000–1300', in P. Andersen et al. (eds), *Law and Disputing in the Middle Ages: Proceedings of the Ninth Carlsberg Academy Conference on Medieval Legal History 2012*. Copenhagen: DJØF Publishing, pp. 123–36.
Taylor, S.K. 2009. *Honor and Violence in Golden Age Spain*. New Haven, CT: Yale University Press.
Tedoldi, L. 2008. *La spada e la bilancia: la giustizia penale nell'Europa moderna (secc. XVI–XVIII)*. Rome: Carocci.
Thauer, J. 2001. *Gerichtspraxis in der ländlichen Gesellschaft: Eine mikrohistorische Untersuchung am Beispiel eines altmärkischen Patrimonialgerichts um 1700*. Berlin: Berlin Verlag Arno Spitz.
Turner, B. 2005. *Asyl und Konflikt von der Antike bis heute: Rechtsethnologische Untersuchungen*. Berlin: Reimer.
Walch, A. 2009. *Histoire de l'adultère (XVIe–XIXe siècle)*. Paris: Perrin.
Wenzel, E. 2008. 'Une autre justice? Les voies "alternatives" dans l'ancienne procedure criminelle', in S. Dauchy et al., *La résolution des conflits. Justice publique et justice privée: Une frontière mouvante*. Lille: Centre d'histoire judiciaire, pp. 74–78.
Wettmann, P. 1987. '"Arbitrator" und "Adjudicator": Zur Bedeutung der englischen Justices of the Peace bei der formellen und informellen Konfliktregelung in ländlichen Gemeinden des 18. Jahrhunderts', *Kriminologisches Journal, Beiheft* 2: 111–30.

Willoweit, D. 1996. 'Vertragen, Klagen, Rügen: Reaktionen auf Konflikt und Verbrechen in ländlichen Rechtsquellen Frankens', in D. Rödel and J. Schneider (eds), *Strukturen der Gesellschaft im Mittelalter: Interdisziplinäre Mediävistik in Würzburg*. Wiesbaden: L. Reichert, pp. 196–224.

———. 2002. 'Richten nach Gnade: Beobachtungen an Hand ländlicher Quellen vom Mittelrhein und angrenzender Landschaften', in H. Schlosser, R. Sprandel and D. Willoweit (eds), *Herrschaftliches Strafen seit dem Mittelalter*. Cologne: Böhlau, pp. 189–205.

Winkelbauer, T. 1992. '"Und sollen sich die Parteien gütlich miteinander vertragen": Zur Behandlung von Streitigkeiten und von "Injurien" vor den Patrimonialgerichten in Ober- und Niederösterreich in der frühen Neuzeit', *ZRG GA* 109: 129–58.

Wright, M., and B. Galaway (eds). 1989. *Mediation and Criminal Justice: Victims, Offenders and Community*. London: Sage.

Würgler, A. 1999. 'Suppliche e "gravamina" nella prima età moderna: la storiografia di lingua tedesca', *Annali dell'Istituto storico italo-germanico in Trento* 30(25): 515–46.

Zekoll, J., M. Bälz and I. Amelung. 2014. *Formalisation and Flexibilisation in Dispute Resolution*. Leiden: Brill.

Zorzi, A. 2001. 'Negoziazione penale, legittimazione giuridica e poteri urbani nell'Italia comunale', in M. Bellabarba, G. Schwerhoff and A. Zorzi (eds), *Criminalità e giustizia in Germania e in Italia: Pratiche giudiziarie e linguaggi giuridici tra tardo Medioevo ed età moderna / Kriminalität und Justiz in Deutschland und Italien: Rechtspraktiken und gerichtliche Diskurse in Spätmittelalter und Früher Neuzeit*. Bologna and Berlin: Duncker & Humblot, pp. 13–34.

Chapter 2

Adjudication or Negotiation

Mediation as Non-modern Element in Conflict Resolution in the Nordic Countries

Pia Letto-Vanamo

Introduction

In European legal literature on developments in conflict resolution, the narrative of so-called modern law dominates. The narrative – partly inspired by the ideas of Max Weber – is referred to especially in discussions of the rationale but also of the legitimacy of current legal order(s). This is the law of the modern nation state, where parliamentary legislation stands at the top of the hierarchy of legal sources. At the same time, the idea of man-made, positive law (and legal positivism) is important, and a quite clear division of labour is drawn between various legal actors (the legislator, the judiciary and legal scholarship). The power of the courts and the legitimacy of adjudication are based on the status of the courts as state institutions, and on the idea of judgement as 'the judge's authoritative command' on the law applicable in the case concerned.[1]

It is easy to agree with this narrative, especially concerning the European continent and the era after the French Revolution – that of national state legislation. During this period, judges (who became state servants) have been obligated or assumed to 'follow' the law, while the university education of legal professionals has focused on training to interpret and apply national, positive law. This also constitutes a foundation narrative for 'no longer modern' law (late modern or postmodern law) discussed by many scholars today. Thus, we seem to be facing the weakening power of nation states, tendencies towards privatized legal regulation and towards alternatives to ordinary (court-based) dispute resolution methods such as mediation.[2]

Again, legal historians are interested in the characteristics of 'not yet modern' law. Scholars seem to agree at least that the so-called pre-modern period included many local and regional variations and was characterized by a plurality of legal orders. However, the main arenas for legal communication, for discussions on justice–injustice (*Recht–Unrecht*) – that is, law applicable in a certain case – were local court sessions. Hence, one can detect early courts or judiciary obtaining their authority from various sources of rule (*Herrschaft* according to Max Weber), but also those whose competences were based on a communitarian and consensual form of conflict resolution. Concerning the latter, which are typical for the history of dispute resolution in the Nordic countries, the most crucial questions – having parallels with the late modern law period, that of the weak(ening) power of the sovereign state – are those of the legitimacy of conflict resolution and of the acceptance of law created by the pre-modern, non-state institutions. Indeed, it is not difficult to draw parallels with modern models of ADR (alternative dispute resolution), especially with the current mediation systems based on the voluntary and active participation – both in the procedure and in regard to the material outcome – of the parties themselves and of other members of the (interest) community.

Hence, in the following I discuss questions related to 'non-modern' dispute resolution. In particular, notions such as the dichotomies of conflict–cooperation and decision–negotiation, which illuminate the relationship between adjudication and mediation, will be dealt with. The main focus is on the history of conflict resolution in systems without any – or with weak – authoritative power above the conflicting parties. First, however, some general issues mainly highlighted by current trends of conflict resolution will be taken up.

From Court Litigation to Mediation

Today, a wide consensus exists as to the central role of the court system in guaranteeing individuals' access to justice. In modern (Western) societies, the courts protect the rights and freedoms of citizens against arbitrary interference, but also ensure that they do not unlawfully interfere with the rights and freedoms of others. However, many other – public and private – institutions resolving disputes and providing legal services also play an important role in the access to justice approach.[3] It can be observed that the increasing use of alternative means of dispute resolution at least partly reflects the problems and low standards of court services and court proceedings. In fact, many have argued that the current Western adjudication system is in crisis. Courts' caseloads have been growing for a long time, but at the same time, the long duration and high costs of court proceedings have prevented individuals from getting justice through the courts. Thus, people have turned their attention to extrajudicial out-of-court alternatives.[4]

More generally, the status and role of ordinary court procedure in dispute resolution reflect the legitimacy and trust that courts enjoy among people in a particular society. Clearly, an increase in differentiation or fragmentation in society seems to weaken the position of the (state) judiciary. Today, in our 'late modern' society, it is quite difficult to speak of one idea of justice; indeed, various meanings are attached to it. At the same time, justice as defined or guaranteed by the ordinary courts does not automatically enjoy acceptance among members of society. The increasing importance of ADR has in many comments been linked not only to problems with court procedures but also to the 'privatization' of the law (with soft law, self-regulation, governance etc.), legal and cultural pluralism, social ruptures and so on.[5]

In the Nordic countries as well,[6] one can recognize the common European tendency to move away from court litigation towards privatized conflict resolution, especially through mediation, which has become popular during this millennium.[7] There are – even in certain criminal law matters – various opportunities for 'amicable conflict solving' outside of courts, organized by ecclesiastical and professional organizations but also by state and municipal authorities. In courts, again, more emphasis has been placed on alternative procedures, the latest (and quite anachronistic) example being court-annexed mediation, with a judge in the role of mediator helping the disputing parties to reach a mutually satisfactory solution. At the same time, the idea of 'procedural justice' has been stressed. In fact, one can speak of a client-centred approach, which emphasizes the parties' subjective experience of (procedural) justice[8] and the interaction between the judge and the parties. Thus, important aspects of the perception of justice today are not only the impartiality and high professional standards of the judge, but also an opportunity for the parties to 'participate' in the proceedings, and the manner in which they are treated during the court procedure.

In mediation[9] – whether it is organized by private institutions or by courts – parties are always the main actors. Mediation is voluntary and requires the parties to agree to it.[10] The purpose of mediation is to help the parties to find a solution that is acceptable to both/all of them. This means that the result of mediation may be based more on what is reasonable under the circumstances than on strict application of the law. Hence, parties' activity in discussions and their ability to listen to each other are crucial for a successful mediation procedure. The mediator is in charge of the process, while the parties are in charge of the outcome: a mutually satisfactory resolution of their conflict, and not an outcome that accords with the substantive law in force.[11] It can in fact be maintained that the legitimacy of the mediation system and the acceptance of its outcomes rests on the active role – or the participation – of the conflicting parties. Nevertheless, they are not only the key actors in negotiating the content of the solution, but at the same time actors in a formalistic procedure administrated by the mediator(s), which also promotes legitimation of the mediation system.

From Consensual to Authoritative Law

A tension seems to exist between the ideal of material justice and a substantively correct judgement (based on the application of the law) on the one hand, and the ideal of 'negotiated law' and a pragmatically acceptable compromise on the other. The former can be understood as a fundament of the 'ideal type' model of Western modern dispute resolution, and the latter as its counter conception. Interestingly, the tension or competition not only characterizes current legal developments but is observable in the history of conflict resolution, too. In the following, examples taken from Nordic legal history serve to illustrate the slow appearance of the ideal of material justice – or the slow disappearance of the consensual element – as the result of adjudication

For a long time, local assemblies were the main arenas for legal communication in the Nordic countries.[12] No big cities existed, and a trained legal profession was a phenomenon that occurred only in the nineteenth century. In rural areas, common – in modern terms, legal and administrative – affairs were dealt with by a local assembly, the *ting*.[13] The *ting* pertains specifically to the self-determination of peasant communities, where communication was oral and documents, or indeed writing, were hardly ever used, and where all affairs became public as soon as they were introduced in a *ting* session.[14] In addition, we know from Sweden and Finland that the *ting*, held twice or three times annually, were the main events of the year. As many people as possible wished to be present when their affairs, and those of their neighbours, were considered and conflicts regulated through practices that resemble modes of arbitration and mediation. Even as late as the beginning of the seventeenth century, it was usual for people to attend the *ting* in large numbers, to arrive at the *ting* house, its yard or other nearby houses. At the same time, it was evident that being present made a difference: the judge/head of the assembly (*häradshövding*)[15] would put questions to the audience, for example on drawing boundaries between pieces of land or on the paternity of a child born out of wedlock, or would ask for their views on such matters as the severity of a criminal penalty or the form in which a penalty should be enforced.

For centuries, the cases in the *ting* sessions were either simple criminal cases or civil disputes relating to the use and ownership of land. Criminal law was act-oriented, with little regard to the motives of the offender. As late as the sixteenth century, every misdeed was regulated through a 'price', which could be characterized as a combination of compensation and fine: it was divided between the (accusing) party, the judge (*häradshövding*, head of the judicial circuit) and the king. A bruise cost three marks, a wound six marks, and the price of manslaughter was forty marks. In most cases, convictions were based on eyewitness reports or confessions. In the absence of a witness or confession, oath taking was the normal procedure. A person suspected and accused (by the plaintiff) of a given act (crime) was given the opportunity to deny any responsibility (and not to pay compensation/fines) by swearing an oath confirmed by the so-called oath-helpers. Civil disputes concerned land, that is, the very basis of all economic activity. These disputes were normally decided with the support of 'assayers', 'jurors' or other groups/panels of laymen – that is, by reference to an act or opinion of the community.

It seems obvious that the participation of community representatives – usually proposed by the parties, and performing in various roles as oath-helpers, assayers, arbitrators or *nämnde*-men – in the decision making could also legitimize solutions adverse to the parties, and make it more likely that the decision would also be observed as 'good law'. Only later did the legitimacy of a judgement become linked to a command or the authority of a judge, and much later still to the authority of (positive) law and to the state judiciary – independent of the legislator and enforcement power – that applied it.

The competition between the 'old' traditional, consensual, negotiated law and the 'new' authoritative law can already be seen in the Nordic medieval laws. One of the most fascinating examples can be found in Article 17 of the Chapter of *Edsöre* in the Law of East Gothland (Östgötaland, ca. 1290).[16] The Article deals (1) with the earlier conflict resolution procedure involving ordeals; (2) with the current, prevailing procedure involving parties' oaths; and (3) with the newer procedure and its idea of examining the 'substantive truth' and making the king's decision on the legal sanction.

It is stated in the Article that, earlier, the 'guilt' or 'innocence' of the accused would have been determined by ordeal, involving holding a hot iron. Birger Jarl (Jarl of Sweden 1248–1266), however, had forbidden ordeal by iron, which was superseded by a new procedure: a procedure at the king's assembly (*räfst* or *ting*) and with a physical and/or capital punishment. Before the penalty was imposed, the investigation and confirmation of the criminal act and of the (actual) killer first had to be made. This was done with the help of testimony, or by the *nämnd.*

The accusers, however, had a choice between various 'procedural forms', and between two kinds of outcome: the death of the defendant and compensation (for restoring a peaceful relationship between the parties) of 40 marks. The accused could then avoid the 40 marks with his oath and the support of three times twelve oath-helpers, as the law stated:

> Now it may happen that a wife kills her husband or a husband his wife. Then he, if he does so, may be executed by the stake and she be stoned if she does so.
>
> Now they are suspected of this crime. It is then said by the law that they shall defend themselves by iron and ordeal, but since Birger Jarl has abolished the proof of hot iron it is so that if he who accuses asks for the law of the king he shall have the person accused caught and have the case investigated by reliable witnesses if reliable witnesses are to be found, and

> by force if he does not admit freely. If such is found that corroborates the truth thereof, or testimony, or if he himself confesses, the man shall be executed by the stake and the woman be stoned.
>
> If he who accuses will not ask for the law of the king but summons and seeks his right, then he who is accused may with the oath of three times twelve men maintain that he did not do it; if he cannot produce the oath he shall pay 40 marks but not lose his life. (Collin and Schlyter 1830; my translation)[17]

The very original idea in cases of manslaughter of a local free man in East Gothland, as in other Swedish provinces, had been to allow the kinsmen of the victim to kill a culprit as retaliation, but only if he was caught red-handed. If they caught him but did not want to kill him themselves, they had to transport him to the assembly (*ting*) and present 'evidence' against him (e.g. asking him to hold a hot iron). After that it was possible to behead him. If the culprit was not already in custody, he was to be summoned to the *ting* and sentenced. However, the kinsmen could make a choice for redress instead of killing. In that case, the 'worth of a man' (40 marks) had to be paid.[18] Article 17 also mentions another, newer way of settling disputes besides referring them to the traditional local *ting*: the accuser/s could choose to have the case dealt with by the so-called *konungens räfst*, a term for the king's involvement in dispute resolution, which encompassed the king's assembly (*ting*) with a panel of men (*nämd*) charged with investigating the crime.

It is possible to argue that the types of procedure depended on the desired outcome, the sanction, which could be either economic redress (in modern terms: first private compensation, later fine; in Swedish *saköre*) or the death (first revenge, later capital punishment) of the accused. Also according to the cited text, the accusers had a choice between procedural forms, but also a choice between redress of 40 marks and the death of the counterparty.

In fact, the procedure entailing 40 marks might be characterized as a type of arbitration or mediation, which would end in reconciliation (in modern mediation terms: in amicable solution). A decision involving 40 marks was more a recommendation than an authoritative judgement. Still, the accused could avoid paying the 40 marks by swearing himself free, through oaths given by himself and by his three times twelve oath-helpers. If he did not manage to find as many as were required to guarantee his probity, he had to pay. But he lost his life (through execution by the stake or stoning) only if the accuser had chosen to bring the case to the king's *räfst*. At the same time, the legitimizing basis of this 'painful' sanction – that is, capital or corporal punishment – was different.[19]

Generally speaking, modern criminal law procedure is not consensual but authoritative. This was also true of the medieval and pre-modern court procedure, in which – in contrast to the early procedure involving compensation and/

or fines and where the parties dominated the procedure – the defendant was subject to the acts of the (church's or king's) authority. In fact, we can argue that death as a punishment appeared along with the involvement of the king in the legal/judicial sphere. This was a new type of retaliation, one that became 'legalized' by the king through the formalities of court procedure. Thus, the retaliation of violence and criminal behaviour became a (real) punishment decided by the court. At the same time, it became important to investigate the criminal act, to know the actual actor in the crime concerned.[20]

Legitimation through Participation

For a long time the sentence was formulated in an old '*ting* community' way: it was impossible to let the king, or his officials, solely decide about the criminal. Help was needed from the panel of men called the *nämnd*, discussed in detail below. According to the Law of East Gothland, the death penalty was imposed by the king's *räfst*. Besides a king's official, the panel known as the king's *nämnd* was elected in the presence and with the consent of the parties from among law-knowing (*rätt-rådiga*) men, who were not the parties' relatives or men who might be partial in other ways.[21] This panel investigated the wrongdoing and decided whether it was a crime against the king's peace (*edsörebrott*), and thus whether the accused should be sentenced to death or freed.

In fact, references to the king's *ting* or nämnd (*konungs räfst*) and the articles of court procedure in cases breaching the king's peace belong to a newer and for a long time narrower layer of law. The category of *edsörebrott* included conflicts over landownership, so-called crimes of treason and other serious crimes, which violated the king's peace, of which killing a family member was one. However, whether the act qualified as a crime against the king's peace had to be determined by the king's *räfst*, which then enabled imposition of a sentence involving capital punishment.

The term *nämnd*, as already used in this chapter, belongs to the history of Swedish court procedure and dates back at least as far as the Middle Ages.[22] At first, these panels of men, drawn from among members of the *ting* community, considered only given types of cases, but later one panel was appointed for the duration of the entire *ting*. At the same time, the composition of the panel became more established, so that some of its members also sat on the panel during the next sessions in the same *ting* district. It is also known that the '*nämnde*-men' were normally selected from among the most respected and wealthiest farmers of the district.

Generally speaking, we can assume that one of the main functions of the *nämnd* was to represent the local community, but also to participate in the settlement of disputes arising between members of the community. These men were aware of local affairs and knew the local people.[23] According to the Law of

East Gothland, the members of the king's *nämnd* swore an oath, but their main function was to pronounce the defendant innocent or guilty of an unlawful act. However, in medieval and early modern Swedish laws and court records, we find *nämnde*-men performing several roles. They were not only 'jurors' (members of a 'jury')[24] but were also active in arbitrating and decision-making: they sat at the *ting* beside the judge (*häradshövding, domare*), and they even acted as judges 'in judging' (*döma*).[25] Simultaneously with the rise in status of local judges and their closer identification with the state judicial authority (in Sweden towards the end of the seventeenth century), the status of *nämnde*-men diminished.

Interestingly, the birth of the modern conflict-solving system seems to be a process of many stages and layers. It might also be too simple to see medieval or early modern legal procedure as a battle for judicial power between a 'bad' state and 'good' local communities. Moreover, the acceptance of solutions came through the actual practices and procedures: through the formalities of dispute settlement but also through participation of the parties and of the *ting* community through formal proof by oaths with twelve or multiples of twelve oath-helpers, or with truth-seeking or other functions provided by the *nämnde*-men.[26] It is also possible to conclude that early Nordic law emerged mainly through judicial practices in local communities rather than through binding precedents or legislation in the modern sense. Thus, the Swedish pre-modern *lag* can be characterized as traditional law that seldom was stated/given. Above all, it is possible to talk of law that was factually applied, and law could also include customs and rites. Hence, this early law cannot be observed by reference to a (modern) system of abstract norms.

Procedural or Substantive Justice

Nevertheless, the early judgement (decision on law) can be labelled mainly as procedural.[27] It did not find or create any substantive legal condition, but it confirmed how to proceed further: for example, that the accused should swear an oath. And this procedural character did not change, although the sentence included the compensation the accused would have to pay if he did not succeed with the oath-giving. At the same time, the difference between norm (law) and fact was small, which is also true in cases where the *nämnd* was used. No authoritative norms (rules) as such forced parties to behave in a certain way. Still, convictions on law – on what was right – guided people's lives in early times, too, and therefore their notion of conflict regulation, dispute settlement, arbitration or mediation.

Thus, the most crucial question is how law or opinions on law could be ascertained. People's ways of thinking in those days were concrete and depended on oral communication. This is also true in dispute settlement, in discussions on law. Legal communication happened in places where the law was dispensed, and the aim was that lost consensus should be recovered through concrete discussions and negotiations.[28] It is possible to maintain that no legal order or legal authority existed outside these judicial communications. One opinion on law was against another opinion on law, and outside the court sessions legal opinions were equal. To have an opinion enforced, it should be shared; and to be imposed as a sentence (which was then the law in the particular case), it should pass a formal procedure: opinions should find each other and reach consensus. Thus, early (non-authoritative) law existed as consensus, the consensus was (re)created by the court procedure, and if the consensus was broken, the law also failed.

The intimate relationship between law and judicial (court) procedure was at least partly a corollary of oral communication, but it also grew from the non-authoritative nature of the law. Because the broken (consensus on) law had to be rebuilt through a certain procedure, the shared opinion of the community was important. Consensus, however, did not mean idyllic harmony. It emerged through negotiations, through participation in court sessions or in inspections. As long as dispute settlement involving state authorities was absent or exceptional, the *ting* sentence needed to obtain authority from forms and rituals, and from participation. Activity by the parties and their kinsmen was needed: the groups of twelve stood with the defendant at oath-giving, and the other panels (*nämnd*) assisted in procedural and substantive decision-making.[29]

Conclusions

This chapter began with references to dispute resolution by the state judiciary as the ordinary way of conflict resolution in modern Western societies. At the same time, a tendency to move away from courts was highlighted. Problems with court proceedings, but also mistrust of courts and of justice produced by court litigation, have promoted out-of-court alternatives. Again, the mistrust has been linked to legal and cultural fragmentation of societies, and to the weakening power of nation states and their laws.

One of the newest and popular alternatives to court adjudication in the Nordic countries is mediation, based on the voluntary and active participation of the conflicting parties, and aiming at a mutually satisfactory (amicable) outcome. Still, a procedure administrated by a mediator is needed. Also, proceedings in courts have been reformed with emphasis on the parties' experience of the procedure. In some countries, the judiciary is also involved in mediation. Thus, a judge plays various roles, the traditional one of the deciding judge and the other of the negotiating mediator. In the former role, the interaction between the judge and the parties is also important – although the outcome of the procedure must accord with the substantive law in force.

After current (postmodern) trends were noted, the history of conflict resolution was discussed. Hence, a tension between 'old' and 'new' law, or consensual and authoritative law in pre-modern court proceedings was highlighted, with examples taken mainly from the Swedish (and Finnish) legal history, characterized by a slow appearance of modern dispute resolution. For a long time, consensual elements dominated conflict resolution and discussions on law, especially in rural areas. Hence, interesting parallels could be drawn between the two non-modern legal systems. For both, the procedural dimension – comprising various modes of participation, negotiation, arbitration and mediation – is crucial. Still, the history of the modern conflict-solving system seems to be a process of many stages and layers. This might also be said about its future.

Nevertheless, the intimate relationship between early law and judicial (court) procedure was at least partly a corollary of oral communication, but it also grew from the non-authoritative nature of the law. The acceptance of solutions came through the legal/judicial procedure: through the formalities of dispute settlement but also through the participation of the parties and of the *ting* community; with formal proof by oaths with twelve or multiples of twelve oath-helpers, or with truth-seeking or other functions provided by the *nämnde*-men.

Again, the current idea of so-called procedural justice can be seen not only in discussions on mediation or other alternatives to court litigation, but also in the concept of fair trial, based on Article 6 of the European Convention on Human Rights. A similar idea is also pronounced by procedures based on the concept of (European or global) governance. This can be understood as one of the consequences of the plurality of ideas on justice, and of the incompatibility of different ideas on foundations of law. Thus, the legitimacy or acceptance of an administrative act or of a court decision, or of the normative order concerned, is thought to be based on fair procedure or on participation of the parties in conflict resolution.

Pia Letto-Vanamo, LL.D., Prof., is a legal historian and comparative lawyer specialized in European legal history, the history of European integration, Nordic legal culture(s) and transnational law. She is Dean of the Faculty of Law at the University of Helsinki. Her main publications include 'Judicial Dispute Resolution and Its Many Alternatives: The Nordic Experience', in J. Zekoll, M. Bälz and I. Amelung (eds), *Formalisation and Flexibilisation in Dispute Resolution* (Brill, 2014) and P. Letto-Vanamo, D. Tamm and B.O.G Mortensen (eds), *Nordic Law in European Context* (Springer, 2019).

Notes

1. See further Weber (1956: 405–12).
2. See the articles in Zekoll, Bälz and Amelung (2014).
3. See further Letto-Vanamo (2014).

4. Arbitration has for a long time been a typical dispute resolution method in business relations. Cases are taken out of the courts and submitted to arbitration for the reason that court proceedings are perceived as too slow and devoid of expertise. The option of non-public proceedings plays an important role here, too.
5. See, e.g., Menkel-Meadow (1996).
6. See articles in Ervo and Nylund (2014).
7. In 2006, court mediation was introduced to Finland, modelled on the experiments carried out in Norway and Denmark.
8. See, e.g., Ervasti (2007).
9. See, e.g., Moore (2003).
10. A main requirement is of course that mediation makes sense considering the claims presented by the parties.
11. Thus, Nordic courts seem to have three different procedural options: traditional trials, concluding with a court decision; the promotion of settlement within civil proceedings; and court-annexed mediation. Promoting a compromise or settlement in civil matters is a traditional part of a judge's work.
12. See further Letto-Vanamo and Honkanen (2005).
13. In towns, administration of justice was a task for the town court.
14. However, this is not to say that an early '*ting* community' for considering common affairs and for disseminating information would have comprised every person in the locality. Instead, the early *ting* was composed solely of able-bodied, tax-paying males.
15. Although precise information detailing the judge's role and functions is absent from medieval laws, we can assume that the head of the assembly, or *häradshövding* in Swedish, chaired the *ting* sessions. Later, he seems to have been in charge of a judicial circuit, which consisted of several *ting* districts, that is, units where sessions were held.
16. On the history of Ösgötalagen see the introduction by Holmbäck and Wessén (1933).
17. See also Holmbäck and Wessén (1933: 39–40).
18. Of which the paternal kin had to pay two-thirds and the maternal kin one-third. See Article 7 of the Chapter on Manslaughter in the Law of East Gothland.
19. See further Weitzel (1994); Gudian (1976).
20. See for instance Härter (2005).
21. Articles 1 and 2 of the Chapter on Procedure (*Räfsta balkär*) in the Law of East Gothland.
22. However, both the term itself and a modified version of the institution remain in use even today. According to the 1734 Code of Judicial Procedure, in force in Sweden until the 1940s and in Finland until the 1990s, a panel of seven laymen was on the court (of whom at least five had to be present); the laymen panel had the authority to override the opinion of the professional judge, but only by unanimity. Since the twentieth-century reforms, they were markedly lay judges; they were given individual votes and subject to the authority of judges.
23. This was important because the head of the *ting* (*häradshövding*) was in charge of *ting* sessions of a *härad* (circuit) with several *ting* districts, and often he was a nobleman living in Stockholm.
24. At the same time, it is very difficult in early court procedure and conflict resolution to draw the line between fact and law – between material questions and legal questions. This is true also when later functions of the *nämnde*-men are analysed.
25. We must take into account that the early term *döma* had a non-legal, non-authoritative meaning. It had the sense of 'to mean' (to make a judgement), similar to the German *meinen* (also *urteilen*), Swedish *mena*, and *tuomjan* in the Finno-Ugric languages. See further: Kulturhistoriskt lexikon för nordisk medeltid 3 (1980: 150–65).

26. Including assayers and other groups and panels of men acting in dispute settlement.
27. On medieval 'law-finding', see Kroeschell (1972).
28. See further Weitzel (2000).
29. Although law(s) could be cast in written form, as was the case with the Law of East Gothland, the legitimacy of the court sentence did not rely on the written norms – even if the sentence had been similar to the text concerned.

References

Collin, H.S., and C.J. Schlyter (eds). 1830. *Samling af Sweriges gamla lagar. Corpus Iuris Sueo-Gotorum antiqui 2:* Östgötalagen. *Codex Iuris Ostrogotici*. Stockholm.

Ervasti, K. 2007. 'Conflicts before the Courts and Court-Annexed Mediation in Finland', *Scandinavian Studies in Law* 51: 186–99.

Ervo, L., and A. Nylund (eds). 2014. *The Future of Civil Litigation: Access to Courts and Court-Annexed Mediation in the Nordic Countries*. Heidelberg: Springer.

Gudian, G. 1976. 'Geldstrafrecht und peinliches Strafrecht im späten Mittelalter', in H.-J. Becker et al. (eds), *Rechtsgeschichte als Kulturgeschichte: Festschrift für Adalbert Erler*. Aalen: Scientia, pp. 273–88.

Härter, K. 2005. *Policey und Strafjustiz in Kurmainz: Gesetzgebung, Normdurchsetzung und Sozialkontrolle im frühneuzeitlichen Territorialstaat*. Frankfurt am Main: Klostermann.

Holmbäck, Å., and E. Wessén. 1933. *Svenska Landskapslagar* I. Uppsala: Almquist & Wicksells Boktryckeri.

Kroeschell, K. 1972. '"Rechtsfindung": Die mittelalterlichen Grundlagen einer modernen Vorstellung', in Mitarbeiter des Max-Planck-Instituts für Geschichte (eds), *Festschrift für Hermann Heimpel zum 70. Geburtstag am 19. September 1971*, vol. 3. Göttingen: Vandenhoeck & Ruprecht, pp. 499–517.

Kulturhistoriskt Lexikon för nordisk medeltid 3. 1980, 2nd edn. Viborg.

Letto-Vanamo, P. 2014. 'Judicial Dispute Resolution and Its Many Alternatives: The Nordic Experience', in J. Zekoll, M. Bälz and I. Amelung (eds), *Formalisation and Flexibilisation in Dispute Resolution*. Leiden: Brill, pp. 151–64.

Letto-Vanamo, P., and T. Honkanen. 2005. *Lain nojalla ja kansan tuella: Moments of Finnish Justice in the 1970s*. Helsinki: Edita.

Menkel-Meadow, C. 1996. 'The Trouble with the Adversary System in a Postmodern, Multicultural World', *William and Mary Law Review* 38: 5–44.

Moore, C.W. 2003. *The Mediation Process: Practical Strategies for Resolving Conflict*, 3rd edn. San Francisco: Jossey Bass.

Weber, M. 1956. *Wirtschaft und Gesellschaft* II. Tübingen: Paul Siebeck.

Weitzel, J. 1994. 'Strafe und Strafverfahren in der Merowingerzeit', *Zeitschrift der Savigny-Stiftung für Rechtsgeschichte*, Germ. Abt. 111: 66–147.

———. 2000. 'Der Grund des Rechts in Gewohnheit und Herkommen', in D. Willoweit (ed.), *Die Begründung des Rechts als historisches Problem*. Munich: Oldenbourg, pp. 137–52.

Zekoll, J., M. Bälz and I. Amelung (eds). 2014. *Formalisation and Flexibilisation in Dispute Resolution*. Leiden: Brill.

Chapter 3

Mediation, Extrajudicial Conflict Regulation and the Privatization of the Criminal Justice System

Hubert Rottleuthner

Under the principle of the monopoly of power, the regulation of criminal conflicts today is dominated by legal provisions applied and enforced by state agencies. The procedure is conducted by a professional judge who does not aim for an agreement between the persons involved and whose decisions can be executed without consent. What, then, could or should be the place of mediation in the realm of criminal issues? Mediation is conceived of as an opposite to official, formalized procedures run by state agents, mainly judges, who, according to given statutes, are in charge of issuing binding decisions that can be enforced by state power. In contrast, mediation excludes officials who are bound by given legal regulations; instead, the 'third' is responsive to the perspectives of the conflicting parties in order to reach a mutually agreed outcome. In Germany, there were attempts in civil cases to combine formal court procedures and mediation, where a judge could transfer the case to a mediator-judge. But this model was abolished by the Mediation Law of the Federal Republic of Germany (*Mediationsgesetz*, Art. 9) in 2012. As a substitute, a *Güterichter*, according to the *Zivilprozessordnung* (ZPO), Art. 278 (5), since July 2012, is permitted to apply 'all methods of conflict regulation including mediation'. However, he/she is not called a mediator because mediation should be in the hands of private persons.

The *Mediationsgesetz* does not mention criminal courts and procedures at all. Does this mean that there is no place for mediation in criminal matters? Or are there mediation procedures applied in state-official criminal procedures? Or could and should they be applied? Is mediation practised in criminal matters 'privately', that is, outside the state Criminal Justice System (CJS)? Or could and should it be practised there? The concern about privatization of criminal conflicts is that it may involve regression to retaliation, self-justice and lynch law. In contrast to this, one could ask whether privatization of the regulation of criminal conflicts via mediation could take place.

This chapter discusses these questions and starts with a look at the official CJS and the role private people play in mobilizing court procedures and in participating in these procedures. The next step will be a look at the regulation of criminal conflicts outside the state system, that is, by private groups or organizations. In both fields, we will find more or less elaborated examples of mediation. Finally, I weigh arguments in favour of and against governmental intervention into criminal conflicts after having considered various models of mediation.

The Role of Private Persons in State Regulation of Criminal Conflicts: Mobilization and Participation

My starting point is the following question: what is the official (legal, formal) and informal role of private[1] agents within the state penal system? The phylogenetic step from private to state conflict management takes place as soon as the role of a 'third' is institutionalized, that is, put in charge of issuing binding decisions. The 'third' becomes a proto-state agency as soon as he (and regularly it is a 'he') is no longer related to the parties in conflict.

However, the 'life of the law' depends on the 'struggle for law' (Jhering 1879); so the 'life' of the penal law basically depends on complaints made by private people to the police. The immense dark figure of crimes is diminished by independent police activities only to a very small degree. Criminology deals with the question: why do people report crimes to the police and other state agencies, and why don't they report? Sometimes people do not realize that they have been victims of a crime, or they do not identify the damage or impairment as a consequence of legally relevant, criminal behaviour. People try to avoid trouble with the police or courts, or they may predict that a charge will be useless because the prosecutor will soon terminate the proceedings.[2] In many cases, people try to manage conflicts among those affected by an offence or, more expanded, among the social in-group. They do not trust outsiders such as state officials; they are convinced that they themselves are able to find ways of solving the conflict more effectively, peacefully and sustainably. This, in consequence, could lead to the use of arbitration, mediation or even retaliation as modes to regulate crimes/conflicts outside the criminal justice system.

As soon as the police and other prosecuting agencies of the state are informed of crimes, private people are, in general, marginalized or even excluded from further proceedings (with the exception of the roles of the accused and of witnesses). However, the German legal system of criminal law has some opportunities for private people to participate in and influence the proceedings which can be characterized by the following points:

- Criminal offences that are prosecuted only upon application by the victim (*Antragsdelikte*).
- In some cases (like trespassing, insult, damage to property), procedural law such as the German *Strafprozeßordnung* (StPO) provides the option of private prosecution (*Privatklage*, Art. 374ff. StPO). The state prosecutor can, if there is no 'public interest' (e.g. in many cases of stalking), transfer the active role in further proceedings to the victims. However, private people rarely make use of this option (Rieß 2000). In the majority of cases in which private prosecution is admitted, arbitrators (*Schiedspersonen*) have to be called in first. This could be a case for mediation, since *Schiedspersonen* are not judges and should have mediation skills.
- There is the possibility of accessory prosecution (*Nebenklage*, Art. 395 StPO).
- On the side of the courts, private people are admitted as lay judges to some criminal courts of first and second instance (*Schöffengerichte* or *Schwurgerichte*),[3] playing a rather decorative role.
- In the German Democratic Republic, social arbitration courts (*Gesellschaftliche Gerichte: Konflikt- und Schiedskommissionen*) were established after 1961/1964 and were in charge of conflicts – including petty offences – within a workplace/'company' or within a neighbourhood. Members of the commissions were colleagues or neighbours, that is, persons from the close social network. Therefore, elements of informal justice or mediation could come into play. However, the *Gesellschaftliche Gerichte* acted under the control of the state prosecutor, who could transfer the case to state courts.
- The role of victims is strengthened in the International Criminal Court. Victims not only participate as witnesses in the proceedings, they have the right to present their views and concerns.[4] They have the right of inspection of the files but no special right of attendance; for example, they are not admitted to proceedings *in camera*.
- The so-called 'deal' (*Absprache, Verständigung*) in criminal procedures[5] brings together officials (judges, prosecutors and lawyers), excluding the 'private' victim and accused, within a medium of contractual relationships, similar to private law arrangements and also former modes of negotiation in early modern and nineteenth-century criminal procedure, particularly concerning verbal and bodily injuries. Because of the communicative structure, especially because of the exclusion of victim and accused, the deal is not a case of mediation.
- In many countries, 'victim–offender (or perpetrator) mediation' was introduced in order to strengthen the position of victims.[6] In fact, this is not a case of mediation in a strict sense because the initiative and the outcome are under state control.[7] The preliminary investigation procedure (*Ermittlungsverfahren*) of the prosecutor must have started; finally, the prosecutor must agree to the

settlement. Only clear cases are admitted, mainly in cases of personal injury and damage to property. There is no open question about causality and the ascription of responsibility. Therefore, no symmetry among the participants exists. The result is not a win-win outcome; instead, the offender has to make restitution satisfactory for the victim. The 'mediator' is not neutral because he/she has to assist the victim. Therefore, the German notion of *Täter-Opfer-Ausgleich* (victim-offender mediation) is more appropriate, although there is no balancing or scaling (*Ausgleich*) of excuse or material compensation and forgiveness. The unofficial character of the *Täter-Opfer-Ausgleich* is given insofar as the 'mediator', at least in Germany, is not engaged in a formal position within the public, state-based criminal justice system. He/she can be a member of a commissioned private agency (mainly social workers) or can be an arbitrator (*Schiedsperson*) or trained mediator.

As a result, we can find within the state CJS two at least rudimentary forms of mediation: communication with a *Schiedsperson* and 'victim–offender mediation'.

The Regulation of Criminal Cases Outside the State CJS

Private Groups and Organizations Dealing with Criminal Issues

Beyond the formal roles private people can play in the mobilization of the criminal justice system, there seems to exist further demand for social groups to solve their conflicts, relevant under criminal law, using procedures such as mediation and arbitration in order to avoid a formal verdict and public punishment. The most prominent groups are churches and firms or companies.

Ecclesiastical or canon law is non-state law. Jurisdiction under this law is restricted to the members of a social, that is, religious group. In many cases of child abuse by priests, state agencies were not informed by the church, which tried to solve the problems within its domain.

Big firms tend to avoid (public) criminal court proceedings, for example in cases of corruption or fraud.[8] Other examples are intra-corporate 'courts' (*Betriebsjustiz*) that deal with petty crimes within firms, for example in cases of theft or property damage.

Another field that shuns the publicity of court proceedings is sports. Quotidian cases of more or less grievous bodily harm in (combatant) sports, doping, misguided decisions by referees or corruption are dealt with among the teams or within a sports association. In rare cases they engage their own sports council (sports arbitration court, sports/sporting tribunal), for example the German Court of Sport or the National Sports Court, which are chaired by professional judges, with state criminal courts as a last resort. The penalties that are issued by the tribunals of the associations can be severe – such as denial of admission to competitions – thus exceeding formal criminal sanctions.[9]

In the USA, many cases of 'campus law', for example cases of rape, filled news reports, revealing a jurisdiction of the universities independent of and even prior to the state CJS.

In the following, I shift from the general analysis of various 'private' groups and organizations in dealing with deviant behaviour and negative sanctions to particular groups in which honour plays an eminent role. Honour conflicts tend to be restricted to the private sphere. Therefore, they are often prone to mediation and arbitration, but also to retaliation.

Honour Conflicts

Conflict theories used to distinguish between conflicts of interest and conflicts of values (Aubert 1972). Honour was, or still is, a prominent and often contested value (before human dignity achieved pole position). The value of honour appears as something to be dealt with personally or by the 'honourable' in-group exclusively. Honour is not only a personal value, like dignity, but is connected to social groups and social reputation and thus to third party involvement. The violation very often is related to the honour of families or mothers and wives. Usually it is a male representative of the family that is formally involved in the regulation of the conflict.

A famous (historical) example is the case of the duel. This is a case of violent solution among those affected; there is no third party involved; the 'second' (*Sekundant*) is, as the name says, not a third person. However, before duels took place, negotiations would be held between the parties, represented by the seconds. Since both represented the parties, they did not act as mediators. Members of the military forces were under an obligation to defend their honour directly. Later on, special military courts of honour (*Militärische Ehrengerichte*) were established (and in 1919 abolished in Germany). Student duels were another issue. In Germany there existed until 1969 an exceptional regulation for duels with lethal weapons in the general criminal code (*Zweikampf mit tödlichen Waffen*, Art. 201–210 *Strafgesetzbuch, alte Fassung*).

The value of honour combines both the material aspect and the procedural one. State agencies have to be kept out of honour conflicts, which traditionally were often dealt with by non-state third parties, for example within guilds or social communities. Honour conflicts among the nobility could not be brought to justice. State intervention establishes a forum in which self-representation as an honourable and deeply insulted person might fail.

There are numerous other social groups that achieve a high degree of integration by internally enforcing codes of honour: criminal and subcultural groups like the Mafia, the Japanese Yakuza, rocker gangs, gangs of robbers, terrorist groups like the Irish Republican Army[10] or the ETA (*Euskadi Ta Askatasuna*) with their own tribunals and sanctions against traitors, and today other groups like youth gangs, migrant groups and so on. As far as empirical evidence on the regulation of conflicts within these groups is available, it rather resembles the procedures of authoritative state courts.

Honour played a major role in the radically anti-universalistic morality of the Nazis, restricting the notion to particular groups. There were 'honour courts' such as *soziale Ehrengerichte* exclusively for company leaders (*Betriebsführer*), *Ehrengerichte des Handwerks* for craftsmen, the *Ehrengerichtshof des Deutschen Handwerks- und Gewerbekammertages, Jägerehrengerichte, Ehrenräte bei den Kulturkammern* and so on. However, *Ehre* became an ideological construct under state (and court) control. Apparently, there was no place for mediation.

Today, 'honour' has been replaced by standards of professional groups. There are socially accepted, prestigious groups with their own codes of conduct, namely traditional professional groups who have, as an indicator of professional autonomy, their own courts, for example for lawyers (in Germany: *Anwaltsgerichte, Anwaltsgerichtshof, Senat des Bundesgerichtshofs für Anwaltssachen*), for civil servants (*Disziplinargerichte*), for soldiers (*Wehrdienstgerichte*), tax advisers, architects, engineers and so on. The medical professions in particular have (in Germany) established a three-step system with increasing state influence, starting from a disciplinary board comprised solely of members of the professional reference group (*Disziplinarausschuss der Landesärztekammer*),[11] then courts of professional conduct (*Berufsgerichte*)[12] affiliated to state courts with state judges, and finally ordinary penal and administrative courts. There is no empirical evidence on the modes of regulation applied by these institutions.

Muslim 'Parallel Justice'

Recently, the practice of Muslim (Turkish, Arab, Lebanese etc.) ways of conflict resolution outside state courts have attracted attention in Western Europe (for Germany, see Wagner 2011 and Rottleuthner 2012). In Great Britain, sharia courts are accepted, for example to regulate conflicts in matters of family law. In Germany, Islamic law is applied by state courts in the frame of international private law under the principle of *ordre public*, which means that foreign law and decisions are only accepted if they do not violate the basic principles of domestic law. Criticism has been provoked by the informal and secret way of dealing with conflicts among Muslim groups. Critics speak of a 'parallel justice' that violates basic principles of the rule of law. But mediation or alternative dispute resolution (ADR) in general are informal and secret; they are forms of private justice, parallel to the state system.[13] However, ADR is not extended to criminal issues officially, with the exception of *Schiedspersonen* acting as arbiters in the case of private prosecution and in the case of victim–offender/perpetrator mediation which proceeds under state control (for both, see above). The critique of parallel Muslim 'courts' concerns not only their informal and secret proceedings, but also the fact that they deal with deviant behaviour that could be prosecuted as crimes, and that by doing so, they keep out state agencies, namely the police, prosecutors and courts, sometimes by obscure means like the threat of exclusion from the community.

These critics rather use the term Islamic 'courts'. In this context they avoid the term 'mediation' as a procedure used by these 'courts' – presumably because 'mediation' has strong positive connotations. In fact, the procedure used by these bodies might come very close to a mediation model. Chaired by an Imam or another person respected by the community, the parties – that is, families or clans – come together in order to discuss conflicts mainly concerning family honour, a wide range of civil law troubles regarding the family, but also conflicts related to criminal issues, ranging from injuries to honour crimes, even honour killings.[14] We are told that they often reach mutually accepted settlements. 'Honour' does not mean that the case will be officially published; only what I would call 'the social field of honour' must be informed of the regulation of the conflict. However, this model of honour crimes and consequential in-group mediation is found not only in Muslim societies, but also in European countries dominated by Christians (and males) on a rather agrarian, pre-industrial level. In all these cases, honour must be achieved and defended by male family members. Women contribute to family honour by behaving in a chaste and pure manner. Their reputation is part of the honour of a family and even of a social community.

The unofficial actors and institutions of private conflict regulation using mediation/arbitration do not operate 'in the shadow of the law'; rather they operate in the dark, because there is no open access to state courts. If they fail to reach a mutual settlement, it is unclear whether the parties will or can possibly resort to formal justice. What is criticized from the point of view of official legality is that state officials – that is, the police or prosecutors – are not informed, as should be the case in most crimes. If the case is brought to court, witnesses obstruct the proceedings; the blame is placed on minors who are not yet punishable, witnesses refuse to give evidence or give false evidence and so on.

It is an open question how such 'courts' of private, social groups operate in Islamic countries, such as Turkey.[15] From an empirical point of view, it is still an open question to what degree Muslim mediation in Germany contributes to sustainable social peace among their 'subcultural' social groups. Is the infinite chain of revenge in fact successfully interrupted, a function that today is ascribed to the state and its courts, vested with the monopoly of power? European history proves that such practices of arbitration/mediation were common in most European countries up to the nineteenth century. Since then, state monopoly of power has become a dominant pattern in legal discourses. Does the revival of non-state modes of conflict regulation indicate that this legitimation pattern no longer persists? The normative point in question with regard to ADR and mediation is whether principles of the rule of law, including state monopoly of power, can outweigh the advantages of private, mutually agreed settlements of criminal conflicts.

Government Intervention vs. Mutually Beneficial Solutions in Criminal Issues

In his famous article, Ronald Coase asked: why do firms exist? (Coase 1937). In his answer, he mainly referred to criteria of efficiency. His findings were generalized in the thesis[16] that a mutually beneficial solution is preferable to government intervention. As preconditions for positive solutions, he mentioned the existence of a market, transparency, symmetry and voluntary participation.

Is it possible to transfer this insight from firms to courts in general, notably regarding the problem of privatization and ADR? Symmetry and voluntary participation are generally required for mediation in civil cases such as marriage mediation, mediation in business or labour disputes, but also in environmental matters, administrative law or conflicts in school education. Is it reasonable to generalize Coase's findings and transfer them to conflict solutions in criminal courts ('government intervention'), in contrast to 'mutually beneficial solutions'? As we have seen, criminal law comes up in the context of state-embedded victim–offender mediation. It is not explicitly excluded from mediation in the Mediation Law of the Federal Republic of Germany (*Mediationsgesetz*) of 2012. However, institutes that offer training in mediation skills keep silent on the issue of mediation in (other) criminal matters.

The fervent critique of (private) mediation among Muslim groups in Germany refers to basic principles of the rule of law. The principle of legality apparently is invalidated; there are no guarantees for equal treatment or for the right to be heard. But one could argue that symmetrical power relations exist as a precondition for informal mediation, otherwise one party would surrender and avoid the procedure. There might be an exit option for state courts, but there is no empirical evidence on whether it is actually used. An essential point of the critique is the secrecy of mediation. But this applies to mediation in general; it applies to legally accepted forms of private mediation in non-criminal matters as well as to victim–offender mediation. We know very little about what is going on in these cases, and even less about whether forms of private justice, mediation and arbitration are relevant regarding the vast dark figure of crimes not reported to the CJS. However, the principle of publicity seems to be of great importance, especially in proceedings of criminal justice. It concerns control and limitation of state power; problems of negative and positive general prevention are involved because published sentences establish essential rules on which a society can rely. In addition, public, publicized decisions and arguments are what legal doctrine feeds on. Publicity of court decisions is a high value.

Just as we have a dark, totally non-public field of crimes, the vast majority of court decisions also remain in the dark. A large number of decisions, even of upper-level courts, are never published. From Thackeray[17] we know what would happen if we knew, like God, of every sin in this world. The life of man would be 'solitary, poore, nasty, brutish, and short'. What would happen if we knew the total outcome of court proceedings, let alone ADR? High values are something to which we should aspire, but we rather want them to become full reality.

The critique of Muslim 'parallel justice' is not only based on principles of the rule of law (legality, equality, publicity); it also refers to the fact that members of an alien culture and/or religion apply their own forms of dispute resolution. Muslim 'courts' are taken as an assault on the identity and integration of the German society and its traditional culture. Muslim legal culture tends to establish a parallel society threatening the homogeneity of the German community (cf. Wagner 2011, 2018).

As problems of cultural diversity are involved, reference should be made, from a normative point of view, to the topic of cultural defence. Forms of private, unofficial mediation in criminal matters practised among Muslim, Turkish, Arab and similar groups are culturally and/or religiously based. The question then has to be answered whether the state is obliged to accept traditional, possibly religious traditions and social norms and practices – or to prohibit what cannot be accepted according to the public policy (*ordre public*) exception mainly regarding principles of the rule of law.

The *International Covenant on Civil and Political Rights* (1966) is quite clear in Article 27: 'In those States in which ethnic, religious or linguistic minorities exist, persons belonging to such minorities shall not be denied the right, in community with the other members of their group, to enjoy their own culture, to profess and practise their own religion, or to use their own language'. The *Indigenous and Tribal Peoples Convention of the International Labor Organization* (1989) states in Article 8: '1. In applying national laws and regulations to the peoples concerned, due regard shall be had to their customs or customary laws'. But, as one might expect, it also draws a line: '2. These peoples shall have the right to retain their own customs and institutions, where these are not incompatible with fundamental rights defined by the national legal system and with internationally recognised human rights'.

We have to balance the principle of cultural defence, which would be in favour of mediation in criminal issues as well, with court principles of the rule of law. This is not an easy case, as we know in Germany from the recent debate about circumcision of young boys. The German parliament accepted this religious and traditional practice among Jews and Muslims although it is a clear violation of personal bodily integrity.[18] Cultural defence shows that there are demands to have ADR/mediation alongside the CJS to deal with specific conflicts and criminal behaviour. Can violations of the rule of law in criminal issues be accepted while paying tribute to alien customs?

Hubert Rottleuthner was Professor of Sociology of Law and Philosophy of Law at Free University Berlin, Honorary Professor at Goethe-University in Frankfurt (Main) and guest professor in Sydney and Brussels. He has published widely on sociology of law and legal theory, on philosophy of law, on theories of legal development, on history of sociology of law, on Nazi law, on law in the GDR and on transitional justice. His main publications include *Richterliches Handeln: Zur Kritik der juristischen Dogmatik* (Fischer Athenäum, 1973), *Rechtstheorie und Rechtssoziologie* (Karl Alber, 1981), *Foundations of Law* (Springer, 2005) and *Ungerechtigkeiten* (Nomos, 2008).

Notes

1. Human reason has the advantage of being self-reflexive. Therefore, I add a brief digression on my multifarious use of 'private' in this chapter. The ambiguity of this concept can be somewhat clarified by introducing its opposites:
   - private, social (societal) vs. state, official (with various conjunctions: official framing of private activities, i.e., state control of input and output; private participation in state activities; steps from private activities to full state procedures; exit options from private activities to state agencies etc.)
   - private, personal, individual vs. social, collective
   - private vs. public
   - (forms) of private law vs. public, criminal law (on this context, cf. the results of the *DFG-Forschungsschwerpunkt* [research focus of the German Research Foundation] 'On the Origin of Public Criminal Law' reported in Willoweit 1999 and Härter 2002)
   - lay people vs. legal professions
   - close relations (family, kinship, neighbourhood, clans, *ting*, guilds), local, rural communities vs. anonymous, distant relations; urban.
2. In many cases, a charge is used only in order to notify the insurance company, as in cases of car or bike theft.
3. Participation of private, non-professional persons or representatives of social groups in German courts outside criminal courts exists only in two cases: (1) lay judges in labour courts as representatives of employers and employees (mainly trade unions), but they are excluded from the *Güteverhandlung* (conciliatory hearing at the start of a proceeding); and (2) *Kammer für Handelssachen*, which have jurisdiction over commercial matters; lay members are elected by the chamber of trade and commerce.
4. Art. 68 (3) of the Rome Statute of the ICC (retrieved 4 January 2015 from https://www.icc-cpi.int/nr/rdonlyres/ea9aeff7-5752-4f84-be94-0a655eb30e16/0/rome_statute_english.pdf): 'Where the personal interests of the victims are affected, the Court shall permit their views and concerns to be presented and considered at stages of the proceedings determined to be appropriate by the Court and in a manner which is not prejudicial to or inconsistent with the rights of the accused and a fair and impartial trial. Such views and concerns may be presented by the legal representatives of the victims where the Court considers it appropriate, in accordance with the Rules of Procedure and Evidence'.
5. This instrument (now Art. 257c StPO) was introduced in 2009, following the jurisdiction of the Federal Supreme Court, in *Gesetz zur Regelung der Verständigung im Strafverfahren*, 29 July 2009 (BGBl I 2352). Empirical findings on this law in action can be found in Altenhain, Dietmeier and May (2013); cf. Höland (2014).

6. In Germany: Art. 46a *Strafgesetzbuch* (StGB), Art. 155a, 155b StPO.
7. According to Recommendation No. R (99) 19 of the Committee of Ministers to Member States of the Council of Europe concerning mediation in penal matters (15 September 1999): '(9) A decision to refer a criminal case to mediation, as well as the assessment of the outcome of a mediation procedure, should be reserved to the criminal justice authorities. . . . (32) The mediator should report to the criminal justice authorities on the steps taken and on the outcome of the mediation. The mediator's report should not reveal the contents of mediation sessions, nor express any judgment on the parties' behaviour during mediation'. Elements of mediation are also included in the ECOSOC Resolution 2002/12 – Basic principles on the use of restorative justice programmes in criminal matters. See under 'use of terms': 'Restorative justice programme', 'Restorative process', 'Restorative outcome', 'Parties', 'Facilitator'.
8. Unusually, Leo Kirch and then his heirs attempted, for more than a decade, to *judicially* enforce their asserted claims against the Deutsche Bank. The struggle ended with an out-of-court settlement in February 2014.
9. Exclusion from sporting events leading to a significant loss of income could not be brought to a civil court.
10. On IRA law and courts, cf. Bittner (2002).
11. *(Landes)Ärztekammern* are public corporations under the legal supervision of the government. Their disciplinary code sets the rules for the non-public proceedings of the *Disziplinarausschuss* and sanctions such as warnings, fines up to €10,000, suspension of medical accreditation etc.
12. The *Berufsgerichte* can decide upon the withdrawal of the authorization.
13. Broadly discussed are phenomena of 'parallel justice' outside the criminal sphere, namely in the field of international arbitration, recent issues of investor–state dispute resolution in the context of TTIP and Ceta, and in the field of consumer protection regarding Directive 2013/11/EU of the European Parliament and of the Council of 21 May 2013 on alternative dispute resolution for consumer disputes. For Germany, see *Entwurf eines Gesetzes zur Umsetzung der Richtlinie über alternative Streitbeilegung in Verbraucherangelegenheiten und zur Durchführung der Verordnung über Online-Streitbeilegung in Verbraucherangelegenheiten (Gesetz über die alternative Streitbeilegung in Verbrauchersachen (Verbraucherstreitbeilegungsgesetz – VSBG))* and the *Entwurf der Verordnung über Informations- und Berichtspflichten nach dem Verbraucherstreitbeilegungsgesetz (Verbraucherstreitbeilegungs-Informationspflichtenverordnung – VSBInfoV)* (both of 10 November 2014).
14. On honour killings see Oberwittler and Kasselt (2011, 2014). The study analyses only cases that were brought to courts (n = 78 cases with 122 perpetrators, in 1996–2005). On the dark figure, see Oberwittler and Kasselt (2011: 56); on the notion of honour, (2011: 15–18). The *Bundeskriminalamt* (Federal Criminal Police Office) defines honour killings thus: 'Bei Ehrenmorden handelt es sich um Tötungsdelikte, die aus vermeintlich kultureller Verpflichtung heraus innerhalb des eigenen Familienverbandes verübt werden, um der Familienehre gerecht zu werden' (Bundeskriminalamt 2006). Agel (2012) analysed twenty-two court cases in Hessen (in 1982–2010). According to her dissertation (Agel 2013), a collectivist understanding of honour (i.e. the honour of the family) is essential for honour killings, thus distinguishing it from killings within partner relationships in which one side feels violated in his (rarely her) honour.
15. My Turkish colleagues, even if engaged in sociology of law, could not provide me with any reliable information on this issue.
16. This is not the 'Coase theorem'.

17. This story has its own tradition in criminology; cf. Merton (1957: 345), Popitz (1968: 4–5).
18. The majority of members of the *Bundestag* did not use the cultural defence argument; instead, they regarded the circumcision of young boys as a manifestation of parental rights. It was Jewish and Muslim parents who made the claim for an exception. In the case of compulsory school attendance, which in five German states is enforced by criminal law, the *Bundesverfassungsgericht* argued that the general public has a legitimate interest that no 'parallel societies' will evolve (2 BvR 920/14, 15 October 2014).

References

Agel, C. 2012. '"Ehrenmord" in Deutschland: Eine empirische Studie', in H.-J. Kerner and E. Marks (eds), *Internetdokumentation des Deutschen Präventionstages, Hannover*. http://www.praeventionstag.de/Dokumentation.cms/1955.

———. 2013. *(Ehren-)Mord in Deutschland: Eine empirische Untersuchung zu Phänomenologie und Ursachen von 'Ehrenmorden' sowie deren Erledigung durch die Justiz*. Lengerich: Pabst.

Altenhain, M.K., F. Dietmeier and M. May. 2013. *Die Praxis der Absprache in Strafverfahren*. Baden-Baden: Nomos.

Aubert, V. 1972. 'Interessenkonflikt und Wertkonflikt: Zwei Typen des Konflikts und der Konfliktlösung', in W.L. Bühl (ed.), *Konflikt und Konfliktstrategie: Ansätze zu einer soziologischen Konflikttheorie*. Munich: Nymphenburger, pp. 178–205.

Bittner, J. 2002. *Rough Justice – Die Justiz der IRA: Eine Untersuchung und Dokumentation zum Begriff des Rechtssystems*. Frankfurt am Main: Lang.

Bundeskriminalamt. 2006. 'Pressemitteilung: Eine Frage der Ehre? Das BKA stellt Ergebnisse einer Auswertung zum Phänomen "Ehrenmorde" vor'. Retrieved 4 May 2020 from https://www.presseportal.de/download/document/55376-2006-05-19-presseinformation-ehrenmorde.pdf.

Coase, R. 1937. 'The Nature of the Firm', *Economica* New Series 4(16): 386–405. http://onlinelibrary.wiley.com/doi/10.1111/j.1468-0335.1937.tb00002.x/full.

Directive 2013/11/EU of the European Parliament and of the Council of 21 May 2013 on alternative dispute resolution for consumer disputes. Retrieved 4 May 2020 from https://op.europa.eu/en/publication-detail/-/publication/2f3efba7-fb97-41b2-953a-69c6080dfbcc/language-en.

ECOSOC Resolution 2002/12 – Basic principles on the use of restorative justice programmes in criminal matters. Retrieved 4 May 2020 from https://www.un.org/en/ecosoc/docs/2002/resolution%202002-12.pdf.

Härter, K. 2002. 'Von der "Entstehung des öffentlichen Strafrechts" zur "Fabrikation des Verbrechens"', *Rechtsgeschichte* 1: 159–96.

Höland, A. 2014. 'Review of Altenhain, Dietmeier and May', *Zeitschrift für Rechtssoziologie* 34(1&2): 340–46.

Indigenous and Tribal Peoples Convention of the International Labor Organization. 1989. http://www.ilo.org/dyn/normlex/en/f?p=NORMLEXPUB:12100:0::NO::P12100_ILO_CODE:C169.

International Covenant on Civil and Political Rights. 1966. Adopted and opened for signature, ratification and accession by General Assembly resolution 2200A (XXI) of 16 December 1966, entry into force 23 March 1976. https://www.ohchr.org/en/professionalinterest/pages/ccpr.aspx.

Merton, R. 1957. *Social Theory and Social Structure*. Glencoe, IL: Free Press.
Jhering, R.v. 1879. *The Struggle for Law.* Chicago: Callaghan.
Oberwittler, W.D., and J. Kasselt. 2011. *Ehrenmorde in Deutschland: Eine Untersuchung auf der Basis von Prozessakten*. Cologne: Wolters Kluwer. Retrieved 4 May 2020 from https://www.bka.de/SharedDocs/Downloads/DE/Publikationen/Publikationsreihen/PolizeiUndForschung/1_42_EhrenmordeInDeutschland.pdf?__blob=publicationFile&v=3.
———. 2014. *Ehrenmorde in Deutschland: Eine Analyse auf der Basis justiziell bearbeiteter Fälle der Jahre 1996 bis 2005*. Retrieved 4 May 2020 from https://csl.mpg.de/de/forschung/projekte/ehrenmorde-in-deutschland/.
Popitz, H. 1968. Über die Präventivwirkung des Nichtwissens*: Dunkelziffer, Norm und Strafe*. Tübingen: Mohr Siebeck.
Recommendation No. R (99) 19 concerning mediation in penal matters adopted by the Committee of Ministers of the Council of Europe on 15 September 1999. Retrieved 4 May 2020 from https://www.euromed-justice.eu/en/system/files/20100715121918_RecommendationNo.R%2899%2919_EN.pdf.
Rieß, P. 2000. 'Über den schleichenden Tod der Privatklage', *SchiedsamtsZeitung* 71(10): 1–7.
Rottleuthner, H. 2012. 'Mediation im Schatten des Strafrechts: Auch eine Auseinandersetzung mit Joachim Wagners Buch "Richter ohne Gesetz"', *Kritische Justiz* 45(4): 444–59.
Thackeray, W.M. 1869. 'On Being Found Out', in W.M. Thackeray, *Works*, vol. 20. London: Smith Elder, pp. 125–32.
Wagner, J. 2011. *Richter ohne Gesetz: Islamische Paralleljustiz gefährdet unseren Rechtsstaat*. Berlin: Ullstein.
———. 2018. *Die Macht der Moschee: Scheitert die Integration am Islam?* Freiburg: Herder.
Willoweit, D. (ed.). 1999. *Die Entstehung des öffentlichen Strafrechts: Bestandsaufnahme eines europäischen Forschungsproblems*. Cologne: Böhlau.

Part II

Mediation

Anthropological Perspectives and Case Studies

Chapter 4

What Is Mediation?

Definitions and Anthropological Discomforts

Andrea Nicolas

> Social theory is built in a dialogue with empirical knowledge . . . When that empirical knowledge derives wholly or mainly from the metropole, and where the theorist's concerns arise from the problems of metropolitan society, the effect is erasure of the experience of the majority of human kind from the foundations of social thought.
>
> —R. Connell, *Southern Theory*

Connell critiques (mainstream) sociology as framing 'its theories as universal propositions or universal tools' but actually just constituting 'an ethno-sociology of metropolitan society' (2007: 226). The specifics and constraints that this self-centredness carries with it (foremost the lack of recognition of ethnographic realities other than the own) raise critical questions not just for the field of sociology but also for other academic fields. Can, for instance, legal theory, which is similarly situated in and nurtured by 'metropolitan society', legitimately be said to be free from 'gestures of exclusion' (ibid.: 46), and uncompromised by ethnocentric biases? Legal theory, in many ways, shares the luggage of 'grand erasure' (ibid.) towards the experiences of people who, for a variety of reasons, do not form part of its definitional core samples. Social marginality, cultural difference, geographic distance, geopolitical 'remoteness' may all result in being out of sight or reach of theory-making, or simply off the political or legal 'radar' that would call for a sophisticated theoretical explanation. Mediation research is no exception to this exclusionary pattern. As this chapter will argue, mediation studies have largely blinded out some of the major, substantive issues so far raised by critical theory, such as problems of centre and periphery thinking, questions of identity, interests and their role in scientific knowledge production. This seems surprising at first, given the fierce debates about power and representation that have emerged over the last decades in the humanities and social sciences (Chakrabarty [2000] 2007: xiii). Upon a closer look, this lack of recognition is symptomatic. Politics of mutual neglect occur between different academic discursive fields, dividing the spheres of expertise and compartmentalizing 'territories' of knowledge production. This chapter attempts to bridge the diversified discourses and professional fields. It will critically review prevailing concepts and definitions of mediation, and situate them among contrasting ethnographic findings that call for a revision of proclaimed universal 'truths' concerning the nature of mediation processes.

Mediation: A Matter of Perspective

Researchers from outside the Euro-American or other 'Alternative Dispute Resolution' (ADR) contexts may occasionally hear professional mediators or legal scholars state, 'that's not mediation', suggesting that they should call their findings 'something else' (whatever that might be). They thus imply that *mediation* is already 'taken', pre-defined by a certain number of specified characteristics.

For comparative sciences, the question arises: *What is mediation? And who says so?* The classic legal definition of mediation is that of a dispute settlement between two individuals or groups with the help of a facilitating or advising, but not a decision-making, third party. Mediation is seen as a kind of negotiation that contrasts to the modes of arbitration and adjudication where, by definition, the right to decide a case lies with the third party, that is, the arbitrator or the judge:

> There may be a mediator in the negotiations who, throughout or in certain phases, acts in some ways to assist in the endeavor to reach an agreed outcome. A mediator has no ability to give a judgment or to make a decision binding on the disputing parties; that is, he is a facilitator but not an adjudicator. (Gulliver 1979: 209)

Gulliver, himself a legal anthropologist, derived his understanding of mediation from his close reading of the work of Harvard law professor Lon Fuller, who some years before had written: 'The primary quality of the mediator . . . is not to propose rules to the parties and to secure their acceptance of them, but to induce the mutual trust and understanding that will enable the parties to work out their own rules' (Fuller 1971: 326). Mediation is thus practically defined as being distinct from other modes of conflict management.[1]

Due to the growing popularity of ADR and the development of the mediation business as a professional niche, an impressive number of publications on mediation have appeared over recent years. An increasing number of these are designed as handbooks and general introductions. Most of these already show in their table of contents that the different 'types' of conflict management can be ordered along the lines of different degrees of third party involvement, measured by the intensity of pressure that is put on the disputants (Menkel-Meadow et al. 2005; Folberg et al. [2005] 2010). It seems worth having a closer look, however, at the underlying premise of this approach. The operational structuring of chapter titles may induce a hermeneutic problem. That is, the three or four kinds of dispute management an author chooses to discuss in a manuscript can lead to the affirmative statement that there are *exactly* three (or four, etc.) *types* of such settlements. Specific ascriptions to categories are then consolidated as inherent properties and group classifiers, for example that arbitration and adjudication jointly constitute one group of phenomena, those of 'adjudicative options', that are on the opposite pole of negotiation and mediation. Together they form a separate group, that of 'non-adjudicative options' (cf. Blake, Browne and Sime 2013: table of contents). Processes that either do not show all parameters of a listed type, or exhibit cross-cutting characteristics, now need justification and an explanation. In a friendly-minded environment, they might get established as 'further' categories in an additive framework, or as peculiar 'subtypes' of already existing main types in a more integrative approach. In a less open context, they are excluded from the monograph.

It is important to note that the terminological use of 'mediation' in jurisprudence is distinguished from other possible usages of the term in other fields. Behrends, Park and Rottenburg, for instance, when using the term 'mediator' (2014: 14), refer to mediators of ideas in the domain of globally travelling models (in particular in African conflict management). Mediators, in their framework, are 'carrier[s]' of models, 'crucial to a model's transfer at all points of its passage' (ibid.), who act as agents of translation in the process of transfer. Their use of the term mediator is close to Merry's 'intermediaries' (2006a: 42–43, 48), whom she understands as 'people who occupy middle positions' (ibid.: 42), translating between different worlds. Merry finds such intermediaries, who can be movement activists, NGO workers, lawyers, government officials or academics (2006b: 134), to be of paramount importance in transnational 'vernacularization' processes of human rights ideas (ibid.: 219), where 'the social position of the messenger is key' (Levitt and Merry 2009: 444). Kapil Raj also applies the term mediation in the sense of intermediation (2009: 105), whereby the terms mediator, intermediary, broker and go-between are used interchangeably. The idea to conceptualize mediators in terms of a linking role has met some criticism. For instance, Firth concludes that the selection of the term 'mediator' is 'unfortunate' in this context (1965: 386, 388). Gulliver adds to this by stating that 'the term *broker* seems preferable in that context and it has become fairly widely established in anthropological writings' (1979: 212).

While a strictly legal usage of the term 'mediation' may help to reduce an abundance of ethnographic data, it may also have disadvantages. Shared characteristics and common fields of interaction, which might underline and twist phenomenologically diverse but perhaps nevertheless analytically related phenomena together, may remain unacknowledged. For instance, diplomats may act, particularly in internationally tense situations, as go-betweens, negotiators or mediators but they also often play the role of socio-cultural brokers.[2] Another example is provided by spiritual experts, monks, saints or priests, who intercede and mediate between the human and supra-natural worlds. They may also act as peace-makers in human conflicts – often precisely because of their intermediate position (Barth [1959] 2004; Pirie 2005).

Notwithstanding such wider notions, mediation in the legal field is exclusively understood as a form of dispute settlement. Marital disputes and divorce procedures may occasionally be included here, but marriage arrangements, as a matter of definition, are excluded from the discussion. However, there are ethnographic contexts in which marriage arrangements *do* form part of the mediators' work (Barton 1930: 109; Nicolas 2011: 88–120). Therefore, the term mediation has to be conceptualized more broadly than merely as a form of conflict settlement. Menkel-Meadow indicates this when noting that mediation can also be used to 'plan future transactions' and to 'improve communications' (2001: xiii). 'The central element of mediation is not that it is used in dispute settlement but that it is intermediated, i.e., that it is done by third parties. . . . It *then* remains to be explained, why mediation as a kind of third party intervention is so often *applied* to cases of dispute settlement' (Nicolas 2011: 6, emphasis in the original). Moreover, mediation, arbitration, negotiation and so on are not mutually exclusive 'types' of processes but strategies that can be applied to different degrees and at different moments, as they can be increased, switched or abandoned within one and the same process (ibid.: 7).

Mediation Taxonomy

Upon reviewing existing classification schemes, Riskin notes that 'a bewildering variety of activities fall within the broad, generally-accepted definition of mediation' (Riskin 1996: 8). Commentators regularly note that in mediation, a variety of 'styles', 'roles', 'strategies', 'categories' or 'models' coexist.[3] Riskin even notes that 'some of these processes have little in common with one another' (ibid.: 8). Yet their belonging to a common category is never questioned. The foundational assumption that 'mediation is facilitated negotiation' (ibid.: 13) remains unchallenged.[4]

Sometimes we find interesting shifts in naming patterns from typologies of *processes* ('facilitative mediation') to typologies of *people* ('the democrat'), or from roles that people fill to strategies that they apply. Specifically, noun production plays a role in the process of objectification. We observe in the descriptions a shift from using a multitude of adjectives, synonyms and verbal constructions 'in good literary style' towards 'clear, unequivocal' terminology, often confined to a few terms eligible to be used in a given context. This is more than a question of stylistic preference; we are here right within the realm of normative knowledge production (Foucault [1969/1971] 1972: 49). We may note that mediation taxonomy, in the words of David Knight (1981: 23), makes an unspoken claim to being a 'natural' rather than an 'artificial' classification with consequences for its ontological status.

No one currently appears to agree upon what exactly a 'proper' mediation taxonomy would look like. This is not a problem of inaccuracy that could be resolved by further refinement of classificatory parameters. In multivariant analysis, there is a potentially open-ended number of factors that could be included, and the fact that even these traits of phenomena that we call factors in the analysis are inevitably abstractions from more complex mediation realities makes it impossible to unambiguously define a category and declare its borders.[5]

In a pointed critique, Michael Moffitt has identified some prevalent patterns in the various existing classification attempts. He observed that some definitions are of a rather 'prescriptive' character, meaning that they tell us what mediation *should* look like, while others are of a more 'descriptive' character, trying to tell us what mediation actually *is*. He also distinguished between 'contextual' and 'acontextual' definitions, whereby contextual would mean historically specific and socially as well as culturally situated, and acontextual as claiming universal validity (2005: 78–79). Noticeably, Moffitt continues by replacing the older taxonomies with his own taxonomical system of mediation 'categories', which he claims to be an 'acontextual' theoretical framework (ibid.: 92).

This, though, is precisely the problem, raised at the beginning of this chapter. Most existing theories about mediation either imply by their subtle way of representation, or explicitly claim to be 'acontextual' and universally valid, while in fact they are 'born' in a highly contextual framework. They are paradigms derived from experiences and observations in specific countries (mainly the US, partly also European countries) in specific historical times (between the 1970s and now), in specific dispute settings (divorce mediation, commercial negotiations, worker–employee disputes etc.) and with specific backgrounds of involved mediators (therapists, professionals, community representatives, court mediators, etc.). These highly specific settings are then *declared* to be acontextual and thus universal. Noticeably, empirical examples deriving from other parts of the world rarely have a chance to influence theory-making. Most definitions of mediation either fully ignore anthropological works that could hint at the need for a different way of theory-making, or, like Alexander's framework of 'tradition-based mediation' (2008: 107, 113–15), put them into a residual category, a sort of 'black box' for the rest, that declares them by definition to be 'other' – all similar to each other in their 'traditionality' but in sum inherently different to the standard Euro-American way.[6]

Does Mediation Equate to 'ADR'? Mediation Myths and Ideology

The problem is mirrored in the popular equation of mediation with ADR. The term 'ADR' itself has a rather recent history, from the 1970s onwards, with a discrete US-American background.[7] The crucial reference here is state law, in the sense of a 'leitmotif', or 'mainstream' way, from which the 'alternative' is then to be distinguished.[8] Twining (1993) rightly notices that this is but another variant of centre and periphery thinking. There are contexts, worldwide, where mediation is not the exception to the rule but perfectly mainstream. Mediation, then, is what is usually done, while addressing historically newer state courts may constitute the alternative option.

Meanwhile, almost every defining trait of the mediation category has been put into doubt in the literature, including 'that mediation is a unique, relatively recent, and peaceful innovation' (Silbey 1993: 350), and 'that mediation is informal, with no specified rules of procedure' (ibid.). Other defining traits called into question are that mediators are bound by 'neutrality' (ibid.: 351), that mediation is an 'unofficial, nonbinding, non-authoritative process' (ibid.), 'that mediators are passive participants in a process shaped by forces they have not deployed' (ibid.: 352), that they 'act without power', are 'unable to impose a decision' (ibid.), and 'that mediation is more efficient, less expensive than other processes, and more effective' (ibid.). Some have even called mediation a 'myth' or 'ideology' (Silbey 1993; Hensler 2002),[9] and Laura Nader has pointed to the ambiguous nature of 'harmony ideology' (1990: xxiii, 307), which may also be at play in 'ADR' contexts (Nader 2002: 151–52). Such critique, however, has not prevented mediation theory from developing along these definitional lines. We are facing a problem that Franz von Benda-Beckmann has called 'submission to legal ideology' (Benda-Beckmann 2009: 30).

Ideology itself is an interesting field of investigation, as it cannot be simply regarded as 'false depiction'. Actors' ideals and conceptions of themselves could become important guidelines for their behaviour. Participants in a process may try to rise up to their own and to other people's expectations. 'Roles', thereby, potentially could become 'identities'.[10] Practising mediators' own views about their profession, accordingly, are of much importance to mediation research. But they should not form the sole reference point of analysis. So far, taxonomies share a fundamental mediator centricity. That is, the overall process is named either after the mediator, who is thought to be at the core of the process, or after the strategies he uses, or the role he plays (as a standard, a mediator is referred to as singular male) and not, for instance, after strategies the disputants might apply. Other actors recede into the background of the definitions.[11] It seems important here to include in empirical research the perceptions, motifs and strategies of disputants and other people involved, and to apply a methodology of cross-perspective, instead of relying on generalized assumptions about their objectives and behaviours. Most importantly, the views and actions of a certain number of mediators in some regions of the globe cannot be taken as being representative of the whole of mankind. They may have their own motivations, interests and procedural particularities.

'Locating' the Context of Theory-Making

Motives and interests are indeed crucial to understanding recent developments in mediation theory. One might ask, who needs the definitions that are so regularly produced and at the same time so fiercely debated? The interest of legal institutions may be to develop theoretical frameworks that deliver practical solutions to the everyday business of legal jurisdiction. Judges need to know what sort of mediatory activity could be acknowledged as proper procedure by the court, and whom they may regard as legitimate mediators in this context.[12] Hereby, the different professional fields and disciplines mutually inform each other. Legal scholars and juridical personnel developing their own definitions may look up the declarations of mediator organizations for guidelines.[13] Professional mediators, on the other hand, may have a particular interest in setting 'the definitional boundaries of their practices' as a strategy of market protection (Moffitt 2005: 78, 93, 98). Mediation research thus also encounters the definition problem as an issue of gate-keeping and exclusion. This certainly also concerns the diverse group of what Volpe and Chandler have called 'pracademic[s]' (2001: 245), authors who write in academic journals '[that seek] to be read both by academics and practitioners' (Menkel-Meadow 2009: 418), and engage in theory production with a profound interest in producing *applicable* definitions and standards for their professional practice. Not least, there are indigenous activists who may have specific concerns about differential power relations and struggle to overcome the silencing of marginalized groups.[14] Socio-legal scholars and anthropologists might enter the debate with their own interest in getting acknowledged in the mediation field by other disciplines, being under pressure to deliver *some theory at all* that could have an impact on recent debates. Some of them seek legal blessing, and directly import theoretical concepts from law studies, like Gulliver who took his definition of mediation from the law professor Fuller. Others oppose existing conceptions provided by state law, perhaps taking the side of social activists, and engaging in the field of action anthropology. The point here is not to state that one interest would be more legitimate than the other, but rather that different goals and interests necessarily generate different conceptions of mediation, and to note that mediation theory is not as innocent as the abstract language of theory may convey.[15]

Concepts, Registers and Translations

The problem of translation now comes into the equation. In exclusively English-speaking contexts, where the language of practitioners and researchers coincides, the differentiation between mediation as an emic term and mediation as an analytical concept may not suggest itself to the analyst. This is particularly relevant where mediation researchers themselves are mediators, and where different possible speech registers may not become apparent. This could profoundly differ from contexts where analytical distance is already established by the 'foreignness' of another language, that is, where concepts have to be translated between different languages and cross various regional contexts, as in many anthropologists' works. From several ethnographies in the field of mediation we learn that mediators could be very differently named in different regions and by different authors. We hear of 'crossers' of the Yurok (Kroeber 1926; US West Coast American Indians), the 'leopard-skin chiefs' of the Nuer (Evans-Pritchard [1940] 1969, Beidelman 1971; South Sudan and West Ethiopia), 'hamlet elders' of the Maya (Collier 1973; Chiapas, Mexico), the 'peacemakers' of the Kipsigis (Komma 1998; Kenya), the 'men of the earth' among the Akan (Kouassi 2000; West Africa: Ghana and Côte d'Ivoire) and so on. Clearly, different observers use different terminologies to describe what they see or hear when translating legal terminology from various languages into English. The varying national backgrounds of observers also implies that their language of publication could vary. A complex net of mutual translations has arisen, producing both terminological standards and a blossoming polyphony.

Concepts and Terminologies: The Gluckman-Bohannan Debate

This lends increasing topicality to a previous discussion among legal anthropologists, commonly referred to as the 'Gluckman-Bohannan debate' (Donovan 2008: 164). Max Gluckman (1955, 1959, [1965] 1972) had applied legal vocabulary from the Roman and English traditions to the Barotse in Sambia (then Northern Rhodesia), a practice that was criticized by Paul Bohannan (1967, [1969] 1997: esp. 402–4), who – inspired by his own fieldwork among the Tiv of central Nigeria (1957) – demanded that the local terminology in the original language be maintained in the description.[16] A subsequent debate emerged about how to ensure comparative work when strictly using local terms.[17] Gluckman refuted the accusation that he had forced concepts and processes of Barotse law into English terminology and/or Roman-Dutch law categories, merely calling for legitimate analysis ([1969] 1997: esp. 352–54). Bohannan, who was accused of being a cultural relativist, who was solely interested in the specifics of the individual ethnographic account and not in cross-cultural comparison, replied that he had nothing against comparison as such, but that he felt uncomfortable with *the way it was done* by Gluckman and others (Bohannan [1969] 1997: esp. 410–18). Thereby, he put a strong requirement upon what theory-building should look like in anthropology – or rather, what it should *not* look like: namely explaining descriptive data of a given ethnographic setting by generalizations derived either from 'Western folk knowledge' or from prevailing scientific theories of other disciplines, like 'Western jurisprudence' (Bohannan 1959, [1969] 1997).[18] Bohannan also warned of possible dangers of a deductive approach (1967: 100).

The result of the debate more or less remained open at the time. Some anthropologists searched for a golden middle way (e.g. Nader 1965: 11). Others concluded that, 'in hindsight, most contemporary legal anthropologists might say that Bohannan had "won." . . . Comparison continues, but it is a different kind of comparison than Gluckman practiced, thoroughly suffused with Bohannan's values and sensibilities' (Conley and O'Barr 2004: 211; cf. Donovan 2008: 166). Anthropologists seem to have become self-confident that 'things have already been said', and authors like Geertz ([1983] 1993: 168–69) seem almost bored by the old debate, or impatient with invocations of disciplinary scepticism towards legal universalisms (Riles 1994). Unfortunately, when it comes to mediation studies, their optimistic conclusions seem doubtful. A considerable part of the mediation literature published over the past years, without discussing the methodological base of this approach, in fact *does* apply pre-existing 'Western' terminology and classification schemes to 'non-Western' forms of mediation, or neglects them altogether in their theoretical discussions. It almost appears as if the Gluckman-Bohannan debate had never taken place.

So, what went wrong? One part of the answer may be found in Gulliver's own assessment: 'What is new, or worthwhile re-emphasizing, to the anthropologist may often not appear so perhaps to the lawyer, and vice versa' (Gulliver 1970: 686). In discursively competitive, interdisciplinary settings, methods and insights are negotiated ever new, and in mediation studies, for the time being anthropological sensibilities are not generally shared. However, as the examples of legal anthropologists like Gulliver, Gluckman and Bohannan have shown, the dividing lines are not simply set between different disciplines, like 'law vs. anthropology' (cf. Riles 1994). Convergences and disagreements about methodological and theoretical issues develop along more complex mutual interactions.

The Go-Between: An Ideal Type?

I shall explain the problem with the example of the 'go-between', which is understood as being the 'most limited form of mediation' (Roberts 1994: 971).[19] Roberts explains that a go-between's role 'is passive in the sense that while he operates as a bridge or a conduit between the two disputants, he does no more than carry messages backwards and forwards between them'; 'He has not actively contributed by tendering advice or urging particular avenues of conduct' (ibid.).

Did the author here describe actual phenomena he had observed? The ethnographic literature on go-betweens is not particularly dense, and some is dated.[20] Roberts himself did not mention in his encyclopaedic article which ethnographic example he particularly had in mind. We can look at one of the 'classics', that of Barton's book on *Ifugao Law* of 1919, as reprinted in Bohannan's compilation of 1967, which seems to be most informative.

In his chapter 'The *monkalun* or *go-between*', Barton writes: 'The *monkalun* should not be closely related to either party in a controversy. He may be a distant relative of either one of them. The *monkalun* has no authority. All that he can do is to act as a peacemaking go-between' (Barton [1919] 1967: 164). This description, indeed, still fits into Robert's definitional framework as outlined above. But later on, in his chapter on the 'Execution of justice', when describing retaliation acts 'in the case of lives lost in feuds, sorcery, murders and head-hunting' (ibid.: 170), which he describes as a form of 'death penalty' (ibid.), Barton explains to the reader that:

> Capital punishment is administered by the injured person and his kin. . . . The culprit is never notified that he has been sentenced to death. The withdrawal of a go-between from a serious case is, however, a pretty good warning. It has about the same significance as the withdrawal of an embassy in an international complication. (Barton [1919] 1967: 171)

The text refers to the *death penalty* as being a consequence of mediators withdrawing (or being rejected, we might assume). One could argue that what Barton describes here is publicly endorsed revenge rather than a 'penality'. After all, it is not the go-betweens themselves who impose a punishment or inflict death on the 'culprit', it is rather a *consequence* of their way of acting (in this case, of no longer intervening) in the settlement process. On the other hand, though, what judge inflicting a penalty on an offender ever carries a weapon, or himself applies physical force on the offender? In a court trial, it is a *consequence* of a judge's way of acting that leads to severe implications for a prosecuted person's life (such as imprisonment, or execution in the case of the death penalty). In both cases of the Ifugao go-between (revenge by the other party) and the court judge (verdict in a trial), a very real threat backs up the authority of the third party – death being the worst-case scenario.

Even when we exclude the consideration of possible consequences in Barton's work, and just look at the actual activities of go-betweens, we stumble across Barton's descriptions. The author writes:

> The *monkalun* is a whole court, completely equipped, in embryo. He is judge, prosecuting and defending counsel, and the court record. . . . His duty and his interest are for a peaceful settlement. . . . To the end

> of peaceful settlement he exhausts every art of Ifugao diplomacy. He wheedles, coaxes, flatters, threatens, drives, scolds, insinuates. He beats down the demands of the plaintiffs or prosecution, and bolsters up the proposals of the defendants until a point be reached at which the two parties may compromise. If the culprit or accused be not disposed to listen to reason and runs away or 'shows fight' when approached, the *monkalun* waits till the former ascends into his house, follows him, and *war-knife in hand*, sits in front of him and compels him to listen. (Barton [1919] 1967: 163–64)

We might agree that this description would not apply to our common understanding of a 'judge', but with Robert's definition of the go-between as a 'most limited form' of third party involvement, who 'does no more than carry messages backwards and forwards' between disputants, this ethnographic description does not fit either. The restricted role of the go-between as a mere medium for transporting information between two parties, without substantially interfering in the process, is doubtful.

The aim of this chapter is not to evaluate Barton's fieldwork and ethnographic descriptions. Rather, it wishes to raise the question of how Roberts and other authors came to formulate their definitional characteristics of the 'go-between'. Did they consult empirical evidence when they postulated their definitions? It seems that, in an admittedly impressive intellectual enterprise, they foresaw the possibility of a whole range of human behaviour in situations of conflict, and formulated definitions for these kinds of hypothetically established situations – definitions ready to be applied to actual cases once these cases were to appear in the ethnographic records. They did describe *ideal types*.[21]

For mediation theory, this raises an important question: do mediation researchers expect the definitional categories they use to represent 'scientific truth' (a concept itself contested in the humanities), 'real-life' occurrences, ideal types or otherwise? The first option would mean that their empirical findings have to fully conform to the qualities of either one or the other form of settlement. The ideal type approach would mean that *tendencies* towards, or *similarities with* these ideal concepts may be found within their materials. A paradox has arisen in the mediation field: the wish to find, or claim to have found, 'objective' categories that represent 'empirical reality' blends with a methodology of ideal ways of defining them.[22]

Revenants of Theory: Modern–Pre-Modern Binaries

The neo-classical trend to classify people, societies, objects or phenomena according to formal taxonomic schemes in parts of the social sciences seems not least to be linked to competition with the natural sciences, and the wish to emulate the latter's apparent success at getting prestigiously rewarded for delivering 'hard scientific facts'. However, a closer look at the realities of taxonomic practice in the history of the natural sciences should serve as a warning against too enthusiastically embracing their early methods. Not only did local knowledge in the new lands of encounter often come under 'erasure' (Fan 2004: 89, 113–14; cf. Foucault [1969/1971] 1972; Knight 1981), but people were also classified according to stages 'of advancement' in social evolution (Staum 2003: 13, 122–57). Different forms of dispute resolution, among other parameters, thereby served as an identifying tool of evolutionary stages.

> Earlier scholarship in anthropology and sociology had ranked dispute resolution techniques on a scale that ranged from self-help to negotiation to mediation to arbitration and finally to adjudication on the most 'civilized' end of the scale. (Nader 2002: 150)

Nader observes this tendency to have reversed over the last decades:

> As 'less civilized' nations achieve what was once the hallmark of civilization, law courts, a new standard for civilization, mediation, replaces the old. (2002: 150–51)

While Nader is mainly concerned with the reasoning and practices of an increasing export of ADR techniques from the US to other parts of the world (aiming at implementing new international 'standard' versions of dispute resolution), this chapter will focus on the question of how mediation is actually *defined* in these globally expansive settings.[23] Although evolutionary stages are no longer widely quoted, a principal, often unspoken divide between 'modern'/'industrial' (Western) and 'pre-modern'/'non-industrial' (non-Western) still underlies much theory-making.[24] Despite the accentuated criticism of the modern–traditional binary and of modernization theory over the last decades, these approaches still seem to substantially inform theory-making in the mediation field.

What profound consequences the postulation of binary societal classifiers could have for mediation theory might become clear when looking at Lon Fuller's classic 1971 text on 'Mediation: Its Forms and Functions'. Having discussed in detail his conceptualization of mediation, Fuller therein, almost in passing, notes that the Ifugao example, as described in Barton's work, does not comply with his theory. The Ifugao description does not conform to the distinction between the six categories of 'legislation, adjudication, administrative direction, mediation, contractual agreement, and customary "law"' (Fuller 1971: 338) which the author previously declares as being paramount. He remarks with respect to the *monkalun*, who according to Barton's description can also act as a 'judge', that 'what appear to us as hopelessly confusing ambiguities of role, were probably not perceived as such . . .' (ibid.). The contradiction is resolved by evolutionary explanation: 'primitive' society had not (yet) reached the same advanced state of functional differentiation as modern state society.[25] Fuller explains the contradiction between theoretical assumption and empirical finding by stating that the Ifugao are 'not modern', and hence he can explain their realities by other standards. Subsequently, they can no longer falsify his theory. I would argue that this approach is not at all peculiar to Fuller's text of 1971, but that the same neglect runs through most contemporary texts on mediation outside anthropology. These contemporary texts simply do not point out to the reader their methodological exclusions.

Johannes Fabian has called the strategy of assigning entire populations, through means of 'sequencing and distancing', a different age, the 'denial of coevalness' ([1983] 2002: 30–31). In his critique of a branch of structuralism within anthropology, Fabian warns of the danger of a 'temporal wolf in taxonomic sheep's clothing' (ibid.: 97). Irrespective of whether or not we agree with Fabian's accusation towards structuralism's aims and consequences, his statement contains a valid warning against the danger of creating social, or cultural 'others' (cf. Salem 1993: 361; Nader 2002: 151).

Allegedly Opposites: Mediation versus Arbitration/Adjudication

The creation of functional opposites, in emphasizing differences rather than commonalities, is a major part of the classificatory enterprise. This is true for the classification of societies as much as for producing taxonomies of conflict settlement. The established distinction between mediation and arbitration in mediation literature is just one example of this.

> Mediation and arbitration [i.e. adjudication of one kind] have conceptually nothing in common. The one involves helping people to decide for themselves; the other involves helping people by deciding for them. (Meyer 1960: 164)

We find here an interesting contrast between the statement of the professional mediator Meyer, which was quoted by legal anthropologist Gulliver (1979: 210), and the ethnographic works of some other anthropologists, including Fredrik Barth. The latter, in his description of 'mediators' (*musipan*) among Swath Pathan in Pakistan (Barth [1959] 2004: 96), interchangeably refers to saints acting in their 'role as mediators and peacemakers' (ibid.: 97) and as 'arbitrator[s]'. Does this qualify as a 'conceptual fuzziness' of Barth? Or is it rather his ethnographically informed insight that the saints' roles and strategies can indeed vary according to the circumstances? The contrast between terminological ideal and ethnographic description becomes even more striking when issues of power are discussed in mediation contexts, such as in Bentley's (1983: 280–81) description of Marano mediators in the southern Philippines.

In addition, in other settings, mediation researchers have noticed that 'effective mediation involves coercion of the disputants by the third party' (Greenhouse 1985: 93). Gulliver himself confirms that 'the mediator may take control such that, in effect, he becomes an arbitrator, dictating the outcome (just as, in reverse, an arbitrator may turn to mediatory advice rather than decision making)' (Gulliver 1985: 37). Roberts and Palmer write that 'the line between the mediator and the arbitrator is . . . clear cut in analytic terms' but at the same time admit that 'this line may be obscured in real-life processes' ([2005] 2008: 158). Roberts even concludes that '*any* form of third-party intervention must transform what would otherwise have been a bilateral process' (Roberts 1983: 549). Then why do we uphold clear-cut definitional borderlines between the categories, and assign mediation 'its place' exclusively within the negotiation sphere?

An expanding body of research articles in legal studies on 'hybrids' shows that there is a growing discomfort with the available set of categories in dispute resolution. As the name 'hybrid' implies, categories of a second order are introduced that show features of more than one of the previously established concepts of negotiation, mediation, arbitration and adjudication.[26] The question, however, is whether we would have needed to introduce them as hybrids if we had not previously rigidly defined mutually distinct 'primary' categories. The tendency in the literature to represent 'hybrids' as a new phenomenon that derives from the late 1970s and 1980s onwards is significant, as the proposition of 'primary' categories and derivative 'secondary' ones carries an implicit sub-narrative of chronological and causal order and conditioning.[27] The scenario neglects the fact that ambiguity and fluidity in people's actions (the so-called 'hybrid' ways of acting) is inherent. It has long been practised, particularly in dispute settlement (Silbey 1993: 350).

The principal categorical distinctions between negotiation and mediation, or mediation and arbitration, adjudication and so forth, we find rarely truly doubted. A set of characteristics is assigned to each category, which are mostly thought of as binary opposites (involuntary vs. voluntary, formal vs. informal, etc.). In Goldberg et al. ([1985] 2012: 4), for instance, a summarizing table of 'primary dispute resolution processes' shows a comparison of their defining traits. Roughly summarized, adjudication as a procedure is said to be involuntary, with an imposed third party; it is described as formal, structured, public, and following principled decisions (reasoning). In contrast, mediation appears to be voluntary, with a selected third party; it is said to be informal, unstructured, private, and based on a mutually acceptable agreement (ibid.). In the following section, I wish to test these assumptions in an ethnographic example derived from my own fieldwork in Northeast Africa.[28]

Testing the Theory: Mediation by Ethiopian Elders

Elders of the Oromo and Amhara ethnic groups regularly act as mediators in cases of insult, brawl, injury, theft, homicide, bride abduction and marriage arrangements. A mediation process is initiated where one side acknowledges its 'guilt' in having done harm or injury to another party. The 'guilty' side consequently contacts two, four, six or more elder men of their surroundings, to act as go-betweens for them. These elders travel to where the victim's family lives, and express the wish to make peace, indicating the offender's readiness to pay compensation. In the case of a marriage arrangement, the same kind of procedure is followed, whereby the elder men and mediators petition on behalf of the prospective husband, at the girl's father's home. It is rare that the petitioned side is pleased with the request, at least not from the outset. Generally, the go-betweens have to return several times to the house of the victim or the future bride before the other side signals that they are ready to enter a settlement process, and gives them an appointment for the peace talks or marriage negotiations. For these talks, the victim's or bride's side nominates its own elders to represent their case.

The encounters between the go-betweens and the representatives of the petitioned side are highly formalized, and much care is taken by the messengers not to offend the petitioned family. Formality is indeed the most effective weapon in the hands of the mediators. In a serious case, like homicide, petitioning takes a special form. As the danger of retaliation by the victim's family is immediate, the go-betweens do not dare to get too close to the victim's compound, and instead stand in a line on a plateau at some distance, shouting two words, *isgoo* and *abet*, repeatedly. These words represent both a plea to God and a call for forgiveness, and they are shouted as long and loud as to be heard by the victim's side. Peace negotiations can only begin when the victim's side sends a messenger to them, telling them that the family is ready to enter peace talks.

The peace talks themselves take place at a later point in time, and at a different place. This is preferably in the shadow of a tree. At these meetings, the victim's side sends its own elders to negotiate with the elders of the other side regarding the compensation sum. Depending on how great the danger is of eruption of mutual hostilities at the meetings, family representatives of one or both parties may or may not be present at these occasions.

At the end of a successful mediation, peace is sealed (or a marriage arrangement affirmed) by means of ritual and ritualized activities such as mutual kissing, swearing peace oaths, ritual slaughtering and mutual feasting. The study of mediation by elders is thus as much a study of mediators and seniority as it is about ritual and law. Law, in the narrower sense of a codified set of rules and prescription, plays a crucial role in the mediation settings among Oromo elders. They follow in their procedures and case decisions the old Oromo law, known as *seera*. The *seera* is comprised of a number of paragraphs that are orally transmitted at the generation-set assemblies, and contain, for instance, detailed prescriptions for compensation sums in case of injuries (the eye, the leg, the teeth, etc.) or the loss of a human life.

The example of the Oromo and Amhara elders provides some interesting aspects. The procedure begins with a literal go-between scenario where messengers travel back and forth between the parties and no one seems to be forced to participate in the process or to accept its outcome. The perpetrator's messengers even plea to the offended party to agree to the talks. The submissive behaviour of the messengers is just one layer of the process, however. The appealed family is in fact put under increasing pressure. Elders may be involved in virtual 'peacefare' in their mediations. Their tremendous formality makes clear that they have come as official envoys, not just on behalf of the appealing family but for the sake of all others around, striving for the public good. Their formal repertoire ranges from ritualized speech and behaviour, clothing and use of holy ritual objects, to implicit or explicit threats of curses and withholding of community support to people rejecting their call for peace. This shows the power, not necessarily of individual elders, but of the formality in procedural contexts and of a highly structured and to some extent purposefully ritualized mediation procedure. Mediation processes, in such contexts, are no longer 'private matters', particularly in cases of homicide, where practically all elders of the surrounding villages, as the most senior representatives of society, are involved in the ritualized, public calls for peace.

It is misleading to refer in such contexts to mediation as 'informal' procedures that are to be distinguished from principally 'formal' court adjudications. In fact, the formal–informal binary has rather arbitrarily been allotted in the literature to an opposition between 'state' (or state-approved) versus 'non-state' forms of procedures.[29] Similar doubts may arise with regard to the principle dichotomy between voluntary and involuntary participation, as a distinguishing marker between mediation and adjudication. As regards adjudication, what for one side may be a choice of action (e.g. bringing charges in court against an opponent), for the other party may be an imposed participation. As to mediation, 'voluntariness' may be a matter of grey shading. How voluntary is the participation in a process when every few days, week by week, some of the most senior members of the community, neighbours, advisors and most respected members of religious associations, stand at a family's door and ask them to agree to talks? While it is true that a police force backing the decision of a judge in an adjudicative process can put substantial force on disputants, the same may occur in processes of mediation or negotiation, where threats of curses, divine sanction, retaliation, social exclusion or the future refusal of help may serve as powerful sanctions against disloyalty to the rules of the procedure.

Intercultural Comparison: Traps and Pitfalls

Clear-cut definitional borderlines between mediation and arbitration, or between mediation and adjudication as substantially different 'types' of processes that mutually exclude each other, appear to be largely self-ascribed, state-centred notions that need to be empirically checked in individual cases, and substantially necessitate cultural comparison, if discussed as universal phenomena. This is not to say that 'culture' so far has been excluded as a factor in virtually all literature on mediation. Indeed, there is a growing body of 'intercultural' or 'cross-cultural' studies that have, over the past years, established their own niche in the wider field of dispute resolution. Unfortunately, many of these 'cultural approaches' suffer from a lack of ethnographic and analytical depth. Most problematic is their almost unified repetition of the motif of 'collectivist' cultures or societies that are held to be inherently different from 'individualist Western' societies.[30] While they set out to recognize those 'other' cultures, they eventually reduce them to traditionalist samples. Not seldom, this is paired with a search for the roots of the true, peaceful nature of human relationships that 'we in the West' have already lost.[31] Such representation may be misleading when we wish to understand what is actually going on in situations of conflict in these societies. The wide absence of criticism on the intercultural conflict resolution spectrum seems to mark anthropologists' strong point of disengagement with, and segregation from, this professional branch. It might be problematic to abstain from engaging in a critical dialogue, as in this rapidly expanding sector, powerful new expertise is being generated.

Conclusions

Defining what is considered to be 'within' or 'outside' the realm of mediation goes beyond a narrower academic interest in 'getting the definition right'. It does, for a whole field of investigation, determine what topics, what regions, what groups and human activities are studied and which are not. Definitions hereby play a crucial role as they have an authoritative character, making a claim to truth, and taking effect as being normative. Once established, they exclude 'deviation', and non-compliant evidence is erased from the list of eligible examples.

Moffitt, in his critical review of mediation definition attempts, has come to the conclusion that we cannot avoid the use of categories, as human language itself is wedded to the making and the use of categories (2005: 91–92). The point is not, however, to avoid the use of words and terms such as mediation, arbitration, adjudication; the question is rather what ontological status they will bear, whether they are seen as emic terms or suitable choices of translation in a transnational dialogue, or whether they claim global, normative validity. We need, in an appreciation of detail and complexity, empirical research that counters the forces of 'disciplining' language, and that produces ethnographically informed, 'thick description', deployable for further analysis (Geertz [1973] 2000: 9–10, 14–15). I believe, in the words of Max Gluckman, that 'it is fatal to become . . . "bored with ethnographic fact"' (Gluckman 1961: 16, quoting Firth [1954] 2001: vii).

The challenge that mediation theory faces is 'the integration of cross-cultural data as a solid foundation for broadly-applicable theory' (Nicholson 1983: 224). The problem is how to do this. Talal Asad has warned us that cultural translation itself may not be free of problems, since it 'is inevitably enmeshed in conditions of power' (Asad [1986] 2010: 163). Sally Falk Moore reminds us that it might not be the synchronic 'characteristics' of different societies (2005: 2) but *processes* that need be compared (ibid.: 10).

This chapter is not merely about criticizing mediation studies and law from an anthropological perspective. Riles is right when stating that the different disciplines are not monolithic blocks that stand in opposition (1994: 606), whereby legal studies would incorporate the 'normative part' (being focused on 'text'), while anthropologists would focus on the 'reflexive', critical part (representing 'empirical, real world investigation' [ibid.: 634]). Common ground, or a moment of 'impasse' (ibid.: 642) can indeed be found in parts of the New Legal Realism and Critical Legal Studies movements. However, critical approaches do not necessarily play a major role in either of the disciplines. As Comaroff and Comaroff allegorically term it, we are still in need of a 'less provincial register' in our theory-making (2012: 49). The call for critical empiricism is as valid in anthropology as it is in legal and mediation studies. It might thus be time to found *Critical-Realist Mediation Studies*.

Andrea Nicolas is a social anthropologist and postdoctoral researcher. She has worked at the Max Planck Institute for Social Anthropology in Halle, the Graduate School of the University of Rostock, and Johann Wolfgang Goethe University, Frankfurt (Main). She has carried out extensive fieldwork in Northeast Africa and is the author of the book *From Process to Procedure: Elders' Mediation and Formality in Central Ethiopia* (Wiesbaden, 2011).

Notes

1. Their agreement constitutes 'common knowledge' among most mediation researchers. Cf., e.g., Della Noce, Baruch Bush and Folger (2002: 39), Kressel (2006: 726).
2. Some discourses about mediation have, interestingly, almost reversed their parameters of inclusion and exclusion over time. Firth, in his critical assessment of 1965, still pointed to the common, and in his eyes legitimate, usage of the concept in religious contexts (1965: 388, footnote 2). He also fully acknowledged diplomacy to belong to the sphere of mediation, and even to be its primary origin (ibid.: 387). For the role of diplomats, see also McGaffey (1987: esp. 102–3).

3. Golann (2000: 42); cf. Silbey and Merry (1986: 7–8, 19), Riskin (2003), Oberman (2008). Gulliver also spoke of different 'roles' that mediators might fill: '. . . from virtual passivity, to "chairman," to "enunciator," to "prompter," to "leader," to virtual arbitrator' (1979: 220). He did not consider these terms 'as principally typological but rather as useful indices along . . . [a] continuum' (ibid.), which is noteworthy, as his previous clear-cut definition of mediation in the book in fact *does* imply the claim of an authoritative typology of processes of dispute resolution.
4. How diverse mediation 'typology' (Kressel 2000: 529) or 'taxonomy' (Jones 1989: 229) could appear can be seen in comparison: Wood (2004: 437) names four styles of mediators (the counsellor, the negotiator, the facilitator and the democrat); Wall and Dunne (2012: 236–37) distinguish six categories of mediation strategies (pressing, neutral, relational, analytic, clarification and multifunctional); and Alexander (2008: 97), aiming to combine several existing typologies into a supra- or 'mediation metamodel', establishes six other models of mediation (expert advisory, settlement, facilitative, wise counsel, tradition-based and transformative mediation).
5. An informing example is Riskin's grid of 1996, as modified in 2003. Depending on what variables are included in the analysis, a sheer endless number of grids and matrices emerge from the 'role-of-the-mediator continuum' (Riskin 2003: 30).
6. Cf. Stuart Hall (1992: esp. 189). We may assume that, in Alexander's framework, historical forms of mediation, though in practice rarely discussed, would be put into the same category of 'tradition-based mediation'.
7. See Menkel-Meadow et al. (2005: xxxv); cf. Menkel-Meadow (2000). The first documented use of the term 'alternative dispute resolution' is accorded to Frank Sander (1976) (Roberts and Palmer [2005] 2008: 46). Barrett argues 'that the movement's roots are much deeper and go back much further' (2004: xiii), and presents an 'ADR timeline' that begins as early as 1800 BC (ibid.: xxv). His timeline suggests a linearity in development, and projects the idea and terminology of ADR back into the past. It is of course important to state that various forms of dispute management already existed long before 'ADR' came to play a role in the US. However, it seems problematic to call the whole of dispute settlement history a 'history of ADR' (Sanchez 1996: 2). Roberts and Palmer, more cautiously, speak here of 'precursors to the emergence of ADR' ([2005] 2008: 9).
8. The term 'alternative' has already been widely critiqued; cf. Twining (1993: 382), Nader (2002: 146). 'Alternative' could be understood in different approaches as a utopian alternative to state law or merely as an exception to the rule. Note the substantial difference between Silbey, who sees ADR as a left-wing phenomenon opposing state law (2002: 176), and Nader, who stresses the opposite, namely the massive imposition of ADR, in a quest for pacification and the countering of a growing number of civil rights pleas, through 'conservative', or liberal forces (2002: 48–49, 52–54).
9. Izumi (2010), in a similar vein, speaks of the 'illusion' of mediator neutrality.
10. De Girolamo, for instance, uses the term 'identities' for mediators, though she regards these identities to be shifting rather than static (2013: 150, 207–8).
11. We see here a problem similar to Nader's call for a 'user theory' of law (2002: 49, 169), which might lead us to the idea of a similar 'user theory of mediation'.
12. From the point of view of law, the discussion about mediation is often about issues of due diligence, duty of loyalty, or problems of liability of mediators (Hopt and Steffek 2008: 60–65). Mediation, in these contexts, is seen through the eyes of law, and talked about in the language of law.
13. For the Canadian context, Ellger gives the 'National Mediation Rules' of the 'ADR Institute of Canada' (2008: 675) and the 'Code d'Éthique des Médiateurs' of the 'Institut

de Médiation et de l'Arbitrage du Québec (IMAQ)' (ibid.: 676) as sources for defining state-law approved mediation. Magnus, in the case of Australia, along with further definitions provided in the literature (2008: 572), names the 'standard definition that is recommended by the National Alternative Dispute Resolution Advisory Council (NADRAC)' (ibid.: 572, my translation). 'Indigenous', 'aboriginal' or other forms of mediation that are not approved by national procedures are absent from these discussions.

14. See, for example, the activist stance taken by Larissa Behrendt (1995: 1).
15. It has, for instance, rarely been explored how far the necessity to search for later employment outside the academic field (NGOs, UN, etc.) has influenced anthropologists' research foci and framed their language of description.
16. Or, if translation would occur, to translate from the local language into the analytical language, and not inversely, so as not to force English terminology upon the local findings (Bohannan [1969] 1997: 411). The argument raised by Bohannan has a parallel in critical translation theory (cf. Asad [1986] 2010: 157).
17. For overviews of the debate, see Nadel (1956); Ayoub (1961); Hoebel (1961); Nader (1965, [1969] 1997); Moore ([1969] 1997, 2005); cf. Donovan (2008: esp. 164–67).
18. Concerning 'Western folk knowledge', we could think of the 'dictionary approach' mentioned by Bohannan, which often finds its way into scientific writing, quoting how a certain term is defined by the British Encyclopaedia – but actually just telling us how a certain term, such as 'law' or 'mediation', is commonly used among British and American native speakers of English. In the same vein, we could open a Tiv dictionary and look up how the term '*jir*' ('which means court, court case, moot' [Bohannan 1959: 292]) is defined. The theoretical discussion would then have to be framed in terms of whether or not, or how far, any other court, dispute-solving session or assembly in the world (e.g. a UN meeting in New York City) would qualify to be called '*jir*'; cf. Bohannan (1959, [1969] 1997).
19. In the case of the 'go-between', just as in the example of the 'mediator', we find different usages of the term in other disciplines. See, for example, Raj, who discusses 'knowledge go-betweens' (2009: 112, 117). In Turnbull's usage, the term go-between may denote not only people (2009: 394–96) but also objects (ibid.: 411–12), or even sicknesses (ibid.: 394).
20. For example, Barton's discussions of the 'go-betweens' of the Kalinga (1949) in the Philippines, and Jones' description (1974) of the 'Waigali' in Afghanistan (see the linguistic critique of the ethnonym by Strand [1976]).
21. Max Weber, in 1904, had developed the notion of 'ideal type': '[An ideal type] is formed by the one-sided accentuation of one or more points of view and by the synthesis of a great many diffuse, discrete, more or less present and occasionally absent concrete individual phenomena, which are arranged according to those onesidedly emphasized viewpoints into a unified analytical construct' (Weber [1904] 1997: 90).
22. Only few mediation researchers apparently admit to the latter, however. Exceptions are Silbey and Merry (1986: 19), who speak of two 'ideal types' of mediation styles that they have found. See also Twining (1993: 388–89), who takes his inspiration from Damaška (1986). The latter was not concerned with mediation processes in the first place, but his method is noteworthy in its open application of ideal types in the Weberian sense to juridical procedures (1986: 5, 10–12).
23. Nader suggests commercial interests and a need for 'pacification' in the world as reasons for the US export of ADR and 'harmony ideology' (2002: 151–52, 156). This discussion is a contested field; see the debate of Neal Milner (2002) with Laura Nader and Elisabetta Grande (2002).

24. For example, Brian Tamanaha, who is actually quite aware of some of the problematics involved, applies a distinction between 'traditional society' versus 'modern society' to his theory on jurisprudence ([2001] 2006: 118–19). Cf. Abel (1983), Merry (1982). With particular regard to mediation studies, Nicholson has already emphasized 'the need for a more adequate heuristic device than the industrial-nonindustrial dichotomy' (1983: 205).
25. See Fuller (1971: 338–39). The same existing tendencies in what he calls 'modern' societies Fuller downplays as exceptions (ibid.: 338).
26. For example, 'med-arb', 'neutral expert', 'mini-trial', 'private judges', 'ombudsman', etc.; cf. Menkel-Meadow et al. (2005).
27. Note the possible evaluative ranking between 'primariness' and 'secondariness' (Said [1993] 1994: 70) concerning status, legacy and recognition. For a critical discussion of the concept of hybridity, see also Young (1995).
28. See Nicolas (2011, 2006 and 2007).
29. For a discussion on the problem of formality, see also Bloch (1975: 3–10) and Nicolas (2011: 12–18). In legal studies, the influential 1982 work by Richard Abel, *The Politics of Informal Justice*, often serves as a blueprint for the notion of 'informality' in non-state contexts (1982: 2). A closer reading of Abel, however, shows that the author himself had some doubts about the undifferentiated characterization of mediation processes as being 'informal' (1983: 181).
30. The idea of dichotomies of 'individualism' versus 'collectivism' goes back to the works of Geert Hofstede ([1980] 2001: esp. 209–78) and Edward T. Hall (1976: esp. 39). The postulated opposition between 'low-context cultures' and 'high-context cultures' (ibid.) is often conjoined with the individualism–collectivism complex (e.g. Ting-Toomey 1988). Commentators have meanwhile voiced criticism against the cultural and gender essentialisms proposed in these works, but proponents of the method continue to apply them. See the critique by Ron Scollon and Suzanne Wong Scollon ([1995] 2001: 167–222), who raise the problem of 'cultural ideology and stereotyping' (ibid.: 167). While some authors of 'cultural' conflict and mediation studies clearly mention their sources of inspiration (Barnes [2006] 2007: esp. 5–8), others keep these allegiances hidden from the reader (e.g. Appiah-Marfo 2013: 338–42).
31. See, e.g., Hook, Worthington and Utsey (2009).

References

Abel, R.L. 1982. 'Introduction', in R.L. Abel (ed.), *The Politics of Informal Justice. Volume 2: Comparative Studies*. New York: Academic Press, pp. 1–13.

———. 1983. 'Mediation in Pre-Capitalist Societies', *Windsor Yearbook of Access to Justice* 3: 175–85.

Alexander, N. 2008. 'The Mediation Metamodel: Understanding Practice', *Conflict Resolution Quarterly* 26(1): 97–123.

Appiah-Marfo, S.Y. 2013. 'Conflict Resolution: The *Faksoro* Custom of the Rotumans of the South Pacific', *Conflict Resolution Quarterly* 30(3): 329–45.

Asad, T. [1986] 2010. 'The Concept of Cultural Translation in British Social Anthropology', in J. Clifford and G.E. Marcus (eds), *Writing Culture: The Poetics and Politics of Ethnography*. Berkeley: University of California Press, pp. 141–64.

Ayoub, V.F. 1961. 'Review of Gluckman's *The Judicial Process in Two African Societies*', in M. Janowitz (ed.), *Community Political Systems, Vol. 1. International Yearbook of Political Behavior Research*. New York: Free Press, pp. 237–50.

Barnes, B.E. [2006] 2007. *Culture, Conflict, and Mediation in the Asian Pacific*, rev. edn. Lanham, MD: University Press of America.
Barrett, J.T. (with J.P. Barrett). 2004. *A History of Alternative Dispute Resolution: The Story of a Political, Cultural, and Social Movement*. San Francisco, CA: Jossey-Bass.
Barth, F. [1959] 2004. *Political Leadership among Swat Pathans*. London School of Economics Monographs on Social Anthropology 19. London: The Athlone Press.
Barton, R.F. 1919. *Ifugao Law*. San Francisco, CA: University of California (= *University of California Publications in American Archaeology and Ethnology* 15(1): 1–186, plates 1–33).
———. [1919] 1967. 'Procedure among the Ifugao', in P. Bohannan (ed.), *Law & Warfare: Studies in the Anthropology of Conflict*. Austin: University of Texas Press, pp. 161–81.
———. 1930. *The Half-Way Sun: Life among the Headhunters of the Philippines*. New York: Brewer & Warren, Inc.
———. 1949. *The Kalingas: Their Institutions and Custom Law*, introduction by E.A. Hoebel. Chicago, IL: University of Chicago Press.
Behrends, A., S.-J. Park and R. Rottenburg. 2014. 'Travelling Models: Introducing an Analytical Concept to Globalisation Studies', in A. Behrends, S.-J. Park and R. Rottenburg (eds), *Travelling Models in African Conflict Management: Translating Technologies of Social Ordering*. Leiden: Brill, pp. 1–40.
Behrendt, L. 1995. *Aboriginal Dispute Resolution*. Leichhardt: The Federation Press.
Beidelman, T.O. 1971. 'Nuer Priests and Prophets: Charisma, Authority and Power among the Nuer', in T.O. Beidelman (ed.), *The Translation of Culture: Essays to E.E. Evans-Pritchard*. London: Tavistock Publications, pp. 375–415.
Benda-Beckmann, F. von. 2009. 'Riding or Killing the Centaur? Reflections on the Identities of Legal Anthropology', in M. Freeman and D. Napier (eds), *Law and Anthropology*. Current Legal Issues 12. Oxford: Oxford University Press, pp. 13–46.
Bentley, C. 1983. 'Marano Mediation and the Reproduction of Social Hierarchy', *Windsor Yearbook of Access to Justice* 3: 270–88.
Blake, S., J. Browne and St. Sime. 2013. *The Jackson ADR Handbook*. Oxford: Oxford University Press.
Bloch, M. 1975. 'Introduction', in M. Bloch (ed.), *Political Language and Oratory in Traditional Society*. London: Academic Press, Inc., pp. 1–28.
Bohannan, P. 1957. *Justice and Judgment among the Tiv*. London: Oxford University Press.
———. 1959. 'Anthropological Theories', *Science* 129(3345): 292–98.
———. 1967. 'Review of *The Ideas in Barotse Jurisprudence*, by Max Gluckman', *Kroeber Anthropological Society Papers* 36: 94–101.
———. [1969] 1997. 'Ethnography and Comparison in Legal Anthropology', in L. Nader (ed.), *Law in Culture and Society*. Berkeley: University of California Press, pp. 401–18.
Chakrabarty, D. [2000] 2007. *Provincializing Europe: Postcolonial Thought and Historical Difference*, new preface by the author. Princeton, NJ: Princeton University Press.
Collier, J.F. 1973. *Law and Social Change in Zinacantan*. Stanford, CA: Stanford University Press.
Comaroff, J., and J. Comaroff. 2012. *Theory from the South: Or, How Euro-America Is Evolving Toward Africa*. Boulder, CO: Paradigm Publishers.
Conley, J., and W. O'Barr. 2004. 'A Classic in Spite of Itself: *The Cheyenne Way* and the Case Method in Legal Anthropology', *Law and Social Inquiry* 29: 179–217.
Connell, R. 2007. *Southern Theory: The Global Dynamics of Knowledge in Social Science*. Crows Nest, NSW: Allen & Unwin.
Damaška, M.R. 1986. *The Faces of Justice and State Authority: A Comparative Approach to the Legal Process*. New Haven, CT: Yale University Press.

De Girolamo, D. 2013. *The Fugitive Identity of Mediation: Negotiations, Shift Changes and Allusionary Action*. London: Routledge.
Della Noce, D.J., R.A. Baruch Bush and J.P. Folger. 2002. 'Clarifying the Theoretical Underpinnings of Mediation: Implications for Practice and Policy', *Pepperdine Dispute Resolution Law Journal* 3(39): 39–65.
Donovan, J.M. 2008. *Legal Anthropology: An Introduction*. Lanham, MD: AltaMira Press.
Ellger, R. 2008. 'Mediation in Kanada', in K.J. Hopt and F. Steffek (eds), *Mediation: Rechtstatsachen, Rechtsvergleich, Regelungen*. Tübingen: Mohr Siebeck, pp. 671–725.
Evans-Pritchard, E.E. [1940] 1969. *The Nuer: A Description of the Modes of Livelihood and Political Institutions of a Nilotic People*. New York: Oxford University Press.
Fabian, J. [1983] 2002. *Time and the Other: How Anthropology Makes Its Object*. New York: Columbia University Press.
Fan, F. 2004. *British Naturalists in Qing China: Science, Empire and Cultural Encounter*. Cambridge, MA: Harvard University Press.
Firth, R. [1954] 2001. 'Foreword', in E.R. Leach, *Political Systems of Highland Burma: A Study of Kachin Social Structure*. London: Continuum, pp. v–viii.
———. 1965. 'A Note on Mediators', *Ethnology* 4: 386–88.
Folberg, J., Dw. Golann, L. Kloppenberg and Th. Stipanowich. [2005] 2010. *Resolving Disputes: Theory, Practice, and Law*. New York: Wolters Kluwer Law & Business.
Foucault, M. [1969/1971] 1972. *The Archaeology of Knowledge & The Discourse on Language*, trans. A.M. Sheridan Smith. New York: Pantheon Books [orig.: M. Foucault. 1969. *L'Archéologie du savoir*. Paris: Éditions Gallimard].
Fuller, L.L. 1971. 'Mediation: Its Forms and Functions', *Southern California Law Review* 44: 305–39.
Geertz, Cl. [1973] 2000. *The Interpretation of Cultures: Selected Essays*. New York: Basic Books.
———. [1983] 1993. 'Local Knowledge: Fact and Law in Comparative Perspective', in Cl. Geertz, *Local Knowledge: Further Essays in Interpretative Anthropology*. London: Fontana Press, pp. 167–234.
Gluckman, M. 1955. *The Judicial Process among the Barotse of Northern Rhodesia*. Manchester: Manchester University Press.
———. 1959. 'The Technical Vocabulary of Barotse Jurisprudence', *American Anthropologist* 61(5): 743–59.
———. 1961. 'Ethnographic Data in British Social Anthropology', *The Sociological Review* 9(1): 5–17.
———. [1965] 1972. *The Ideas in Barotse Jurisprudence*. Manchester: Manchester University Press.
———. [1969] 1997. 'Concepts in the Comparative Study of Tribal Law', in L. Nader (ed.), *Law in Culture and Society*. Berkeley: University of California Press, pp. 349–73.
Golann, Dw. 2000. 'Variations in Mediation: How – and Why – Legal Mediators Change Styles in the Course of a Case', *Journal of Dispute Resolution* 41: 41–61.
Goldberg, St.B., F.E.A. Sander, N.H. Rogers and S.R. Cole. [1985] 2012. *Dispute Resolution: Negotiation, Mediation, Arbitration, and Other Processes*, 6th edn. New York: Wolters Kluwer Law & Business.
Greenhouse, C.J. 1985. 'Mediation: A Comparative Approach', *Man* (N.S.) 20(1): 90–114.
Gulliver, Ph.H. 1970. 'Review of *Ideas and Procedures in African Customary Law*, ed. by Max Gluckman', *Bulletin of the School of Oriental and African Studies* (London) 33(3): 685–86.
———. 1979. *Disputes and Negotiations: A Cross-Cultural Perspective*. New York: Academic Press.
———. 1985. 'Arbitration and Mediation', in A. Kuper and J. Kuper (eds), *The Social Science Encyclopedia*. London: Routledge, pp. 36–37.

Hall, E.T. 1976. *Beyond Culture*. Garden City, NY: Anchor.

Hall, S. 1992. 'The West and the Rest: Discourse and Power', in S. Hall and B. Gieben (eds), *Formations of Modernity: Understanding Modern Societies*. Cambridge: Polity Press, pp. 184–227.

Hensler, D.R. 2002. 'Suppose It's Not True: Challenging Mediation Ideology', *Journal of Dispute Resolution* 2002(1): 81–99.

Hoebel, E.A. 1961. 'Three Studies in African Law', *Stanford Law Review* 13: 418–42.

Hofstede, G. [1980] 2001. *Culture's Consequences: Comparing Values, Behaviors, Institutions, and Organizations across Nations*. Thousand Oaks, CA: Sage Publications.

Hook, J.N., E.L. Worthington and S.O. Utsey. 2009. 'Collectivism, Forgiveness, and Social Harmony', *Counseling Psychologist* 37(6): 821–47.

Hopt, K.J., and F. Steffek. 2008. 'Mediation: Rechtsvergleich, Regelungsmodelle, Grundsatzprobleme', in K.J. Hopt and F. Steffek (eds), *Mediation: Rechtstatsachen, Rechtsvergleich, Regelungen*. Tübingen: Mohr Siebeck, pp. 3–102.

Izumi, C. 2010. 'Implicit Bias and the Illusion of Mediator Neutrality', *Journal of Law and Policy* 34(71): 71–155.

Jones, Sch. 1974. *Men of Influence in Nuristan: A Study of Social Control and Dispute Settlement in Waigal Valley, Afghanistan*. London: Seminar Press.

Jones, T.S. 1989. 'A Taxonomy of Effective Mediator Strategies and Tactics for Nonlabor-Management Mediation', in A. Rahim (ed.), *Managing Conflict: An Interdisciplinary Approach*. New York: Praeger, pp. 221–29.

Knight, D. 1981. *Ordering the World: A History of Classifying Man*. London: Burnett Books.

Komma, T. 1998. 'Peacemakers, Prophets, Chiefs and Warriors: Age-Set Antagonisms as a Factor of Political Change among the Kipsigis of Kenya', in E. Kurimoto and S. Simonse (eds), *Conflict, Age and Power in North East Africa: Age Systems in Transition*. Oxford: Ohio University Press, pp. 186–205.

Kouassi, E.K. 2000. 'West Coast Diplomacy among the Akan and Their Neighbors', in I.W. Zartman (ed.), *Traditional Cures for Modern Conflicts: African Conflict 'Medicine'*. Boulder, CO: Lynne Rienner Publishers, pp. 67–77.

Kressel, K. 2000. 'Mediation', in M. Deutsch and P.T. Coleman (eds), *The Handbook of Conflict Resolution: Theory and Practice*. San Francisco, CA: Jossey-Bass Publishers, pp. 522–45.

———. 2006. 'Mediation Revisited', in M. Deutsch, P.T. Coleman and E.C. Marcus (eds), *The Handbook of Conflict Resolution: Theory and Practice*, 2nd rev. edn [1st ed. 2000]. San Francisco, CA: Jossey-Bass, pp. 726–56.

Kroeber, A.L. 1926. 'Law of the Yurok Indians', in *Proceedings of the 22nd International Congress of Americanists*, Vol. 2. Rome, pp. 511–16.

Levitt, P., and S. Merry. 2009. 'Vernacularization on the Ground: Local Uses of Global Women's Rights in Peru, China, India and the United States', *Global Networks* 9(4): 441–61.

Magnus, U. 2008. 'Mediation in Australien', in K.J. Hopt and F. Steffek (eds), *Mediation: Rechtstatsachen, Rechtsvergleich, Regelungen*. Tübingen: Mohr Siebeck, pp. 569–85.

McGaffey, D.C. 1987. 'Negotiation and Mediation: A Diplomat's Perspective', in D.J.D. Sandole and I. Sandole-Staroste (eds), *Conflict Management and Problem Solving: Interpersonal to International Applications*, foreword by K.E. Boulding. London: Frances Pinter, pp. 100–103.

Menkel-Meadow, C. 2000. 'Mothers and Fathers of Invention: The Intellectual Founders of ADR', *Ohio State Journal on Dispute Resolution* 16(1): 1–37.

———. 2001. 'Introduction', in C. Menkel-Meadow (ed.), *Mediation: Theory, Policy and Practice*. Aldershot: Ashgate, pp. xiii–xxxviii.

———. 2009. 'Chronicling the Complexification of Negotiation Theory and Practice', *Negotiation Journal* 25: 415–29.

Menkel-Meadow, C.J., L. Porter Love, A. Kupfer Schneider and J.R. Sternlight. 2005. *Dispute Resolution: Beyond the Adversarial Model*. New York: Aspen Publishers.
Merry, S.E. 1982. 'The Social Organization of Mediation in Nonindustrial Societies: Implications for Informal Community Justice in America', in R.L. Abel (ed.), *The Politics of Informal Justice, Volume 2: Comparative Studies*. New York: Academic Press, pp. 17–45.
———. 2006a. 'Transnational Human Rights and Local Activism: Mapping the Middle', *American Anthropologist* 108(1): 38–51.
———. 2006b. *Human Rights and Gender Violence: Translating International Law into Local Justice*. Chicago: University of Chicago Press.
Meyer, A.S. 1960. 'Functions of the Mediator in Collective Bargaining', *Industrial and Labor Relations Review* 13(2): 159–65.
Milner, N. 2002. 'Illusions and Delusions about Conflict Management: In Africa and Elsewhere' (Commentary to Laura Nader and Elisabetta Grande 2002), *Law and Social Inquiry* 27(3): 621–29.
Moffitt, M.L. 2005. 'Schmediation and the Dimensions of Definition', *Harvard Negotiation Law Review* 10(69): 69–102.
Moore, S.F. [1969] 1997. 'Comparative Studies', in L. Nader (ed.), *Law in Culture and Society*. Berkeley: University of California Press, pp. 337–48.
———. 2005. 'Comparisons: Possible and Impossible', *Annual Review of Anthropology* 34: 1–11.
Nadel, S.F. 1956. 'Reason and Unreason in African Law', *African* 26(2): 160–73.
Nader, L. 1965. 'The Anthropological Study of Law', *American Anthropologist* 67(6), Part 2, (Special Issue: The Ethnography of Law): 3–32.
———. [1969] 1997. 'Introduction', in L. Nader (ed.), *Law in Culture and Society*. Berkeley: University of California Press, pp. 1–10.
———. 1990. *Harmony Ideology: Justice and Control in a Zapotec Mountain Village*. Stanford, CA: Stanford University Press.
———. 2002. *The Life of the Law: Anthropological Projects*. Berkeley: University of California Press.
Nader, L., and E. Grande. 2002. 'Current Illusions and Delusions about Conflict Management in Africa and Elsewhere', *Law and Social Inquiry* 27(3): 573–94.
Nicholson, M.E.R. 1983. 'Modern Mediator in Cross-Cultural Perspective', *Windsor Yearbook of Access to Justice* 3: 204–27.
Nicolas, A. 2006. 'Governance, Ritual and Law: Tulama Oromo Gadaa Assemblies', in S. Uhlig (ed.), *Proceedings of the XVth International Conference of Ethiopian Studies, Hamburg July 20–25, 2003*. Wiesbaden: Harrassowitz Press, pp. 168–76.
———. 2007. 'Founded in Memory of the "Good Old Times": The Clan Assembly of Hiddii, in Eastern Shewa, Ethiopia', *Journal of Eastern African Studies* 1(3): 484–97.
———. 2011. *From Process to Procedure: Elders' Mediation and Formality in Central Ethiopia*. Wiesbaden: Harrassowitz Press.
Oberman, S. 2008. '*Style* vs. *Model:* Why Quibble?', *Pepperdine Dispute Resolution Law Journal* 9(1): 1–62.
Pirie, F. 2005. *Feuding, Mediation and the Negotiation of Authority among the Nomads of Eastern Tibet*. Working Paper No. 72. Halle/Saale: Max Planck Institute for Social Anthropology.
Raj, K. 2009. 'Mapping Knowledge Go-Betweens in Calcutta, 1770–1820', in S. Schaffer, L. Roberts, K. Raj and J. Delbourgo (eds), *The Brokered World: Go-Betweens and Global Intelligence, 1770–1820*. Sagamore Beach, MA: Watson Publishing International, pp. 105–50.
Riles, A. 1994. 'Representing In-Between: Law, Anthropology, and the Rhetoric of Interdisciplinarity', *University of Illinois Law Review* 1994(3): 597–650.

Riskin, L.L. 1996. 'Understanding Mediators' Orientations, Strategies and Techniques: A Grid for the Perplexed', *Harvard Negotiation Law Review* 1(7): 7–51.
———. 2003. 'Decisionmaking in Mediation: The New Old Grid and the New New Grid System', *Notre Dame Law Review* 79(1): 1–53.
Roberts, S., and M. Palmer. [2005] 2008. *Dispute Processes: ADR and the Primary Forms of Decision-Making*, 2nd edn. Cambridge: Cambridge University Press.
Roberts, S.A. 1983. 'Mediation in Family Disputes', *The Modern Law Review* 46(5): 537–57.
———. 1994. 'Law and Dispute Processes', in T. Ingold (ed.), *Companion Encyclopedia of Anthropology: Humanity, Culture and Social Life*. London: Routledge, pp. 962–82.
Said, E. [1993] 1994. *Culture and Imperialism*. London: Vintage Books.
Salem, P.E. 1993. 'A Critique of Western Conflict Resolution from a Non-Western Perspective', *Negotiation Journal* 9(4): 361–69.
Sanchez, V.A. 1996. 'Towards a History of ADR: The Dispute Processing Continuum in Anglo-Saxon England and Today', *The Ohio State Journal on Dispute Resolution* 11(1): 1–39.
Sander, F.E.A. 1976. 'Varieties of Dispute Processing', *Federal Rules Decisions* 70: 111–34.
Scollon, R., and S. Wong Scollon. [1995] 2001. *Intercultural Communication: A Discourse Approach*. Malden, MA: Blackwell Publishers.
Silbey, S. 1993. 'Mediation Mythology', *Negotiation Journal* 9(4): 349–53.
Silbey, S.S. 2002. 'The Emperor's New Clothes: Mediation Mythology and Markets', *Journal of Dispute Resolution* 2002(1): 171–77.
Silbey, S.S., and S.E. Merry. 1986. 'Mediator Settlement Strategies', *Law & Policy* 8(1): 7–32.
Staum, M.S. 2003. *Labeling People: French Scholars on Society, Race, and Empire, 1815–1848*. Montreal: McGill-Queen's University Press.
Strand, R.F. 1976. 'Review of *Men of Influence in Nuristan: A Study of Social Control and Dispute Settlement in Waigal Valley*, by Schuyler Jones', *The Journal of Asian Studies* 35(4): 712–13.
Tamanaha, B.Z. [2001] 2006. *A General Jurisprudence of Law and Society*. Oxford: Oxford University Press.
Ting-Toomey, S. 1988. 'Intercultural Conflict Styles: A Face-Negotiation Theory', in Y. Kim and W. Gudykunst (eds), *Theories in Intercultural Communication*. Newbury Park, CA: Sage, pp. 213–35.
Turnbull, D. 2009. 'Boundary-Crossings, Cultural Encounters and Knowledge Spaces in Early Australia', in S. Schaffer, L. Roberts, K. Raj and J. Delbourgo (eds), *The Brokered World: Go-Betweens and Global Intelligence, 1770–1820*. Sagamore Beach, MA: Watson Publishing International, pp. 387–428.
Twining, W. 1993. 'Alternative to What? Theories of Litigation, Procedure and Dispute Settlement in Anglo-American Jurisprudence: Some Neglected Classics', *The Modern Law Review* 56: 380–92.
Volpe, M.R., and D. Chandler. 2001. 'Resolving and Managing Conflicts in Academic Communities: The Emerging Role of the "Pracademic"', *Negotiation Journal* 17(3): 245–55.
Wall, J.A., and T.C. Dunne. 2012. 'Mediation Research: A Current Review', *Negotiation Journal* 28(2): 217–44.
Weber, M. [1904] 1997. *The Methodology of the Social Sciences*, trans. and ed. E.A. Shils and H.A. Finch. New York: Free Press [orig.: M. Weber. 1904. 'Die "Objektivität" sozialwissenschaftlicher und sozialpolitischer Erkenntnis', *Archiv für Sozialwissenschaft und Sozialpolitik* 19: 22–87].
Wood, J. 2004. 'Mediation Styles: Subjective Description of Mediators', *Conflict Resolution Quarterly* 21(4): 437–50.
Young, R. 1995. *Colonial Desire: Hybridity in Theory, Culture and Race*. London: Routledge.

Chapter 5

Mediation in Circumstances of the Existential

Dispute and Justice in Rwanda

Stefanie Bognitz

Vignette – Émilienne

Émilienne is an elected mediator in the cell of Nyamirama in the Southern Province of Rwanda. Before becoming a mediator, she had already been an elected judge – *inyangamugayo*, literally, a trustworthy person who can stand against humiliation – of the Gacaca Court in her place of residence. In her capacity as *inyangamugayo*, she adjudicated genocide-related cases and earned the nickname 'prosecutor', given to her by people who experienced her impartiality and tireless encouragement to seek truthful accounts of what happened during the genocide in 1994 and what needs to be known for her community to live on. When asked about how she was accepted and trusted as a mediator, Émilienne points out the significance of the sashes that mediators wear during their sessions. These appear in the colours of the national flag, green, yellow and blue and are provided to mediators by the Abunzi Secretary in the Ministry of Justice. Émilienne recounts that 'the small flag we put on with our sashes gives us power'. When I inquire further about the need for mediation, she responds that 'there are many heads in Rwanda, many bad things happened here and people don't trust each other. Mediation is like your intelligence and we can show people how it can repair our broken hearts. When we go into mediation, the mediation committee, together with the disputing parties and their witnesses become one thing'. Émilienne frankly states her task of mediating under the auspices of the state, when she describes her embodiment of power in situations of mediation as related to the visible signs of the nation state. Her estimation of being in the position of a mediator alludes to an involved self-interest (Gulliver 1977: 16), but also accounts for the common good of mediation.

Vignette – Désiré Émmanuel

Désiré Émmanuel is elected vice-chair of the Mediation Committee of second instance of Gasaka Sector in the Southern Province of Rwanda in which he is responsible for mediating appeal cases. He acknowledges the inscription of mediation into law since 'it was important to establish a law on mediation to guide people and make them take mediation seriously'. The promise that mediation brings with it lies in its unifying goals, because 'people don't have similar understandings, but if there is a law encouraging them to better understand a certain principle, it helps them to reach a common understanding and to move forward'. He believes that 'mediation is to make people understand each other. One party can be in dispute because he thinks only on his own behalf and has no other advice. A good outcome is when all the parties are convinced and agree to leave the dispute, instead of people not agreeing and pushing us to enter into the case'. Apart from being challenged by people to bring about more legal consciousness, understanding and sensitivity for ordinary Rwandans, Désiré Émmanuel aims to look beyond the force of law and sets mediation apart, stating: 'We don't go deep into the laws, mediators – *Abunzi* – are not like judges, our aim is mediation'.

The Promise of Mediation

Alongside the advent of extraordinary transitional justice instruments, Rwanda's ordinary legal system was extended to include a historically and locally embedded mechanism for mediation. On the one hand, mediation establishes access to justice and relieves ordinary courts of law from heavy caseloads and backlogs. On the other, mediation contributes to a more effective functioning of courts, since certain cases are sorted in mediation before they move on into the courtroom (Rwanda Governance Review 2012). Since 2004, community-elected mediation committees have been a substantial component of the Rwandan justice system. These committees are situated at the lowest, most accessible levels. Thirty thousand mediators are elected by their local communities. Mediation, which is mostly known as an alternative dispute resolution mechanism (cf. Nader 1980; Palmer and Roberts 1998; Busingye 2014), was adapted to become a decentralized, widely spread and locally established institutional form. 'The settlement, mediation, conciliation and arbitration can be especially recognized as the actual need for another decentralised justice; less frightening, more communicative and therefore closer and more human' (Rwanda Governance Review 2012: 14). In the Rwandan context, however, mediation is not an alternative to adjudication, but a foregoing supplement in the sense of an addition. A case below a certain value can only move into court when it has undergone mediation beforehand and mediators have decided upon its classification for appeal in court.

The institutional form of mediation enforces mandatory or so-called obligatory mediation for civil (below 3m RWF/$3,200) and criminal (petty) cases below a certain value. This limits access to courts for cases and litigants in order to refer them or restrict them to mediation only (see also Lankhorst and Veldman 2011: 25). The difference in costs on behalf of the justice system for a mediated case at appeal level (20,000 RWF) and a court case at first instance (280,000 RWF) has been calculated at 260,000 RWF (ibid.: 54–56). This excludes the costs to be incurred by litigants once a claim is addressed in a court of law. Given this background to the introduction of mediation in Rwanda, ruling mediation by jurisdiction within the premises of formal statutory law and including the mediation committee in the judiciary, the model applied can be termed *mandatory mediation*. However, the question of whether the mediation committee is an integral part of the Rwandan judiciary or separate from it can be debated, since any deliberations and decisions made by the mediation committee at the appeal level are not considered by the court of first instance when the case is pursued further, that is, appealed in an ordinary court of law, or Primary Court (see also Abel 1982: 299). Following from this, the legal practice and competence of mediators weighs less than the jurisdiction of a court of law and the expertise of a judge. Still, mediation is a new and unprecedented process in the institution of the Rwandan justice system. Even though it was introduced as an amendment to courts rather than a replacement, mediation committees are organizational extensions (Rottenburg 2009: 105, 140) of the established judiciary and strongly rely on such a structure, keeping old structures in place but extending them by adding new aspects to emphasize discontinuities or obsolescence of the organizational apparatus under scrutiny.

The Rwandan model of mediation, specifically, has been enthusiastically implemented throughout the country. Its popular purchase is based on effective and efficient outcome-oriented mediation practice. It is a legal service rendered to ordinary people cutting across categories such as class, age, gender, origin and ethnicity. When John Comaroff considers law as a fetish in its becoming a common denominator, he observes that citizens everywhere are increasingly encouraged to deal with their everyday problems by making use of legal means (Comaroff 2006: 6). This is a challenging suggestion if we expect that the transformation of problems into disputes simultaneously implies the achievement of more justice. Comaroff continues with this scenario: 'And heterogeneity begets more law. Why? For one thing, because legal instruments *appear* . . . to offer a means of commensuration: a repertoire of standardised terms and practices that, like money in the realm of economics, permit the negotiation of values and interests across otherwise intransitive lines of difference' (Comaroff 2006: 11, emphasis in the original). The legal means that Comaroff points out – be it in this case mediation as a truth and agreement-seeking institutional practice – offer a common language for the common place of law, a space where ordinary people render their common complaints and everyday problems into disputes situated in a public arena (see also Snyder 1993: 17).

The suggestion to establish mediation as an institution is laid out in the 2003 Constitution of Rwanda in its Article 159: 'There is hereby established a "Mediation Committee" responsible for mediating between parties to certain disputes involving matters determined by law prior to the filing of a case with the court of first instance. The Mediation Committee shall comprise of persons of integrity and acknowledged for their mediating skills'. Following the Constitution, consecutive Organic Laws were adopted to regulate the structure, competence and functioning of mediation committees. These laws comprise Organic Law N° 17/2004 of 20 June 2004, Organic Law N° 31/2006 of 14 August 2006, Organic Law N° 02/2010/OL of 9 June 2010 as the latest amended law governing mediation committees (*Komité z'Abunzi*), Presidential Order N° 49/01 of 6 July 2010 specifying modalities for electing the mediation committee members, as well as Ministerial Order N° 82/08.11 of 2 May 2011 determining internal rules and regulations of the mediation committee.

To strengthen the capacity of Abunzi, the Ministry of Justice and its Abunzi Secretary organize training to improve mediators' knowledge of existing and governing laws as well as their application in everyday mediation. Following Organic Law N° 02/2010 of 9 June 2010 mentioned above, the Ministry of Justice (2012) published guidelines for Abunzi – *Inyigisho Zigenewe Abunzi* – in order to outline the ways in which mediation is carried out and translate the Organic Law for the mediators.

The 2010 amended 'Organic Law on the Organisation, Jurisdiction, Competence and Functioning of the Mediation Committee' states in its Article 20 on hearings that 'when settling a case, Mediators shall hear claims from each of the parties in conflict and from witnesses if any. They may have recourse to advice by any person who can shed light on the matter'. The procedure of how to go about mediation is outlined in Article 21: 'To settle the dispute submitted to them, Mediators shall seek *first* to conciliate the two parties. *In case of non-conciliation*, they take *decision consciousness according to their hearts' advice* and in accordance with the Laws and local customary practices provided it is not contrary to the written Law' (capital letters in the original, my emphasis).

These two articles capture the cardinal point in the law on mediation, laying out the regimes of action for mediators and disputing parties. Article 21 thus sensitizes mediators to consecutively move from the primary regime of action, *conciliation*, to the secondary, *decision*. If the imperative to reconcile peacefully fails, the mediators decide on the dispute based on their legal consciousness and considering the parties' claims of justice (see also Doughty 2014). The article introduces a qualitative aspect to the mediation process. The easier and desired regime of action in mediation is laid out in the practice of conciliation. Following from this, the more challenging aspect of bringing parties together in mediation shall be achieved through the practice of decision. In a regime of action in mediation within which mediators seize their decision consciousness, disputing parties must hand over their agency to reconcile to the mediators, who will come to a decision on a necessary conciliation. To achieve these two distinctive regimes of action in mediation, it is required for the mediation committee to be elected from among a group of locally known persons of integrity – *inyangamugayo*, literally, someone who stands against humiliation. Citizens acknowledge them publicly for their trustworthiness and their mediating skills (Bognitz 2017).

Connotations of the word mediation in Kinyarwanda – *kunga* – draw on several areas of ordinary practice. In the realm of medicine, it describes the re-joining of a broken bone. In ordinary handicraft, it captures the process of connecting two cords into a longer one. A third connotation testifies to mediation as described here, when the relationship between people is re-established and parties enter a situation of conciliation. The emphasis here is re/conciliation through mediation. The law on mediation sets the basis for the creative capacity of parties in mediation shifting between regimes of action. Article 21 signposts mediation, but mediation as such is not a law. The process of mediation can take at least three substantial forms, shaped by the expectations of the parties and the position of the mediators towards the parties. First, engaging in a mutual agreement is equivalent to conciliation between the disputing parties. Second, an agreement reached through mediation is a result of re/conciliation facilitated by the mediators. Third is the case of non-agreement, in which mediators begin a mediation-like process, accompanied by cross-examination, classification – that is, rejection or acceptance of evidence – and hearing of witnesses, resulting in a decision made by the mediators, but not the disputing parties. What is stipulated in the law on mediation, however, is distributive and procedural justice, as will be further explored below. Mediation relies on a certain dynamic and openness among all participants. Parties in dispute as well as the mediators, who shape and remake mediation as an open-ended dispute resolution mechanism, always depend on the dynamics between the involved actors.

It is never self-evident at the outset of mediation how it will be concluded, and nor are regimes of action in mediation to be understood as discrete competences. What mediation, as observed in Rwanda, shows is a dynamic dispute resolution mechanism, which holds the possibility of an *alternative* in its procedural character, but is not an *alternative* to adjudication (cf. Benda-Beckmann, this volume). If there is a 'Rwandan model' of mediation, it is a blend of the ideal types of dispute resolution, namely negotiation, arbitration, mediation or adjudication. These alleged boundaries quickly fade away in the everyday practice of mediation.

The new institutional form of mediation committees enforces mandatory mediation for certain civil and criminal cases. This curtails access to courts for cases and litigants in order to access mediation only.[1] I will explore the re-institutionalization of what the Rwandan legislator calls home-grown initiatives to contemporary challenges (Rwanda Governance Review 2012) further in the following section. In this sense, legal practitioners employ 'hybrid models' with a certain flexibility and creativity and reshape these in the making of law (de Sousa Santos 1984). This hybridity of mediation – bringing a dispute resolution model from the past and introducing it into contemporary law – has its limits. Even though practices of mediation are embedded in Rwandan legal and cultural history (Reyntjens 1990; Sarat and Kearns 1998), most of the involved actors in the contemporary system – volunteer mediators and parties in dispute – experience mediation as a legal institution in the realm of the state, rather than under the control of local legal knowledge regimes and practices. The cultural justification for the practice of mediation cannot overwrite the mandatory force of mediation in Rwanda (Doughty 2016; Provost 2017). This condition surfaces when disputing parties during mediation sessions tirelessly claim broader conceptions of access to justice and challenge their mediators, arguing that: 'You are the custodians of the law', 'You are obliged to read the law to us', 'You have to educate us about the law' or 'You have to share with us what is on your mind about this case' (mediation at Gasaka Sector, Southern Province of Rwanda, 2012). In this regard, citizens pursue access to justice by means of legal knowledge in general, and demand access to knowledge about land, succession and inheritance law in particular, which are all issues at the heart of ordinary citizens' everyday existential concerns. Their demands shape an understanding of access to justice as legal practice rather than access to the legal system.

Mediation in the Wake of Post-Transitional Justice in Rwanda

In the wake of post-transitional justice, procedural justice occupies an imperative space for disputing parties in mediation. It implies the actors' perception of fairness of the inherent rules and procedures that regulate a decision-making process and result in the making of agreements. Justice is measured according to the application of the rules, that is, the degree to which they are complied with (Peachey 1989: 301). Moreover, procedural justice is practised and entered into by seizing the right to voice disagreement. This strengthens the aspect of popular participation, which is of substantial value for the mediation procedure. Often, claimants' complaints address the aspect of procedural injustice: 'Mediators don't care, at least in court, they write down your case and set a date' (disputing party, Nyamagabe, Southern Rwanda, 2012). To some extent, such ambiguities in the perception of mediation may arise from the legal constellation of the mediation committee – mediation is mandatory, whereas mediators deliver a voluntary service, dedicating time and effort for a small remuneration of annual health insurance coverage (see Organic Law N° 02/2010/OL, Article 3 on Mediation Organ). This shortcoming can render mediation uncertain, and challenges the promise of mediation as a hybrid dispute resolution mechanism.

Another emerging form of justice can be traced regarding the litigation or matter of dispute enabled through the mediation committee. Property, succession and inheritance-related matters of dispute make up the biggest number of cases mediated in respective committees. In order to settle such cases to the satisfaction of the involved parties in dispute, and therefore prevent future disputes, the aspect of distributive justice is imperative for the mediators (Doughty 2014). It is for this reason that distributive justice can often be traced in disputes related to resource allocation for which different criteria can be applied in order to agree on a fair and just distribution. Such criteria have to be negotiated and allocated throughout the process of mediation, often involving witness accounts and knowledge from within the community in which a dispute over land or property is located. Equality, proportionality and need are significant variables in the achievement of distributive justice (Peachey 1989: 301–2). In summary, distributive justice and the prospect of mediation share an intrinsic relationship.

People in different social arrangements share the need to address problems and resolve their disputes. Practices, networks, organizations and institutions are established that help participants to work towards reaching impartial agreements. To be legitimate, comprehensive and fair, their conditions need to be flexible enough to allow for competing views. In this regard, mediation is one way to achieve the articulation of problems and the negotiation of agreements. Mediation has materialized as a form, model, practice, paradigm, concept and ideology that has attracted the attention of a multitude of scholars and ignited debates across different disciplines (Fuller 1971; Nader 1980; Felstiner et al. 1980–81; Merry 1989; Palmer and Roberts 1998).

Before any mediation process stands a disagreement aggravated to a dispute. There are various responses to states of crisis. Someone's feelings of discontent and perceptions of injustice could remain unarticulated. But when actors express their experiences of infringements of rights, they want to set things right and articulate their discontent openly. When a problem is in the world and framed as a claim, parties in dispute often recur to long established processes when they situate a dispute in a public forum, possibly with a third party intervener – as the mediation process suggests (Gulliver 1977: 15). This process relies on justifications, probably of accusations, which were until then ignored or silenced by various other forces at play, and grafted on the initial disagreement. The unfolding dispute relies not only on linking accusations with experiences of injustice, but disputes evolve around material objects of desire or loss that establish equivalences in relations. A dispute is the articulation of perceived injustices addressed as a claim to a public forum (Snyder 1993: 13). As acceleration of an unanswered claim or an unresolved disagreement between persons, a dispute is addressed to a public forum possibly staffed by a third party (Gulliver [1969] 1997: 14). There is another correlation at play regarding the quality and scale that is hidden underneath 'the duration of disputes that depends on the intensity of bonds that unite victims with those against whom they clamour for justice' (Snyder 1993: 13). Of anthropological concern is the gradual transformation from disagreement to dispute. At the time when a dispute crosses the threshold demarcating the private from the public, the intimate from the open, it enters the public forum of mediation. It is beyond this threshold that the substantial elements of the underlying disagreement become abstract in such a way that they turn into a general, legible form of processed dispute. The processed dispute is replete with arguments that are put to the test by the parties involved and scrutinized by mediators for their worth and significance with regard to whether they are approximations of the truth or facts. Studying dispute resolution mechanisms opens a perspective on what matters in cases enacted in the judicial sphere in regard to respective assemblages, rules, institutions and stabilizing objects (Boltanksi and Thévenot 1999: 360).

I depart from a general understanding that mediation is a way of dealing with disputes. It is enacted as a significant form of dispute resolution when ruptures in the social or normative order amount to perceptions of discontent that can be articulated by disputing parties in the presence or under the guidance of the facilitative capacity of a third party. As a practice, mediation connects resolution of a dispute and its prevention in a twofold process, in which the settlement of past injustices has a similar significance to expectations of the future as part of negotiating a mutual agreement. It is thus necessary to consider different approaches towards the processes and prospects of mediation.

Mediation can be traced throughout human and legal history as part of human interaction (Gulliver 1977: 16), for social organization and even in the non-human material world, in human-environment-technology interactions and interfaces (cf. Haraway 2016). 'An important role for institutions becomes the normative mediation between conflicting representations, technologies, and rhythms in time' (Bear 2014: 7).

Mediation also suggests an understanding of dispute resolution in light of creative, dynamic and inclusive processes in dealing with wrongs and establishing social order. Mediation as a form to address injustices redirects our focus to the production of legitimacy, not only in an agreement but also of emerging social and legal institutions. This directly relates to the range and scale of mediation as a field of practice that has brought about various models of mediation. In light of existential concerns in post-transitional justice Rwanda, the inquiry into mediation considering practices of critique, justifications and dispute alludes to how mediation is questioned and reshaped.

Legal scholars situate mediation as an alternative dispute resolution (ADR) model, with the premise of mediation as an 'alternative' to law (Fuller 1971). Such alternatives to adjudication show a wide variety and range, for example from negotiation to mediation to arbitration. In aiming for restorative justice, ADR approaches are established to exclude retribution in the form of punishment, as a result of adjudication, and instead emphasize mutuality, compliance and reintegration. Mediation as an alternative dispute resolution earns its justification due to its emphasis on the restoration of bonds, mutual trust and consent between parties. As a practice, mediation promises to embrace and reinforce reciprocity as foundational in the organization of the social.

Mediation has been implemented as a legal fix in many post-conflict settings in transition, including tendencies of increasing professionalization and legalization of mediation. Some legal scholars have argued that mediation is not about compromise (Menkel-Meadow 2001) and that models of ADR in general are not necessarily neutral (Nader 1993). What can be said of mediation is that it is situated at the heart of maintaining social control in situations of rupture, dispute, uncertainty or conflict (Gulliver 1963; Greenhouse 1985: 91). There are other practices that could be treated as mediation when they are – explicitly or implicitly – about the production of social order and offer creative approaches to overcome situations of disaccord, animosity or conflict in their broadest sense. Studying mediation in this broader sense as a specific form of negotiation can generate insights into how agreements are reached (Boltanski and Thévenot 2006).

Mediation constitutes a diverse and pluralistic field of study. Literature on mediation roughly follows four different plots, narrated along the lines of *satisfaction* in terms of its effectiveness and quality of justice, *social justice* with regard to its agency in helping people to achieve fair and equal treatment, *oppression* in reference to social control and surveillance, and *transformation* of human conflict and interaction as well as interconnected institutions (Bush and Folger 2005). Mediation may offer an orientation towards the future that lies in its anticipation of pacified relations, the partial forgetting of aspects of litigation and the ongoing making and remaking of the dispute, so that it is never fixed or explicit at any moment, but rather undergoes constant transformation and reiteration (Menkel-Meadow 2004: 101).

Mediation in Circumstances of the Existential: Clémentine Muhawenimana

In the vignette at the start of this chapter, Désiré Émmanuel differentiates possible situations in the process of mediation. Mediation can succeed and reach a good conclusion when a dispute is overcome and laid to rest. This is the case when disputing parties under the guidance of mediators gradually take distance from their initial claims, accusations and justifications as they stand at the inception of the mediation process. The disputed matter and the dispute as such move into the background, while mutual relations and empathy for each other gain more emphasis throughout the situation and are brought into the foreground. This dynamic process of mediation is almost always anticipated by mediators at the outset and unfolds during the course of mediation. Often, mediators emphasize their understanding of what should be achieved through mediation with the help of physical space that forces the disputing parties into proximity. Lack of space and the restrictions of the tight locations in which mediation committees gather have an enabling capacity given the mediators' strategy to move a dispute into the realms of mutual recognition of the parties. The mediators can limit the physical distance between parties: 'come and sit together', or consciously create situations of proximity: 'embrace each other' (mediation committee, Gasaka Sector, Southern Province of Rwanda, 2013).

Gradual shifts in the application of the rules of engagement for mediation depend on speech acts, practices, strategies and tactics in mediation and the degrees of intervention by the mediators, who have the capacity to create conditions for mutual understanding in order to move collectively into a realm of recognition.

Against this background, I trace some of the everyday endeavours of Clémentine Muhawenimana from Nyamagabe District in the Southern Province of Rwanda as she sets off to turn a family matter of contested land into a dispute that draws on a sense of injustice. In the mediation setting, Clémentine encounters Désiré Émmanuel, who speaks in the earlier vignette, as he takes the lead in mediating her claim of access to family land. Clémentine is in her early twenties, she is illiterate, has a disability and lives temporarily with her child in an adobe tool shed entrusted to her through someone's goodwill. She reports that after giving birth to her child, she had already been homeless several times. Even now, her living situation is uncertain, neither safe nor appropriate for her and her child. When we enter the tool shed together, I realize that the rice and sugar I brought along in neatly enveloped brown paper bags are almost the only staple foods in the shed, despite some shrivelled sweet potatoes scattered on the bare floor. There are neither food supplies nor distinct traces to show that mother and child have been living in the shed. Everything seems makeshift and transitory. Clémentine puts the bags on the clammy mud floor, where they will soon be dampened by humidity and examined by curious ants. In the absence of any furniture, I can only assume that mother and child spend their nights on the ragged cloth spread out on the floor. While looking for a place to sit down for our interview, we are surrounded by innumerable farming tools. These are not only reminders of the bare life led in the tool shed, but are strangely reminiscent of a time of killing (cf. Hatzfeld 2006, 2008), a sight and emotion I would often encounter due to the plethora of accounts of genocidal violence available in witness and survivor accounts of the Gacaca Courts. I do not ask further about the living conditions in the tool shed, but Clémentine interrupts my quiet concern and starts to talk about the rain. During the rainy season, she would not sleep but sit through the night under an umbrella waiting for the rain to stop.

The tool shed, besides being a marker of poverty, exclusion from the local community and the absence of neighbours, and therefore a makeshift space that is even contested by the local authorities who oblige every resident to register in designated residential spaces, such as *umudugudu* (agglomerations of households) rather than tool sheds turned living spaces, is far from the only indignation that Clémentine continues to experience. She spent two and a half years of her early childhood in the infamous Gikongoro prison, which is only a stone's throw from her current tool shed shelter. When Clémentine's mother was prosecuted for the homicide of her husband, she took the four-month-old baby with her to serve the sentence. After her mother's release from prison, Clémentine remembers her being careless of the well-being of her children. Together with her siblings, she would have to struggle to make a living on her own. Clémentine's biography carries a certain weight of accumulated impurities, humiliation and hardships. She believes that her physical disability – one of her legs is completely stiff and she already feels that this impairment has taken its toll on her whole body – is related to her mother's crime, a guilt for which Clémentine would repent physically through suffering pain and indignation. She imagines this tragedy in her family to be transposed onto her present living conditions, of which she is reminded with every step she takes. In the following, I lay out some of the problems and predicaments Clémentine continues to bring to the attention of responsible authorities at different levels in the decentralized administrative structure and legal system.

Only recently Clémentine moved to Gasaka Sector located in Nyamagabe District in the Southern Province of Rwanda, where the family land and house of her parents are located. A sector is an administrative unit established through Rwanda's decentralization policy, based on the 2003 Constitution as an initiative to promote good governance, accessibility of administrative infrastructure and accountability of local governance on the premises of proximity between citizens and local authorities in respective institutions (see also Bierschenk and Olivier de Sardan 2014). It was Clémentine's intention to open a case to gain access to the land and house of her parents with the responsible authorities, the local mediation committee and with the assistance of the Access to Justice Bureau of Nyamagabe District (see also Bognitz 2013). Meanwhile, Clémentine also addresses her uncertain living conditions and denial of access to her parents' land to the executive secretary of the cell[2] for assistance in improving her housing situation. In Rwanda, such assistance could be organized either through the occasion of *umuganda*, which is a form of voluntary but regular and organized community work, or through *ubudehe*, which is a form of social assistance and support based on a voluntary effort achieved through the involvement of the local community.[3] The executive secretary, however, refuses to organize either of the supporting schemes to improve Clémentine's situation. What is more, *umukuru w'umudugudu*, a local authority of the village, the smallest administrative unit within which Clémentine currently resides, also denies her requests. This authority justifies its denial based on Clémentine's uncertain living circumstances, her not having a decent address and place of residence, which in turn make it impossible for Clémentine to be known and eligible for any supporting schemes. Her encounters with the authorities have become a vicious circle in which her predicaments are taken up by authorities as justifications not to care for her condition and to deny her underlying request for assistance and support. Clémentine attempts to generalize her claim by asking the authorities about the number of days and nights they want her to spend out in the open without shelter before receiving any attention or help from them. With this strategy, she challenges the local authorities' sense of what vulnerability entails for Clémentine, who is mother to a child without a residence or a proper home to live in.[4]

Clémentine nevertheless continues to take her claim further, to the administrative level of the district, and addresses the mayor. Before she was able to talk to the mayor, however, she staged a public protest against the local authorities who had neglected her. As a mode of resistance, she remained in front of the district office until late into the night; citizens do not generally frequent public offices outside of working hours, or publicly display their disobedience to state authorities. By the time of nightfall, she was forcefully taken to the police station by a night watchman. From the police station, she was referred back to the district mayor, but her claim continued to be played back and forth between authorities at different levels of local governance, making it impossible for Clémentine to situate her claim in a public arena.

When she recaps the last two and a half years, the time it took for her claim to unfold, she believes that her appearance, her disability, her childhood as an orphan and the fact that she falls in the social category of a vulnerable person are certainly among the reasons for her repeated rejection by the responsible authorities. She compares herself to other claimants she had observed before mediation committees. She has seen a father who came to a mediation session together with his son for the first time. After only a short time, they left with a written decision in their hands with which they could then proceed to other instances of local administration and governance – they had been served well, she believed. Clémentine, however, would have appeared before the same mediation committee for the second time without even having had the chance to address the mediators or convey her claim so that they could register her and schedule a session for mediating the involved parties. From these experiences, she concludes that if she had a brother, or anyone better off to support her, the claim would have taken a different route. She also does not have the means or self-assertion to follow up on the matter. From the local authorities that Clémentine had addressed during the last few years, she came to understand that she was neglected because of the quantity of problems she brought forth. The multiple entanglements of her claims in relation to her vulnerable living conditions could not be processed by the established legal-administrative apparatus. Moreover, Clémentine alone was not in a position to generalize her attempts to turn her multiple entanglements into a singularly circumscribed claim.

There are normative principles at the heart of people's critical actions, opinions and articulations. Among such critical practices are people's claims in moments of denunciation of social injustices or the critical moments in which injustices and inequality surface. Veena Das (1995) refers to critical events, as it is yet uncertain what these moments may hold for the future. For Clémentine, bureaucratic and administrative injustices were most likely reproduced because of her exclusion from the local community for reasons of family relations and the perceived threat of her causing disorder due to broken family ties and disintegration. It is noteworthy how Clémentine has come to understand what is considered legitimate critical capacity in justification. As of now, it is necessary to trace the competences Clémentine employs as her sense of injustice goes along with experiences of neglect and exclusion she made in the context of local legal – mediation committees and governance – structures. She disentangles her claim, initially replete with multiple entanglements of problems and shortcomings, in order to situate a sharply cut out claim in the realm of justice. Having undergone significant degrees of abstraction and generalization, Clémentine brings a land-related dispute to the attention of the responsible mediation committee. With this achievement, it is yet a different set of normative principles, forms and procedures against which she will test her critical capacity on the premises of justifications referring to generalized values, ordering practices and established laws. In order to keep alive the critical capacity of an actor's justification in a situation of crisis or dispute, the legitimacy of someone's claims towards someone else, be it a person who is already familiar with the situation or someone external to it, can only be maintained with reference to general principles, that is, a process of generalization is set in motion (Boltanski and Thévenot 1999: 364). The legitimacy of critique or justification therefore depends on the level of generalization. Clémentine submits the existential human condition that holds her hostage to a reality test. She addresses her claim to a number of authorities, organizations and institutions, trying to mobilize others in order to turn her claim into a delineated dispute that qualifies for mediation or can eventually be submitted to court. Only if she is successful in mobilizing supporting persons and abstracting her claim to rephrase it in the sense of injustice with a general validity, can the claim turn into a dispute, which again relies on the critical capacity of justification shared by others such as mediators and the public. Clémentine lays out her attempts to mobilize others on the level of local-legal governance and the administrative apparatus.

> I engaged the court, legal aid and the district authorities. I spent one night on the steps to the district office in search for justice until I was arrested by the police. But finally, the district mayor listened to my problems and wrote down my claim for the consideration of local authorities. That is how the matter was brought about. They [local authorities] turned it into a case and referred it to the mediators. That is how I entered the mediation and we started to go deep into the heart of the matter.

Clémentine first appeared in mediation in August 2012, by which time I had already started to regularly participate in mediations with the Gasaka Sector committee. Désiré Émmanuel served in the capacity of vice-chair of the mediation committee and regarded my presence during mediations as beneficial to the mediators' deliberations, probably because of my experience in numerous such committees in the Southern Province, some of which would hand over their appeal cases from the first instance mediation to the second instance located at Gasaka Sector. Initially, Clémentine formulated her claim, taking on the identity of a claimant against three elderly men, her paternal uncles, of illegally crossing the boundaries onto her family's plot of land.[5] The notion of family land herein refers to a plot owned first by Clémentine's parents and after their passing communally owned by all the children, female and male, that is, Clémentine and all her siblings. At the beginning of mediation stands an accusation. Before opening the mediation procedure, an unexpected inquiry into the relationship between both parties in dispute by one of the mediators aptly switches the register of engagement in mediation. The answer is surprising: 'She is our child', mentions one of the defendants, who turns out to be Clémentine's uncle, one of her father's brothers. Immediately, the mediators are filled with hope and attempt to re-establish peaceful relations between the relatives. They appeal to the parties' mutual recognition of their relationship and existing family bonds. 'There is no need to be in dispute with your child, you can find an agreement. Here, we encounter many people who reconcile and leave their case', argues Désiré Émmanuel. Not letting too much time pass, to comply with this rhetoric, Clémentine swiftly reiterates her sense of injustice and lays out her claim by referring to her general state of destitution and marginalization. 'I do not have a place to stay. They occupy my property. What can I do if I do not have a field to live from?' This evokes the existential concern at the centre of her claim and her ongoing search for security, well-being and future certainty (Jackson 2013: 25). She employs the more general forms of exclusion and poverty to validate her claim. How can she be asked to ignore equivalences when the distribution of goods and properties remains uneven? She reinforces, without referring to shared family bonds, that '*they* occupy the *whole* land and I have *nothing*'. In response to Clémentine's general claim, Désiré Émmanuel, still convinced of the principle of shared humanity and empathy, seeks the possibility of reconciliation with the three elderly men. 'As mature and wise people that you are, do you really want to exclude her from the family land and your common property?' The mediator refers to the elderly defendants' integrity and experience. He points out that they are themselves responsible for their families. The three uncles are well past their sixties. The mediator wants to know one thing at that point: 'Could you instead share the land with her?' The mediators' attempt to establish a situation that has the capacity to hold all involved parties together based on their family bonds fails (cf. Gulliver 1977). The three defendants harshly reject this suggestion. Thus, they repetitively put forth justice claims. They employ the language of accusation supported by proof and denunciation (cf. Boltanski and Thévenot 2006: 228–31). Their tone gets rough.

Defendant: She lies.
I bought the land.
Here is the contract of purchase.
She even wants to go to Kagame![6]

The mediators' initial ambition to put the affair to a reality test under the regime of recognition and mutual trust fails. Taking several turns, the parties in dispute repeat their claims of justice. Again, the opposition of the disputing parties is thereby emphasized by what I have already referred to as the central variables of a dispute process. Imbued with temporality, morality and bargaining powers, verbal exchanges alongside the continuous formulation and utterances of new truth and justice claims continue (Boltanski 2012: 203–4). Suddenly, another incident drives the mediation to yet another deadlock. A strong denunciation of morality puts at risk the truthfulness of Clémentine and promptly stirs up the mediators.

Defendant:	Alas, even her mother killed her father with her own hands.
Clémentine:	(Silence.) (Bows down to reach out for her child.)
Lead Mediator:	*No*. This is *not* the case here!
Second Mediator:	Can this girl be liable for that?
Lead Mediator:	This is not *our* case. If there is such a case and her mother committed that crime, it has to go to court.

The defendant's surprising accusation introduces Clémentine's family history to the mediators and the public. It refers back to broken family bonds and brusquely transposes her mother's criminal responsibility for murder in cold blood onto Clémentine's claim submitted to mediation. As of now, she is certainly no longer the defendants' child, as the mediator evoked only a short while ago at the outset of mediation. She carries on and probably embodies the lingering guilt of her mother, who brought unaccountable loss to the brothers and relatives of her husband, the father of Clémentine. This loss stands as it is acclaimed to rather impair the family of the deceased than Clémentine as a daughter. However, the defendant's reiteration of past circumstances outlining a family tragedy is instantaneously and unequivocally rejected by the mediators. In the semi-professional socio-legal practice of mediation, the mediators know well that they are not a competent body, given their situatedness on the threshold of the legal system, to mediate or in this case adjudicate serious criminal matters that fall under the auspices of the Penal Code.[7] The lead mediator turns to Clémentine and inquires again: 'So, without going into the case, what can they [your uncles] do according to you in order to put the dispute to rest? We wanted you to mediate among yourselves. Now, I think we have to enter the case'. The disputants remain with their initial justifications so the mediators see themselves confronted with taking account of their 'decision consciousness in accordance with the laws' (Organic Law N° 02/2010/OL of 9 June 2010, Article 21, p. 25). This implies that the dispute is unlikely to be laid to rest.

Since the mediation process between Clémentine and her elderly uncles is irreversibly framed by justifications from the moment of mobilizing allegations of a crime in the family, the mediators have to withdraw to material objects in support of the parties' justice claims and mutual accusations. As mentioned earlier in Clémentine's case history, she fails to present underlying material evidence because of a number of unwilling actors who refuse to support her cause. After weeks of bargaining over the case, the mediators take a decision that will neglect Clémentine's claim. Speaking in 'accordance with the law', the mediators could not find a basis for her to gain access to the land as she had originally anticipated. Moreover, the mediation re-emphasizes her precarious living conditions and leaves her trapped in a marginal state without any prospect to access land as a very basic means of survival. What is more, mediation has taken away the chance to share the family land from which Clémentine could have made a rightful and legitimate living. The decision taken by the mediators stating that she has no access or inheritance rights actually situates Clémentine as a person deprived of a childhood, disconnected from the family from which she descended, and excluded from her parental shared property of which she should have inherited her share as eligible and rights-bearing offspring of a legal marriage.

Concluding Remarks

Taking mediation as a magnifying glass enables us to look at judicial and administrative structures in the wake of post-transitional justice in Rwanda. Through decentralization, bringing with it new bureaucratic and institutional forms, processes of dispute are put in the hands of people in the same context in which their disagreements and disputes occurred in the first place, ensuring that agreements are reached at the lowest institutional capacities possible at almost no cost, at least by the calculations of the state. In mediation, disputes are decentralized and embedded in the local context, situated beyond the sight of higher legal or state authority. However, bearing in mind that the alternative of mediation, commonly known as a local legal practice, has been blended into law under the order and auspices of the state, it is transformed into a central codified dispute resolution process of the state, expected to decentralize disputes that are undesirable for central state consideration. Access to justice and access to the legal system are disconnected and newly evaluated by actors in mediation, as has been shown in detail in the case of Clémentine. In the ethnographic outline of Clémentine's experience of mediation, her existential human condition could not be altered by dispute processes, as suggested in the transformative model of mediation by Bush and Folger (2005). Instead it was only reinforced. Clémentine cannot succeed in freeing herself from victimhood. 'It is in the nature of a victim not to be able to prove that one has been done a wrong. A plaintiff is someone who has incurred damages and who disposes of the means to prove it. One becomes a victim if one loses these means' (Lyotard 1988: 8, quoted in Das 1995: 174).

When entering mediation, disputing parties may display resentment and deep hostility towards each other. This is not only manifested in body language or reticence between antagonists inside cramped mediation rooms, but moreover in their strategies to invent facts and tamper with arguments or in their tactics to bring critique to light and let mistrust appear on the surface of a situation (Bognitz 2018). But the triadic constellation of the mediation process can contribute to the recreation of trust, mutual bonds between families or neighbours in dispute and cooperation for the achievement of satisfying and sustainable solutions (Bognitz 2017). Moreover, equivalences amplified when the actors seized the emphatic aspects of language which they conveyed in the practice of mediation. Mute or tacit equivalences can only develop force as critiques, excuses or justifications when they are given a voice or stand in for people who defend their respective justice claims (Boltanski 2012: 70–71). Boltanski would thus argue that there is no closure for disputes that cannot reach beyond justice:

> Indeed, the persons involved in this process will constantly seek new objects, new arguments, new persons deemed trustworthy, to defend them, support their cause and provide evidence. This is why the regime of justice is always insufficient in itself. It can channel disputes at least for a while by subjecting them to its own order. But it is powerless to stop them. To end a dispute in justice, one always has to seek out something other than justice. (Boltanski 2012: 91)

Assuming that language also maintains disputes by giving equivalences a voice, it would seem impossible to settle disputes under the regime of justification (Boltanski 2012: 159). And indeed, the regime of justification in which all involved actors situate themselves led to the impossibility of mediation and the refusal of access to land for Clémentine. Jean-François Lyotard adds that 'the plaintiff becomes a victim when no presentation is possible of the wrong he or she says he or she has suffered' (1988: 8). Being in the position of the claimant, suffering from an existential condition evokes the memory of experiences of injustice and may even recall some aspects of it more vividly because of her continuous situation of suffering, deprivation and humiliation.

Acknowledgements

I thank Fazil Moradi, Sally Engle Merry, Richard Rottenburg, Bertram Turner, Jean and John Comaroff for their critical discussion of and engagement with my ethnography on promises of access to justice in Rwanda on which this text is based. This chapter matured in discussions at the International Max Planck Research School on Retaliation, Mediation and Punishment with Keebet and Franz von Benda-Beckmann, Günther Schlee, Karl Härter and many others. I would also like to thank Carolin Hillemanns for her continued support of this publication project and her tireless commenting on this text.

Stefanie Bognitz is faculty member and lecturer at the Institute for Social and Cultural Anthropology at the Martin Luther University Halle-Wittenberg. She is also a fellow at the Research Network on Law, Organization, Science and Technology and associate at the Max Planck Institute for Social Anthropology. Her recent publications include 'Mistrusting as Mode of Engagement in Mediation: Insights from a Socio-Legal Practice in Rwanda', in F. Mühlfried (ed.), *Mistrust: Ethnographic Approximations* (transcript, 2018), pp. 147–68.

Notes

1. The notion of access to justice as I will refer to in the course of this chapter therefore suggests a somewhat hidden double bind in the sense that in a situation of granting access to the institution of mediation, access to courts is ruled out. It is moreover noteworthy to differentiate between access to justice as opposed to access to the legal system. But this is not to suggest that access to mediation falls short of achieving justice.
2. In Kinyarwanda, people refer to this authority as *umunyamabanga nshingwabikorwa w'akagari*, which literally describes a person who attends to the tasks entrusted to her in secrecy.
3. For Clémentine to be eligible to receive social assistance from *ubudehe*, she must fall within one of the *ubudehe* categories. Following the poverty categorizations of the National Ubudehe Programme, Clémentine is among the poorest, living under conditions of extreme poverty. She is categorized as someone 'who doesn't have something to eat, is homeless, begs, doesn't even have a nail and is lucky when he dies' (Poverty Category 1 – the Poorest, National Ubudehe Programme in EDPRS2 Social Protection Strategy).
4. According to the Participatory Poverty Assessment (Government of Rwanda 2001), Clémentine would fall under the category of 'vulnerable', i.e. 'no sufficient propriety of his own, his and his family's living standards are not commendable and are characterised by bad

food, uncomfortable and small house, begging, lack of access to health care, children do not attend school, and dirt.' (Government of Rwanda 2001: 25, see also Sommers 2012).

5. The enigma of land distribution and access is at the core of mediation in Rwanda. In a country-wide performance survey of mediation committees in 2012, a majority of 86 per cent of claims submitted to mediation were land-related. These consisted of 47 per cent of claims relating to inheritance of land and properties, followed by 39 per cent of claims relating to movement of field boundaries (Rwanda Governance Board 2012: 35). However, I must mention that land-related claims and disputes are only shaped as such during the mediation process specifically and during the time of accessing the legal system by passing certain obligatory passage points of local governance, executive secretaries and local authorities who bear responsibility for naming a claim and inscribing it in registration books that are handed on to mediation committees. In this regard, disputes are abstracted forms of claims constructed after multi-layered claims have been sorted out from prolonged precursory conflicts and translated to disputes with the assistance of a third party, the mediators.
6. The reference to 'going to Kagame' here relates to the occasions when the president of Rwanda would tour the countryside and install himself in a particular place for a number of hours to listen to citizens' concerns directly. People can seize the opportunity to bring matters of concern personally to the attention of the president. However, people also refer to others who take this opportunity to talk to the president in an ironic way, to belittle a person's claim as being too marginal a matter to deserve the attention of the authoritative president. Quite similar perceptions circulate about bringing people's affairs to the office of the ombudsperson or the president's legal office. Many who experienced injustices and misdemeanours, especially on behalf of decentralized instances of administration and governance, take this course of action.
7. The competence of mediators is restricted to petty criminal offences in which the value of the loss suffered by the injured party does not exceed 3m RWF, which equals 3,400 EUR (Organic Law N° 02/2010/OL of 9 June 2010, Article 9, pp. 14–16).

References

Legal Sources

Constitution of the Republic of Rwanda of 04 June 2003. Amendment n° 2 of 08 December 2005. Retrieved 14 September 2015 from http://www.wipo.int/edocs/lexdocs/laws/en/rw/rw032en.pdf.

Ministry of Justice. 2012. *Inyigisho Zigenewe Abunzi* [Instructional guidelines concerning mediation committees]. Kigali, Rwanda.

Organic Law N° 17/2004 of 20 June 2004 on the Organisation, Jurisdiction, Competence and Functioning of the Mediation Committee. *Official Gazette of the Republic of Rwanda*. Retrieved 19 July 2018 from http://www.primature.gov.rw/fileadmin/user_upload/documents/Official%20Gazettes/2006%20Official%20Gazettes/Official_Gazette_no_Special_of_16.08.2006.pdf.

Organic Law N° 31/2006 of 14 August 2006 on the Organisation, Jurisdiction, Competence and Functioning of the Mediation Committee. *Official Gazette of the Republic of Rwanda*. Retrieved 19 July 2018 from http://www.primature.gov.rw/fileadmin/user_upload/documents/Official%20Gazettes/2006%20Official%20Gazettes/Official_Gazette_no_Special_of_16.08.2006.pdf.

Organic Law N° 02/2010/OL of 09 June 2010 on the Organisation, Jurisdiction, Competence and Functioning of the Mediation Committee. *Official Gazette of the Republic of Rwanda*. Retrieved 19 July 2018 from http://www.primature.gov.rw/fileadmin/user_upload/doc

uments/Official%20Gazettes/2010%20Official%20Gazettes/Official_Gazette_no_28_of_12.07.2010.pdf.
Rwanda Governance Review. 2012. *Documenting Home-grown Initiatives: Assessing Performance of Mediation Committees*. Rwanda Governance Board Kigali, Rwanda. Retrieved 02 April 2020 from http://www.rgb.rw/fileadmin/Publications/Rwanda_Governance_Review/Rwanda_Governance_Review_2012__Mediation_Committees.pdf.

Published Sources

Abel, R.L. 1982. 'The Contradictions of Informal Justice', in R.L. Abel (ed.), *The Politics of Informal Justice*. New York: Academic Press, pp. 267–320.
Bear, L. 2014. 'Doubt, Conflict, Mediation: The Anthropology of Modern Time', *Journal of the Royal Anthropological Institute* 20(S1): 3–30.
Bierschenk, T., and J.-P. Olivier de Sardan. 2014. 'Ethnographies of Public Services in Africa: An Emerging Research Paradigm', in T. Bierschenk and J.-P. Olivier de Sardan (eds), *States at Work: Dynamics of African Bureaucracies*. Leiden: Brill, pp. 35–65.
Bognitz, S. 2013. 'Crafting Transitional Justice: Significations of Rights-Based Organisations and Legal Aid in Rwanda', *Nouvelles Études Pénales* 24: 269–83.
———. 2017. 'Trusting Mediators: On Becoming *inyangamugayo* in Rwanda', *POLITIKA*.
———. 2018. 'Mistrusting as Mode of Engagement in Mediation: Insights from a Socio-Legal Practice in Rwanda', in F. Mühlfried (ed.), *Mistrust: Ethnographic Approximations*. Bielefeld: transcript, pp. 147–68.
Boltanski, L. 2012. *Love and Justice as Competences: Three Essays on the Sociology of Action*. Cambridge, MA: Polity Press.
Boltanski, L., and L. Thévenot. 1999. 'The Sociology of Critical Capacity', *European Journal of Social Theory* 2: 359–77.
———. 2006. *On Justification: Economies of Worth*. Princeton, NJ: Princeton University Press.
Bush, R.A.B., and J.P. Folger. 2005. *The Promise of Mediation: The Transformative Approach to Conflict*, revised edn. San Francisco, CA: Jossey-Bass.
Busingye, J. 2014. 'Alternative Dispute Resolution: Quest for Affordable, Accessible Justice', *The New Times Rwanda*, 8 September.
Comaroff, J. 2006. 'Reflections on the Anthropology of Law, Governance, and Sovereignty in a Brave Neo World', Keynote Lecture at the conference 'Law and Governance', Max-Planck-Institute for Social Anthropology, Halle.
Das, V. 1995. *Critical Events: An Anthropological Perspective on Contemporary India*. Delhi: Oxford University Press.
de Sousa Santos, B. 1984. 'From Customary Law to Popular Justice', *Journal of African Law* 28(1/2): 90–98.
Doughty, K.C. 2014. '"Our Goal Is Not to Punish But to Reconcile": Mediation in Postgenocide Rwanda', *American Anthropologist* 16(4): 1–15.
———. 2016. *Remediation in Rwanda: Grassroots Legal Forums*. Philadelphia: University of Pennsylvania Press.
Felstiner, W.L.F., et al. 1980–81. 'The Emergence and Transformation of Disputes: Naming, Blaming, Claiming. . .', *Law & Society Review* 15(3/4): 631–54.
Fuller, L.L. 1971. 'Mediation: Its Forms and Functions', *Southern California Law Review* 44: 305–39.
Government of Rwanda. 2001. 'Participatory Poverty Assessment'. Retrieved 30 June 2017 from http://www.devpartners.gov.rw/fileadmin/templates/docs/EDPRS/Key%20Analytical%20Studies/Overarching%20Studies/Participatory_Poverty_Assessment_Report_2001.pdf.

Greenhouse, C.J. 1985. 'Mediation: A Comparative Approach', *Man* 20(1): 90–114.
Gulliver, P.H. 1963. *Social Control in an African Society. A Study of the Arusha: Agricultural Masai of Northern Tanganyika*. London: Routledge and Kegan Paul.
———. [1969] 1997. 'Case Studies of Law in Non-Western Societies: Introduction', in L. Nader (ed.), *Law in Culture and Society*. Berkeley, CA: University of California Press, pp. 11–23.
———. 1977. 'On Mediators', in I. Hamnett (ed.), *Social Anthropology and Law*. London: Academic Press, pp. 15–52.
Haraway, D.J. 2016. *Staying with the Trouble: Making Kin in the Chthulucene*. Durham, NC: Duke University Press.
Hatzfeld, J. 2006. *Machete Season: The Killers of Rwanda Speak*. London: Picador.
———. 2008. *A Time for Machetes: The Rwandan Genocide – The Killers Speak*. London: Serpent's Tail.
Jackson, M. 2013. *Lifeworlds: Essays in Existential Anthropology*. Chicago: University of Chicago Press.
Lankhorst, M., and M. Veldman. 2011. *Legal Empowerment and Customary Law in Rwanda: Report of a Pilot Project Concerning Community-Level Dispute Resolution and Women's Land Rights*. Leiden University: International Development Law Organization.
Lyotard, J.-F. 1988. *The Differend: Phrases in Dispute*. Minneapolis: University of Minnesota Press.
Menkel-Meadow, C. 2001. 'Introduction', in C. Menkel-Meadow (ed.), *Mediation: Theory, Policy and Practice*. Dartmouth: Ashgate, pp. xiii–xxxviii.
———. 2004. 'Remembrance of Things Past? The Relationship of Past to Future in Pursuing Justice in Mediation', *Law & Society Review* 5: 97–115.
Merry, S.E. 1989. 'Mediation in Nonindustrial Societies', in K. Kressel and D.G. Pruitt (eds), *Mediation Research: The Process and Effectiveness of Third Party Intervention*. San Francisco, CA: Jossey-Bass, pp. 68–90.
Nader, L. (ed.) 1980. *No Access to Law: Alternatives to the American Judicial System*. New York: Academic Press.
———. 1993. 'Controlling Processes in the Practice of Law: Hierarchy and Pacification in the Movement to Re-form Dispute Ideology', *The Ohio State Journal on Dispute Resolution* 9: 1–25.
Palmer, M., and S. Roberts. 1998. *Dispute Processes: ADR and the Primary Forms of Decision Making*. London: Butterworths.
Peachey, D.E. 1989. 'What People Want from Mediation', in K. Kressel and D.G. Pruitt (eds), *Mediation Research: The Process and Effectiveness of Third Party Intervention*. San Francisco, CA: Jossey-Bass, pp. 300–21.
Provost, R. 2017. 'Centaur Jurisprudence: Culture before the Law', in R. Provost (ed.), *Culture in the Domains of Law*. Cambridge: Cambridge University Press, pp. 1–20.
Reyntjens, F. 1990. 'Le Gacaca ou la Justice du Gazon au Rwanda', *Politique Africaine* 40: 31–41.
Rottenburg, R. 2009. *Far-Fetched Facts: A Parable of Development Aid*. Cambridge, MA: MIT Press.
Sarat, A., and T.R. Kearns. 1998. 'The Cultural Lives of Law', in A. Sarat and T.R. Kearns (eds), *Law in the Domains of Culture*. Ann Arbor: University of Michigan Press, pp. 1–20.
Snyder, F. 1993. 'Law and Anthropology: A Review', *European University Institute Working Paper Law* 93(4): 1–46.
Sommers, M. 2012. *Stuck: Rwandan Youth and the Struggle for Adulthood*. Athens: University of Georgia Press.

Chapter 6

Mediation and Truth

Günther Schlee

Mediation takes place in the context of negotiation. Two or more parties who are involved in a conflict ask a mediator to help them reach an agreement. The mediator then has to reconcile their perceptions of what is at stake, to assess the interests of the parties and to find a compromise.

Truth, on the other hand, has a definite ring of non-negotiability and hostility to compromise. The 'truth' that is negotiated is not credible; the truth that is based on a compromise is compromised. Constructivists may teach us that all our convictions and beliefs are the result of social interaction and the process of finding a shared language and shared procedures to establish 'facts', but people who use the word truth without inverted commas usually take it as something out there, independent of their wishes, interests or biases.

In this chapter I take two apparently quite different domains into consideration, in order to explore the relationship between truth and mediation: penal law procedures in North America and Europe and elections in Africa. The comparison of these two quite disparate fields in which 'mediation' is practised reveals close structural parallels, which suggests a more general 'logic' of mediation.

The language of German law is unambiguous about truth. What a penal process has to find out is *materielle Wahrheit*,[1] literally 'material truth'. As this does not appear to work in English, an English press release of the German Federal Constitutional Court has 'the real facts'[2] in its place. 'Materielle Wahrheit' is not perceived as a collective mental construct, nor is it a matter of negotiation. As it is not a matter of negotiation, there is no place for mediation in matters of truth.

There are different fields of activity in which the tension between mediation and truth is played out. One obvious example of such an activity is plea bargaining in the context of criminal trials. Plea bargaining seems to be more widely practised in the USA than, say, in Germany. Take, for example, a murder case. There is evidence against the accused, but it is not quite compelling. The accused risks being sentenced nevertheless. Despite the remaining doubt, he faces, say, a 40 per cent risk of being sentenced to death. For the prosecution this translates into a 60 per cent risk of having to accept an acquittal. The accused is then offered the option that the murder charge is dropped in favour of some lesser charge, say manslaughter, second degree murder, inflicting some bodily harm where death as a consequence was not intended but accidental. All parties, the defence and the prosecution and the judge may know that this charge is factually untrue, although they may abstain from saying so. But several years of prison for the defendant are better than a 40 per cent risk of execution and for the prosecution they may be preferable to a 60 per cent risk of acquittal on a murder charge.

According to the German legal system, this is not possible and is prohibited by law. Although a decision of the German Federal Constitutional Court[3] allowed plea bargaining (*Verständigung im Strafprozess*), it also obliged the judge to check the results of the agreement for factual truth (*materielle Wahrheit*). Although it seems that this decision gave evidence that in the German legal system the negotiated 'truth' cannot differ substantially from the factual truth, I took it as evidence for the opposite. The verdict must have been necessitated by the existence of such discrepancies.

My point is that whatever may be proclaimed on the normative level, plea bargaining must by its very logic lead to departures from truth. Of course, it is possible that the result of the bargain coincides with the truth, but this is not essential for the process of bargaining. Predictably, the legal regulations that try to prevent these departures are not fully applied in practice. A study by Karsten Altenheim[4] showed that only 28 per cent of the judges even claim to check the results of plea bargaining, the pleas of being guilty of lesser charges, for factual truth. So 72 per cent admit not meeting this legal requirement. And who knows what percentage of those who claim to make such inquiries actually do so, and do so seriously?

Another effect of mediation on truth is that questions about factual truth are simply dropped under the influence of mediation. Right and wrong are simply the wrong categories if one wants to identify the interests of contestants, their relative influence, flexibility or lack thereof, and try to find areas of possible agreement by compromise.[5] One could also paraphrase this as a shift of paradigm from systems of knowledge concerned with 'truth' (science, including forensic science or expert knowledge, 'positivist' history, i.e. the branch of history interested in reconstructing factual events etc.) to 'politics'.

Prominent examples in this regard are African elections. For the present chapter I will focus on the Kenyan case, but there are numerous examples from the past decade in which election results were contested, counting and recounting led to more and more confusion (or was said to be inconclusive by those who did not want to cede power although it was pretty clear to neutral observers that in all likelihood they *had* lost the election), and then the question of who had actually won was dropped and a process of political bargaining assisted by mediation known as *power sharing* set in.

Apart from these two scenarios – in which actors either agree on a fake version of events or drop the concern with truth altogether – there is also the possibility that mediators temporarily assume the role of experts or advisors and question the evidence or try to convince one of the parties with evidence-based arguments. So facts may come into the proceedings. But for any successful outcome of a mediation – for the simple reason of the absence of an adjudicator and the impossibility of imposing a resolution on anyone – 'truth' tends to be negotiable and insistence on a factual reality out there (beyond our subjectivities) a harmful attitude to a negotiation process.

Apart from these general characteristics, many mediation processes have specific features that make it even more unlikely that they result in anything like 'truth'. International peace conferences in Africa are often sponsored by Western powers with governments who are answerable to electorates who have expectations about constitutionalism and legal norms. This means that the Western mediators may have an agenda that differs from the agendas of both or all parties among whom they want to mediate. They have to produce texts for a foreign readership in an often legalese but invariably politically polished language, taking into account international norms about constitutionalism, human rights, civic rights, gender rights, minority rights and so on. After many years of observing 'peace processes' in and about the Sudan (since 2011 split into Sudan and South Sudan), Alex de Waal has come to the conclusion that 'the proceedings within the conference hall' are often 'a sideshow to bargaining conducted elsewhere' (de Waal 2015: 193). This bargaining may be on totally different issues like dividing rent from mineral resources, income from internationally sponsored anti-terrorism programmes, control of export infrastructure, control of foreign 'development' aid, trading ethnic voting blocs or impunity for human rights violations. In the '14th Somalia Peace Process' in Kenya (2002), there were 'technical committees' that discussed constitutional drafts, property restitution, the obligatory DDR (demobilization, disarmament and reintegration),[6] land rights and property restitution, international relations and economic policy under the guidance of foreign experts and in the presence of an international audience. Parallel to this there was a 'leaders' committee' composed of 'warlords' trying to strike a power sharing deal without even waiting for the constitutional committee to define state powers and levels of administration. So the 'powers' to be defined by the constitution did not appear to be the same thing as the 'power' to be shared by the entrepreneurs of violence (Schlee 2006, 2008).

African Elections

I will focus on the Kenyan experience of post-election violence with subsequent mediation resulting in power sharing. This example can be put in a wider context and we even have some rough quantitative measurement of the importance of this phenomenon. In an analysis of all presidential and parliamentary election results and their acceptance in Africa from 2010 to mid 2012, Judith Vorrath shows that there were fifteen elections the results of which were not called into question and that thirteen of these led to a change of power. She lists twenty-eight cases as contested, and of these twenty-six have not led to a change of power. The five cases she calls 'hotly contested' (*äußerst umstritten*) show a similar pattern: three of these have not led to a change of power (Vorrath 2013: 15). In twenty-one cases, the countries in question had experienced a violent conflict within the preceding ten years. In seven, or one-third of these cases, the elections led to an aggravation of this conflict (Vorrath 2013: 20). Vorrath concludes that elections, especially if carried out in deficient ways, can be a mixed blessing, but that, on the whole, their effects are not as bad as one might have expected. But does that not depend on one's expectations, including expectations about the African experience? What would one say if, for example, in Europe, one-third of all elections led to an escalation of violence, even if that applies only to cases with a recent history of violence? Elections even lead to violent conflicts if before the elections the setting had been quite peaceful in over 10 per cent of cases (two of nineteen) (Vorrath 2013: 20).

Vorrath also gives us a clue as to why this violence occurs. In twenty-nine of thirty-one cases in which elections did *not* lead to a change of power, this result was 'contested' or 'highly contested' (Vorrath 2013: 15). This means in many cases that presidents who were voted out of power did not leave office. This is the situation where 'peace makers', 'moral authorities', 'senior statesmen', the mysterious 'International Community' and other *mediators* come in and arrange *power sharing*.

Power Sharing

Power sharing is often just about cutting the 'national cake' down the middle. It is an unpolitical solution if we define politics as the struggle for better programmes, about public welfare and the competition for wider acceptance and winning debates. Better programmes suddenly are no longer the issue. The *content* of political debates loses importance or gets completely lost. Everyone and their enemies, as long as they are potentially harmful, that is, able to obstruct a negotiated solution, form a government and get their share of the ministries and other leading positions.

Often it is not just about government positions. It is about owning the state, including the civil service and parastatals. I have observed cases in which civil servants, even teachers, or employees of parastatals like a junior clerk in a state-owned bank were forced to resign if they wanted to run in an election. If they were opposition candidates and their party failed to win, after the election they were not hired again into their prior positions. One of them reported that he was told, 'Wait for your turn. Now it is still our time to eat' (for the 'eating' metaphor, see Bayart 2006; Wrong 2009). When I told my Kenyan friends that in Germany the composition of the civil service, including a large proportion of the senior staff in federal ministries, does not change with a change of government, they were quite astonished. That so many livelihoods in Kenya depend on who is in power is one explanation for the bitterness of political struggles. The winner takes it all.

Power sharing has the effect of modifying the principle of 'the winner takes it all' and incorporating broader segments of the political class. Regularly governments formed by power sharing are blown up to provide many positions, of course at the expense of the taxpayer.

We now proceed with a brief chronology of the Kenyan case of post-election violence and subsequent power sharing. I will try to use as few names as possible and to do without the acronyms of political parties, but a few key persons and the names of their ethnic groups need to be mentioned, because much of Kenyan politics is based on trading ethnically defined blocs of votes. This book has a theoretical focus. It aims to explore the relationships between retaliation, mediation and punishment. In this chapter I therefore keep the description of historical events slim and focus on what I need to make my more general points. The following account aims to be objective and to avoid misrepresentations, but it is far from being detailed or exhaustive. For a broader and more detailed picture, the reader may refer to Carrier and Kochore (2014), Lynch (2014), Moss and O'Hare (2014) and Mueller (2014).

27 December 2007

In the elections the incumbent President Mwai Kibaki (Kikuyu, from central Kenya) stood against Raila Odinga (Luo, from western Kenya), the opposition leader and son of a former vice-president under the first president of Kenya, Jomo Kenyatta (Kikuyu). The son of Jomo Kenyatta, Uhuru Kenyatta, was a minister in Kibaki's government. The opposing alliance, apart from Odinga, comprised William Ruto (Kalenjin,[7] Rift Valley) on Odinga's side against Kibaki and Uhuru.

Well into January 2008

The election results were narrow and hotly contested. Elections were followed by mass violence. In Nairobi there was warfare between slums, which were to a large extent ethnically segregated. In the Rift Valley, Kikuyu farmers who had settled there as squatters on White-owned farms in colonial times and later acquired property there were massacred or expelled by Kalenjin and others who thought the land should have been given back to them, because they owned it before the Whites.[8] In retaliation, Kikuyu manned road blocks, for example at Naivasha, dragged people out of cars and buses and killed Kalenjin (in retaliation for the Rift Valley massacres) or those whose name started with O (Luo, Luhya from western Kenya), for presumably having voted for Raila Odinga. What needs to be remembered to appreciate later twists to the story is that Uhuru's people (Kikuyu) and Ruto's people (Kalenjin) massacred each other on a grand scale.

January and February 2008

Shortly after the eruption of violence, the then chairman of the African Union (AU), John Agyekum Kufuor, the president of Ghana, came to mediate. A little later he was joined in these efforts by the General Secretary of the United Nations, Ban Ki-moon. The latter then asked his predecessor, Kofi Annan, to chair the mediation effort.

April 2008

The result of these efforts was power sharing. A grand coalition was formed to include both contestants, Mwai Kibaki as president and Raila Odinga as prime minister, an office that was newly created to accommodate his wishes.[9] The number of ministers was forty-four, an all-time record.

Parallel to these developments, there was much debate about how to apprehend and punish the perpetrators of mass violence and the massive abuses of human rights that had taken place early that year. The options were the International Criminal Court (ICC) in The Hague or a trial in Kenya. At one point, parliament expressed its mistrust of the Kenyan judiciary and its preference for The Hague (ICC).

As late as October 2010, 68 per cent of Kenyans wanted the trial to be held at the ICC. By mid July 2013 this number had fallen to 39 per cent, with only 7 per cent in Central Province, Uhuru's stronghold, and only 24 per cent in the Rift Valley, where Ruto's Kalenjin make up a large share of the population (Mueller 2014: 36). What happened in this period to turn the country against the ICC? The answer is a combination of government tactics to make the ICC look bad, delaying tactics by the defendants and the fact that the ICC had overstretched its powers, not its judicial competencies but its factual power. Not having an executive branch, and lacking police or military power, the ICC can only carry out its mission when those who hold these powers have a modicum of goodwill, and that was lacking.

The government preferred a trial in Kenya but dragged its feet. In July 2009, Kofi Annan handed a sealed envelope with the names of the six main suspects, identified by the ICC on the basis of evidence collected originally by the

Waki Commission,[10] also known as CIPEV (Commission of Inquiry into the Post-Election Violence), set up by the Kenyan government, to the president, exhorting him to take steps against them.[11] If he did not do so, the names would be disclosed and the ICC urged to take over. The six suspects came to be known as the Ocampo Six, after the chief prosecutor of the ICC. In order to keep the discussion brief, in the following we will focus on two of them. When the names were disclosed, it turned out that they comprised Uhuru Kenyatta and William Ruto. They were accused of instigating and masterminding mass violence against each other's ethnic constituencies.

That a new common adversary had come into play must have had a positive effect on their personal relationship. During the following elections, in 2013, they jointly stood against Raila Odinga, Uhuru as the presidential candidate, Ruto as his running mate, that is, prospective vice-president.

The new alliance was first met with great scepticism, both among Kikuyu and Kalenjin. To cite just one voice: a Kalenjin elder interviewed by Lynch explained that the basis of the new unity was '*purely* The Hague' and that 'animosity among Kikuyu and Kalenjin' cannot be wiped out overnight (Lynch 2014: 97, emphasis mine). Later, the ethnic followings closed ranks behind their leaders. The victims of the post-election violence were no longer the focus of attention, although thousands of Internally Displaced Persons (IDPs) were still living in provisional camps and not a single perpetrator had been brought to justice. The 'Alliance', the 'Three Os' (Ocampo, Obama, Odinga), were now perceived as the adversaries. US President Obama was inserted into this enumeration because he was perceived as just another Luo and as partial, at least since the visit of his foreign secretary Hillary Clinton, to Kenya.

William Ruto followed a summons to The Hague in August 2011. As agreed in advance, he was then allowed to return to Kenya. In January 2012 the charges against him were confirmed. The press was full of reports about public prayer meetings for the accused.

Uhuru and Ruto had become heroes. What their followers had done to each other suddenly played no role. Displaced people and victims of human rights violations had become a disturbing factor. Protection of witnesses became a major concern for The Hague, but was not achieved. Witnesses felt threatened, recanted and came out with stories of how they had been bribed by The Hague. They were shown on television, talking for their lives. As a consequence, charges against some of the six were dropped, but not those against Uhuru and Ruto.

Long before the next elections there was much concern in the media about a possible renewal of community violence. Governmental and nongovernmental organizations, churches and religious leaders exhorted Kenyans to remain peaceful. No doubt, this reinforced a genuine desire for peace, but it also kept fear alive. To vote for one's own people seemed to be the safest option. To vote for a leader who had struck a deal for peace with a potential adversary also looked like a safe option. This was the case for the Kikuyu and Kalenjin. They would not vote for Odinga in this climate of fear. Were some of his grievances possibly not legitimate? This did not elicit sympathy for him but only raised fear. Legitimate grievances make people more likely to seek revenge.

April 2013

The results of the elections were that Uhuru Kenyatta won by a narrow margin and became the new president. He made William Ruto his deputy president. The unanimous expert opinion is that the impending ICC trial had actually helped the suspected perpetrators to win the elections. It is tempting to call this the Ocampo effect. Earlier, this effect could be observed in the Sudan.[12] The ICC has gained a reputation in Africa as an 'instrument of imperialism' and as having a bias against less powerful nations, as no human rights abuses by major world powers have ever been on its agenda.

2013/2014

Uhuru and Ruto, having won the election and been installed in high office, now had a stronger position in regard to the ICC. They now claimed more convincingly that they would have to check their busy calendars and that they could only follow summons to The Hague if their government duties allowed. At one point they proposed video conferences as an alternative to a trial in The Hague. They also suggested that the trial could be held in Nairobi, or perhaps Arusha.

This sent the ICC into a tailspin. In June 2013, the Trial Chamber (TC) 'ruled that Ruto did not need to be physically present continuously'; in October, this ruling was overturned by the Appeals Chamber. The same month, Uhuru's TC ruled that he would have to be present only at key sessions. In late November, the ICC member states, among them Kenya and most other African countries, 'amended its rules and procedures to permit trials by video conferencing and high level officials to be represented by council' (Mueller 2014: 36f). It is up to the accused to decide whether they want to appear in court or not. If the trial does not go their way, they can stop attending procedures.

At the same time, many of the victims of the expulsions of Kikuyu from the Rift Valley, the IDPs, 'remained in old and battered tents on small scraps of land awaiting resettlement five years after their initial displacement' (Lynch 2014: 98). No perpetrators had been brought to justice in Kenyan courts. Some victims complained not so much about impunity but about the lack of truth. There was a longing for the truth to come out, independent of punitive sanctions. A Kikuyu woman complained: '[my] neighbour still has my cow that he stole three years ago. He burnt my property and killed my husband. In the peace forum we are sitting together and he doesn't confess!' (Lynch 2014: 99).

In December 2014, the ICC dropped the charges against Uhuru. BBC News (2014) cites the prosecution as claiming that bribing and intimidation of witnesses had made the collection of sufficient evidence impossible. The charges against Ruto were dropped in April 2016.

August to October 2017

'Uhuruto' (Uhuru plus Ruto) won the presidential elections of 8 August 2017, with 54 per cent of the vote against Raila Odinga. The Supreme Court nullified these elections on 1 September. The surprise was not that the elections were found to be rigged but that a court of law dared to rule against the government of the country. An anecdote has it that the president of Uganda, Yoweri Museveni, expressed his astonishment to Uhuru by saying, 'How can you lose in your own court?' Since then much has been done in Kenya to silence independent voices.

The elections were repeated on 26 October 2017, but Raila Odinga withdrew, anticipating more rigging, and asked his supporters to boycott them. Predictably, 'Uhuruto' won by a wide margin.

2018

Raila mobilized his supporters to boycott pro-government commercial firms and had himself sworn in as 'the people's president' at a huge rally. On 9 March, however, he and Uhuru formed a new alliance, the objective and content of which has remained rather vague and has left many groups of people unsure of the situation. Ruto's supporters wondered what happened to Ruto's prospects of succeeding Uhuru as the president of the country in 2022, a prospect they believed to be part of the deal. Raila's supporters wondered if the boycott was still on and whether Raila was still the leader of the opposition or whether he had informally become part of the government, and who or what they were still expected to oppose. Foreign observers and international politicians had reason to wonder in what capacity Raila had started to represent Kenya. Obviously, a new deal had been struck by the leaders, leaving not only the broad masses but also large segments of the political class, comprising their own followers and (former) allies, in the dark.

Lessons from this Case

An important function of penal procedures is that – unless their logic is perverted by plea bargaining, political considerations, lack of independence of the judiciary or other obstructing factors – they first have to establish the facts of the matter, before they mete out punishment. Of the products delivered by punitive justice, truth is just as important as punishment. Of course, penal courts are not the only means to arrive at the truth. There can be 'truth and reconciliation committees', to cite the South African name of one of many similar instruments of 'Transitional Justice', which has turned into an international industry. Very often, however, those who accuse the ICC or other courts of 'over-emphasis on punitive justice to the neglect of peace and reconciliation' (Lynch 2014: 105), especially if they are partisans of suspected perpetrators, want 'peace and reconciliation' without putting the truth on the table first. They want forgiveness for crimes that are not specified and perpetrators who are not named. They want an amnesty. Amnesty for what? Simply to forget things, to leave the victims in their battered tents by the roadside and to leave crimes uninvestigated, is not amnesty but amnesia.

We will never know who won the elections in 2007. The truth was put aside and a negotiated solution was reached through mediation: power sharing. The cause of the mediation was international concern about mass violence. The truth about this mass violence is known on the general and collective level. It is known which ethnic groups had voted for whom and who retaliated against whom for having voted for the other side, even if this was wrong in millions of individual cases; the general patterns are clear. It is also known that there was a land issue behind the electoral violence in the Rift Valley. After all, this was not the first outbreak of violence. It is known that in the Rift Valley, many perpetrators were Kalenjin and that Kikuyu prevail among the killed and displaced. All this and much more is generally known and accepted. But truth is not brought down to the individual level. The Kikuyu woman cited above knows that the neighbour who killed her husband still has her cow, and she can do nothing about it. There are no institutions to help establish the murder and the theft and to return the cow to the woman. Instead, people are asked by NGOs and other 'mediators' to go to the peace forum and to talk about peace in general terms. This is not only an insult to the human mind, which is inquisitive by nature, it is also an insult to justice and a recipe for keeping grudges alive at the risk of renewed violence.

A Comparison with the USA

While in both Kenya and Zimbabwe and elsewhere (Ivory Coast) messy elections with unclear results led to mass violence and the demand for mediation, in America, in the same general period, equally narrow and hotly contested elections did not lead to mass violence and were not resolved by mediation. While in both Kenya and Zimbabwe the younger contestants who saw themselves as winners of the election had to share power with the incumbents (Tsangirai with Mugabe in Zimbabwe and Odinga with Kibaki in Kenya), there was no mediation between Al Gore and George W. Bush after the 2000 presidential election and there was no power sharing. Kenya, which had always had a president and never a prime minister, created the office of prime minister in 2008 so that Odinga could have his share of the power. No such office was created in the USA to give Al Gore the chance to rule alongside President George W. Bush.

Applying the African model to the US borders on the comical, because it would clearly overstretch our imagination about what could happen under any circumstances in the USA. So is the African model funny? I am sure that many

Africans would fail to see the funny side. They would have liked to know who had won the elections and they would have preferred the American solution.

So what was the American solution? The American solution was counting and recounting the votes. Nevertheless, no agreement on the results was reached and a court ruling was required. According to some commentators, in the end one candidate, Al Gore, probably had most of the popular votes, but because of the bundling effect by voting through electors, George W. Bush won the election and became president. This led to some criticism of the voting system, which had led to somewhat paradoxical results, but no-one claimed that the rules should be changed post-hoc to deal with an exceptional case.

The next question is: how? How could the Americans achieve a solution different to the African one? One reason is that they stuck to procedures. While in Africa the question of who had actually won was dropped when it became too hot, that is, when people began resorting to violence, 'Americans trust their democratic institutions and, in this case, legal avenues were sought to clear the mess'.[13] In the end the matter was resolved by the Supreme Court (whose critics do not tire of pointing out that it is controlled by Republican Justices), whose decision allowed a previous vote certification to stand, made by the Florida Secretary of State, Katherine Harris, a Republican. Harris's certification gave Bush more votes than Gore and awarded him the presidency. It halted further recounts. Media organizations subsequently analysed the ballots and found that further recounting would have given Gore more votes.

This caused criticism, but not violence. The effects of the voting system through electors and the paradox that it may produce results quite different from the popular vote was problematized. Rules were criticized by some and there was discussion about changing them for the next time, but they were accepted by all as being valid this time. (In fact, the voting system was never reformed and sixteen years later, in 2016, Donald Trump with the majority of electors won against Hillary Clinton who received the majority of the popular vote.) The same think tanks that would have advocated 'mediation', ad hoc solutions and changing the rules in the middle of the game for Africa would never have dreamt of giving the same advice to Americans.

Conclusions

This chapter began with plea bargaining in penal procedure and ended with elections in Africa. The topics sound rather different, but their structure is the same, and a core question that arises from the study of both fields is about the relationship between mediation and truth.

Both in plea bargaining in the US (as the country where it is most common and accepted) and in mediated negotiations after contested elections which lead to power sharing in Africa, the situation that triggers the process shares one key feature: uncertainty. Alternatively, we can speak of a lack of sure knowledge or ignorance of a certain kind or of more than one kind. In the case of plea bargaining, the suspect knows whether she has committed the crime and the prosecutor strongly suspects that she has committed it; he does not have enough evidence to be able to prove it, but enough to make her fear that he might, rightly or wrongly, convince the jury of her guilt. We here assume a female suspect and a male prosecutor for easier pronominal reference: 'he' stands for the prosecutor, 'she' for the suspect. The latter might be innocent, but because of the risk of being sentenced for a serious charge, she pleads guilty to a lesser charge. Alternatively, she may be guilty and profit from the lack of certainty on his side by getting a lighter punishment than she deserves. Ignorance on his side consists of a lack of certainty of her guilt, a kind of ignorance that she does not share because she knows what she did. Ignorance on her side consists of a lack of knowledge of how the jury will assess the existing but not entirely conclusive evidence against her.

Which kinds of ignorance characterize the other case, that of the contested African elections that lead to power sharing? There might be chaos and disorganization and fraud by all sides, and no one knows who has actually won the elections. Alternatively, the incumbent, with his closer relationship to the state apparatus and the electoral commission, knows whether or not he has cheated, while the challenger can only strongly suspect that he has cheated, but she cannot be sure. (Note the pronouns – they are used for easy reference; no gender bias is intended: he = incumbent, she = challenger.) But there are stronger reasons to suspect him, as he has the wherewithal to cheat because of his access to the apparatus. On the other hand, he might also suspect her of cheating, because there are ways in which the opposition might also manipulate elections, for example by multiple registration of the same voters or by registering voters who are foreigners or under age. If he has cheated, he knows it. She may know it or not. If she has cheated, she knows it; but he may know it or not. In come the electoral committee and the foreign observer. The former may be involved in the cheating and therefore knows about it, it may not be involved but have found out about it, or it may not know. The foreign observer and later the mediator, as persons from outside, tend to know less than the local actors. They ask questions and consult the evidence. The evidence may not be conclusive. The resulting ignorance is of the type: unable to know, therefore don't know. Or there may be evidence that there was no cheating or only cheating to an extent low enough not to affect the outcome of the elections, and the incumbent is declared the winner. No time will be wasted in declaring the incumbent the winner, to avoid unrest and potential violence. Alternatively, there may be evidence that the challenger has won the elections but is denied her victory. In an ideal world she is then declared the winner, the incumbent gracefully concedes defeat, and she takes power. If the incumbent is not giving in, however, and there is no one to force him to do so, foreign observers and later mediators might be tempted to pretend to be less sure of the results of the elections than they actually are, because they want to open a dialogue. The ignorance involved here is of a different kind: not wanting to know, pretending not to know, or denial. Incentives for this may be the public interest, namely avoiding violence. They may also be of a private kind. After all, a mediator wants to mediate and derives prestige from doing so. (In the case of senior statesmen, monetary incentives like per-diems paid by international institutions may not play a decisive role, but there may be cases in which they do.) The former kind of incentive will be admitted, the latter not.

Forms of knowledge, including forms of ignorance, are not the only results of our search for points of comparison. Heydebrand (1993: 603) describes plea bargaining as a form of exchange. A confession of guilt is traded for a less severe punishment. There are other aspects to this exchange. As the misdeed confessed might not have been committed at all, one can also say that truth is sacrificed for the speedy completion of the trial. Can we transfer the idea of exchange to our other case, contested elections in Africa? What is traded for what in the mediated power sharing arrangements we have described?

The incumbent who refuses to quit after (presumably) losing the election, in the power sharing arrangement is handed back a proportion of the power he would have lost entirely if he had conceded defeat. Assuming a deal that splits power half and half (an arbitrary assumption for the sake of a mental experiment because power can be split in different proportions), he goes for the 50 per cent deal instead of accepting the zero option. To go for the other option, sticking to 100 per cent, would have required a lot of violence and would have led to uncertain results: at worst defeat, at best very bad press, since he would have to enforce his will by force of arms on a justly enraged electorate. So he trades half of the power, which he is not sure he would be able to keep anyway, for enhanced secure tenure of the other half and a degree of legitimacy in keeping it. Another way to phrase this is that he renounces the violent option and receives 50 per cent of the power as a reward.

Trading the renunciation of violence for some benefit is not limited to mediated power sharing negotiations after contested elections. There is a whole field of activities defined by just this form of exchange: racketeering, blackmail ('I know where your family lives'), extortion of money by taking hostages, robbery at gunpoint (here the abstention from shooting is rewarded by a monetary payment or a transfer of other valuables), rape (here the beating stops when the victim gives in) and possibly others. I leave the extension of the list to the criminal imagination of the reader. What all these activities share is that they are illegal. This makes power sharing mediated by the UN or some other international agency stand out as something singular. In this field of related activities defined by this feature, power sharing is the only one that is not only regarded as legal but even deserving of applause by peace-loving people. One may object that violence by the state, if indeed the state machinery is used by the incumbent who does not want to leave, is legitimate. According to the Weberian model of the nation state, it is even the only legitimate form of violence, because the state holds or should hold the monopoly on violence. But can this legitimacy be extended to violence ordered by a president who has been voted out of office and does not want to go?

The challenger who has reason to believe that she has won the elections and now feels deprived of her victory, in a power sharing deal also gives up the option of violence. But the means of violence at her disposal might have been lesser anyway. Unless parts of the armed forces defect to her, or she is linked to some militia in her home region, she might have only unarmed civilians who are ready to protest in the streets on her side. Renouncing violence in such a case might amount to little more than avoiding a massacre of her own followers.

Different as the cases we have examined may be, the logic of mediation plays a role in all of them, and is detrimental to truth. The pacifying effect of mediation, which sacrifices truth, is often short lived.

Günther Schlee is one of the Founding Directors of the Max Planck Institute for Social Anthropology in Halle, Germany. His main publications include *Identities on the Move: Clanship and Pastoralism in Northern Kenya* (Manchester University Press, 1989) and *How Enemies Are Made: Towards a Theory of Ethnic and Religious Conflict* (Berghahn Books, 2008).

Notes

1. Das Bundesverfassungsgericht, BVerfG, 2 BvR 2628/10 vom 19.03.2013, Absatz Nr. 1, https://www.bundesverfassungsgericht.de/SharedDocs/Entscheidungen/DE/2013/03/rs20130319_2bvr262810.html, accessed 4 May 2020.
2. Federal Constitutional Court, Press Release No. 17/2013 of 19 March 2013, 'Legal Regulation of Plea Bargaining is Constitutional – Informal Agreements are Impermissible', https://www.bundesverfassungsgericht.de/SharedDocs/Pressemitteilungen/EN/2013/bvg13-017.html, accessed 4 May 2020.
3. See note 2, above.
4. Jochen Neumeyer, 'Deals im Strafprozess: Wenn die Wahrheit vor Gericht verhandelbar ist', 18 March 2013, https://www.wz.de/politik/inland/deals-im-strafprozess-wenn-die-wahrheit-vor-gericht-verhandelbar-ist_aid-30059833, accessed 3 February 2020, Jochen Neumeyer, 'Kuhhandel im Richterzimmer', 6. November 2012, https://www.wz.de/politik/inland/kuhhandel-im-richterzimmer_aid-30222185, accessed 3 February 2020.
5. On the different logics of guilt and punishment on one side and interest and accommodation on the other, and about the power sensitivity of African customary law, see Schlee (2013, 2017).
6. See Sureau (2017) on DDR in South Sudan.
7. The Kalenjin are the ethnic group to which former president Daniel T. arap Moi belongs (1978–2002). Moi was vice-president (1967–78) under Kenyatta after the elder Odinga (1964–66) and a brief intermezzo.
8. While the former White Highlands and the conflicts between their present dwellers and those who claim to have lived there before the Whites no doubt is the longest collective

land issue, ethnic territorialism and elite-driven subdivisions of administrative units along ethnic lines are a trend throughout Kenya and beyond (Schlee and Shongolo 2012).

9. This made Raila Odinga the formal counterpart of the British prime minister Gordon Brown, who visited Kenya in July. The shared interests of the two countries mentioned included combating drug trafficking, military cooperation, and construction of a nuclear power plant in Kenya (which so far has not materialized) (*Daily Nation* 2008).
10. The Waki Commission had begun hearings in July 2008 (*Sunday Nation* 2008a). From the start there were suggestions that the work of this commission would not make a trial at the ICC superfluous but might secure evidence that would contribute to the success of such a trial, in view of the Kenyan executive being involved on one or the other side and the new coalition government being reluctant to deal with the post-election violence in a serious way (*Sunday Nation* 2008b).
11. Some headlines from 10 July 2009, illustrate the commotion this caused: 'Annan's thunder: Unhappy Kofi hands envelope over to Ocampo triggering panic in government and parties' (*The Standard*, p. 1); 'Government in crisis talks as Annan hands over secret envelope to the ICC' (*The Standard*, pp. 8, 9).
12. Many people think that the popularity of president Omar Al-Bashir in the Sudan was on the decline when Ocampo issued the international arrest warrant against him in 2009, and received an immediate boost by this very act. Soon after, Bashir went on a visit to Gulf countries and received red-carpet treatment everywhere, as if to demonstrate that no-one would arrest him.
13. Abdullahi Shongolo, report for the Max Planck Institute for Social Anthropology on 'The Dynamics of Political and Ethnic Violence in Kenya', January 2008, p. 8.

References

Bayart, J.-F. 2006. *L'Etat en Afrique: La politique du ventre*. Paris: Fayard.

BBC News. 2014. 'ICC Drops Uhuru Kenyatta Charges for Kenya Ethnic Violence'. Retrieved 24 November 2011 from http://www.bbc.com/news/world-africa-30347019.

Carrier, N., and H.H. Kochore. 2014. 'Navigating Ethnicity and Electoral Politics in Northern Kenya: The Case of the 2013 Election', *Journal of Eastern African Studies* 8(1): 135–52. doi://dx.1080/17531055.2013.871181.

Daily Nation. 2008. *UK Visit: Brown Praises Kenya's Recovery*, 24 July, 9.

De Waal, A. 2015. *The Real Politics of the Horn of Africa: Money, War and the Business of Power*. Cambridge: Polity Press.

Heydebrand, W. 1993. 'Neue Formen der Justiz in den USA zwischen formellem Prozeß, Verhandeln und Vergleich', in H. Mohnhaupt and D. Simon (eds), *Vorträge zur Justizforschung: Geschichte und Theorie*, vol. 2. Frankfurt am Main: Klostermann, pp. 599–625.

Lynch, G. 2014. 'Electing the "Alliance of the Accused": The Success of the Jubilee Alliance in Kenya's Rift Valley', *Journal of Eastern African Studies* 8(1): 93–114. doi:10.1080/17531055.2013.84438.

Moss, N., and A. O'Hare. 2014. 'Staging Democracy: Kenya's Televised Presidential Debates', *Journal of Eastern African Studies* 8(1): 78–92. doi:10.1080/17531055.2013.869929.

Mueller, S.D. 2014. 'Kenya and the International Criminal Court (ICC): Politics, the Election and the Law', *Journal of Eastern African Studies* 8(1): 25–42. doi:10.1080/17531055.2013.874142.

Schlee, G. 2006. 'The Somali Peace Process and the Search for a Legal Order', in H.-J. Albrecht, J.-M. Simon, H. Rezaei, H.-C. Rohne and E. Kiza (eds), *Conflicts and Conflict*

Resolution in Middle Eastern Societies: Between Tradition and Modernity. Berlin: Duncker & Humblot, pp. 117–68.
———. 2008. *How Enemies Are Made*. Oxford: Berghahn Books.
———. 2013. 'Customary Law and the Joys of Statelessness: Idealised Traditions versus Somali Realities', *Journal of Eastern African Studies* 7(2): 258–71.
———. 2017. 'Customary Law and the Joys of Statelessness: Somali Realities beyond Libertarian Fantasies', in B. Turner and G. Schlee (eds), *On Retaliation: Towards an Interdisciplinary Understanding of a Basic Human Condition*. Oxford: Berghahn Books, pp. 208–35.
Schlee, G., and A.A. Shongolo. 2012. *Pastoralism and Politics in Northern Kenya and Southern Ethiopia*. Woodbridge: James Currey.
Sunday Nation. 2008a. 'Post Election Violence: Waki Team Starts Hearings this Week', 6 July, 48.
Sunday Nation. 2008b. 'Election Violence Probe: Grand Coalition on the Spot', 25 July, 6.
Sureau, T. 2017. '"The Last Bullet": South Sudan's Emerging State', Ph.D. dissertation. Halle (Saale): Martin Luther University Halle-Wittenberg.
Vorrath, J. 2013. 'Wahlen in Subsahara-Afrika: Segen oder Fluch?', *SWP-Studie S 7*. Berlin: Stiftung Wissenschaft und Politik. Retrieved 4 May 2020 from https://www.swp-berlin.org/fileadmin/contents/products/studien/2013_S07_vrr.pdf.
Wrong, M. 2009. *It Is Our Turn to Eat: The Story of a Kenyan Whistleblower*. New York: Harper Collins.

Chapter 7

Crossing the Boundaries of Mediation

Keebet von Benda-Beckmann

Introduction

Over the past decades, mediation has become quite popular worldwide. It is an obligatory or voluntary alternative to adjudication for a great variety of disputes, ranging from large-scale, violent international conflicts to small-scale conflicts within local communities. Mediation is used in family disputes (including domestic violence), disputes among neighbours, labour disputes, commercial and consumer issues, and even in disputes between citizens and agencies of state administration. In keeping with the rising interest in mediation, the field of persons acting as mediators is also expanding. Often, judges are legally obliged to try mediation before they may pass judgement. But there is also more and more out-of-court mediation by lay persons as well as professionals for whom a plethora of training courses is on offer. In the US, judges offer their service as mediators outside of the courts, as an 'off-state' private business.[1] There is a growing transnational industry of mediation that offers its services around the world for a broad array of issues and under vastly changing political constellations. Insight into how mediation works is not only of scientific interest; mediation has become big business and has become politically relevant.

This chapter discusses the dynamics that modes of disputing were undergoing during the first decade of Indonesia's constitutional reforms after the fall of the Suharto regime in 1998, when decentralization was taken seriously, and before much of decentralized authority was taken back again by the central government. It explores the temporal coincidence of a rapid expansion of modern communication technologies, of the active introduction of a particular type of mediation, and of decentralization policies that were initiated at the turn of the century. One of the unintended and unexpected outcomes of these processes was that traditional mediators began to cross the boundaries of mediation, thereby generating new modes of dispute processing. In Indonesia, the mediation business was booming, with strong support from the USA and Australia. However, vigorous insistence on a particular form of mediation on the part of international organizations often clashed with quite different local forms of mediation, thereby creating much confusion among both the mediators and those for whom mediation was intended. At the same time, local forms of mediation, in the eyes of local populations, sometimes became adulterated by modes of conflict processing that resembled adjudication by state courts.

The next section will provide a conceptual background against which the remarkable rise of mediation in Indonesia has to be understood. After the fall of the autocratic and highly centralized Suharto regime in 1998, the country undertook fundamental constitutional reforms, thereby mutating into a more open society with decentralized political structures. In the wake of these reforms, Indonesia experienced a proliferation of a broad array of modes of mediation, often under the heading of reconciliation, with which people began to experiment.[2] Three types of mediation stand out: (1) religiously inspired mediation; (2) something that I will call American-style mediation for lack of a better term; and (3) local forms of mediation that are usually called 'traditional' but which, in fact, have been adapted to a changing political and economic environment since early colonial times. Recently, some have begun once again to undergo remarkable change. I will present, briefly, examples of each of these three types of mediation, drawing on research that I carried out together with Franz von Benda-Beckmann among the Minangkabau in West Sumatra, Indonesia between 1999 and 2009 and on the work of other anthropologists in other parts of Indonesia. The examples will serve as points of departure for discussing the political contexts in which a diverse field of mediation was emerging. I shall suggest that the new styles of mediation can only be understood by taking into account the broader political and social changes that were going on. The new modes of mediation were a result of the political freedom and decentralization policies that came with the reforms. However, the political constellations in which mediation was put into practice varied a great deal, and each mode seems to have found its own niche, serving different sets of actors in addressing different issues.

Conceptual Approaches to Mediation

Despite the great differences in what mediation is and what it can do, there is general agreement that people opt for mediation where the formal judicial system does not work, because it is unavailable or too expensive, or because people lack trust in it, because it is corrupt, or dysfunctional, and biased towards the powerful. Some actors prefer mediation as a strategy to avoid the punishment they would face if the conflict were to be submitted to a court. Others prefer mediation to avoid publicity or establishing a precedent. And many are simply unacquainted with the state judicial system. For them, mediation is the most familiar form of dispute management. Beyond this, the literature on mediation differs markedly.

There are at least four different yet partly overlapping strands of literature on mediation, including literature on national and international conflicts, small-scale conflicts, comparative work, and practical dos and don'ts.

As a prominent mode of dispute management in large-scale violent conflicts, mediation has been the subject of a growing body of scholarship that analyses the conditions under which it has been successful. Woolford and Ratner (2010) analyse the transformative potential of mediation and discuss the advantages of mediation for restorative justice as compared with other out-of-court methods of dispute management. Greig (2001) argues that mediation can only be successful if the conflict is ripe, and he analyses the factors that make an international, violent conflict ripe for mediation. Beber, also writing about large-scale, international conflicts (2010: 11), discusses three waves of scientific literature on mediation. In the first wave, analyses of the 1970s and 1980s saw the idiosyncratic qualities of mediators as the core factor for success. Bercovitch and Schneider (2000: 149) found trust in the mediator and his credibility and personal skills to be necessary prerequisites for successful mediation. In a second wave, Beber (2010: 11–12) argues that the 'contingency approach' of Bercovitch and others is dominant. In this type of analysis, 'leverage' is diagnosed as a prime predictor of success. In the third wave, Beber makes a plea for a closer examination of the structural factors of international mediation. He distinguishes three clusters of factors: (1) the procedural framework; (2) ascertaining facts, providing information, facilitating communication, managing and screening information; and (3) recommendations regarding the willingness to make 'concessions, moderate extreme demands, and propose possible settlements', which can lead to 'substantive compromises'. Based on his analysis of a large range of international conflicts, he suggests that, of these three factors, the latter two form the core of mediation (Beber 2010: 5–7). He concludes that access to privileged information is perhaps the key factor for successful mediation in international conflicts. That is, only mediators who are perceived to have such privileged information are acceptable and have a chance for success (2010: 184). Beardsley et al. (2006: 64) emphasize that a mediator, to be successful, should not only facilitate and communicate, but be capable of shifting the 'reservation point' of disputing parties.

The literature on mediation in small-scale disputes is also expanding, reflecting the increasing range of issues for which mediation is becoming a preferred mode of dispute management. Neighbourhood mediation emerged in the 1970s, drawing on examples from socialist countries, as well as Africa and Asia as it was known from anthropological literature (Abel 1982; Merry 1982; Merry and Milner 1993). These earlier studies are particularly strong in the analysis of the parties, and the role and background of mediators. In the initial phase there was considerable critical discussion about the problem of power differentials between parties and the lack of procedural protection of the weaker party (Abel 1982; Merry 1982). This kind of criticism has retreated to the background.

There is a vast amount of practice-oriented literature that primarily discusses the dos and don'ts, which I shall not discuss here. It has taken from the research on mediation that it works best when the power relation between the parties is relatively balanced and mediators learn to be aware of the problem of power and how to make sure the powerful party does not become too dominant. But how and to what extent this is to be achieved is not so clear.

Finally, comparative studies that include mediation in the US and in Asia and Africa suggest that there are fundamental differences in techniques used in mediation throughout the world. Comparative studies such as de Girolamo (2012) often focus on cultural differences in mediation styles. Cremades (1998), comparing arbitration and mediation in different countries, enquires into cultural differences in dispute management and looks into the conditions under which arbiters may engage in mediation. Comparative studies have shown that one kind of mediation cannot be easily transplanted and some companies seem to have become more sensitive to this insight. As useful and important as comparative studies are, many suffer from some serious problems. First, the analysis is generally based on national characteristics and provides no space for the sometimes vast regional differences.[3] Thus, Callister and Wall (2004) compare Japanese and Thai styles of mediation based on national characteristics, glossing over regional differences. It is telling that they do not refer to the work of David Engel (1978; Engel and Engel 2010), who writes about the ethnically diverse northern part of Thailand with different attitudes towards hierarchy. Secondly, some scholars discuss 'environment' factors (Wall, Stark and Standifer 2001: 372, 377), such as legislation, expected benefits and familiarity with mediation, and, of course, culture, but these factors mainly serve to explain whether mediation is used or not. The relevant environment is not used to analyse differences in modes of mediation and to explain why certain modes are more successful than others. Most notably, the broader socio-political environment that may help explain modes of mediation is rarely addressed in these kinds of comparisons. A third problem is that this body of scholarship treats mediation styles as static and does not consider the possibility that mediation styles may undergo change, let alone question under what conditions this may occur and what the changes might be. And a final problem concerns the often ambiguous way in which mediation is conceptualized, mixing mode of disputing with purpose or outcome. While most authors agree that mediation is a mode of dispute management in which a third – relatively – uninvolved party facilitates negotiations among disputing parties who make the final decision, the concept is often also used to denote one specific, desirable outcome such as reconciliation, peace, harmony, or the restoration of social relationships. This is confusing, for reconciliation and peace, or any other goal, may be reached by other means than mediation. Besides, there are many other reasons for opting for mediation, such as simply ending a dispute; speeding up a disputing process; making optimal use of one's privileged position; avoiding publicity; preventing persecution of crimes, to name only a few. These points of critique were already formulated in the 1970s and early 1980s, when a focus on power differentials between parties also brought to light that parties may have other interests than what current proponents assume.[4]

The clearest conceptualization is still found with Gulliver (1979), who distinguished modes of dispute management on the basis of three axes: (1) constellation of involved actors (disputing parties only or the involvement of a 'third' to distinguish negotiation from all mediation, arbitration and adjudication); (2) authority of decision-making: who makes the ultimate decision and may impose this on the disputing parties (the disputing parties or the 'third', to distinguish negotiation and mediation from arbitration and adjudication);[5] and (3) compulsion of rules: are substantive and procedural rules prescribed or not (to distinguish adjudication from all others). Reconciliation in this typology may be but is not necessarily a goal for any type of dispute management and is not a distinctive feature that sets mediation apart from other forms of dispute management. This formal framework is a useful basis for asking questions about what the potential alternatives might be, why the involved persons opt for mediation and what they wish to achieve, rather than including the purposes in the concept itself. It is a good starting point from where to look into the extremely diverse field of mediation, to explore the range of actors, their motivations, and the diverse procedures and discourses that are involved, and to understand the fuzzy practices of what is glossed over as mediation. Gulliver's conceptualization also allows for a clearer view of the hybrid forms of mediation that are emerging, in which the 'third' party may switch roles from mediator to arbitrator or adjudicator and back.

Religiously Inspired Mediation

The end of the Suharto regime in 1998 and the period immediately following had been rife with violent conflicts, which were generally labelled as religious conflicts. Calling them religious conflicts conveniently glossed over the fact that competition over resources between local and immigrant groups and between ethnic groups, as well as attempts by the armed forces to hang on to their political power, were at least as important factors in many of these conflicts.[6] These 'religious' conflicts had drawn deep rifts in Indonesian society. General distrust in a corrupt judiciary that is unwilling or incapable (or both) to persecute powerful alleged perpetrators of crimes had rendered the courts an inappropriate venue to deal with these issues. Past conflicts and the fear that more might emerge gave rise throughout Indonesia to the establishment of what was called 'interreligious dialogue'. The 'dialogues', which were actually forms of mediation, were meant to prevent or put an end to religious conflicts by drawing on religious discourses rather than on the judicial system or on discourses of local traditions and legal norms called *adat*. Interreligious and interethnic tensions were not new, and some regional governments had established institutions for dispute management in such conflicts as early as the 1970s. Thufail (2012) discusses the religious and *adat* politics around the various institutions for interreligious dialogue that were to deal with conflict prevention, peace and dispute resolution in Northern Sulawesi. On the island of Java there were a number of privately initiated institutions of interreligious dialogue that with more or less success tried to mediate in conflicts among persons of different faiths (Thufail 2010: 17–18). In 2006, the Indonesian minister of religious affairs and the minister of the interior issued a Joint Decree (*Surat Keputusan Bersama*), to establish the Forum for Religious Harmony (*Forum Kerukunan Umat Beragama*) on the levels of province and district. The Forum was to serve conflict prevention, resolution and peace-making. It dealt with building permits for religious buildings, seemingly mundane, but with the potential to polarize society considerably (Thufail 2012: 363–64). However, the general purpose of such state or privately initiated mediation was to facilitate retaining or re-establishing working relations among groups of different faiths, or of groups sharing the same faith but of different ethnic backgrounds. These modes of mediation shared the characteristic that they were geared towards communication, reconciliation and forgiving, and towards mending social ties, thereby employing a religious discourse, while avoiding references to legal discourses.[7] In the mediation process, commonality of religious tenets among persons of the same faith, and mutual respect for differences, was stressed. Fact-finding was of subordinate importance and perpetration of crimes tended to be decentred. Recourse to a legal discourse and the judicial system was considered less appropriate for two reasons. Legal discourse is prone to intensify rather than mitigate violence and conflict. Besides, there was a lack of trust in the Indonesian judicial system, which was deemed both corrupt and incapable.

Religious mediation was also used in attempts to deal with mass atrocities committed by the armed forces, most notably those of 1965–66 and the Tanjung Priok riots of 1984. But in these constellations, mediation showed its more problematic side. The political freedom allowed for a more open discussion about the highly sensitive 1965–66 massacres, when mass killings, targeting (alleged) communists, were committed as Suharto seized power.[8] The issue was particularly sensitive because the killings had not only been committed by the armed forces but also by religious militia associated with political parties, and because some religious parties had been deeply implicated in both killings and land seizure. Some called for an ad hoc human rights trial, while others supported a reconciliation approach and called for a Truth and Reconciliation Commission (TRC) after the examples of Chile and South Africa. A TRC had the support of Syarikat, an NGO affiliated to the Nahdatul Ulama (NU), the Islamic party whose militia had been deeply involved in the 1965–66 massacres. The former Indonesian president Abdul Rahman Wahid was a prominent member and the apologies he made as president of Indonesia were also understood as an implicit apology by NU. The movement for a TRC was also supported by Elsam, a human rights NGO, and the Asian Foundation. However, the victims and their families were no match for the strong opposition from among the perpetrators. Fear of renewed persecution was also deep seated among the victims and their families (Thufail 2010). These attempts at mediation by a TRC have remained unsuccessful. The National Human Rights Commission has also not been able to deal fully with this issue.

Religiously inspired mediation was also used in the aftermath of the Tanjung Priok riots of 1984. In that year, riots broke out when a high military officer allegedly entered a mosque without taking his shoes off, a serious insult towards the Muslim believers. The Suharto regime considered the protesters radical Muslims and moved in with what many considered disproportionate violence (Thufail 2010: 11–15). Attempts to press for persecution had been effectively suppressed as long as Suharto was still in power. But after the political freedom that began in 1998, calls for persecution became louder and victims and their relatives began to organize with the help of civil society organizations. When the public pressure reached a level at which it could no longer be ignored or suppressed, and an ad hoc human rights court on Tanjung Priok was established, General Tri Sutrisno who had been commander of Jakarta during the riots, took steps to keep the issue out of court.[9] In 2001, he began to promote a religiously inspired form of mediation, called *islah* (literally, 'to repair' or 'to reform'),[10] which frames conflicts in religious terms of ethics and morality and focuses heavily on forgiveness and reconciliation. What is more, General Tri Sutrisno acted as a mediator rather than an involved party, claiming that he had been unaware of the violence committed at the time and that he only wanted to facilitate dialogue. There was, he insisted, a 'need to forget the troubled past' and to emphasize, instead, 'the normative and ethical value of building a peaceful future' (Thufail 2010: 13). *Islah* was thus intended to fend off criminal persecution of members of the armed forces that had been actively involved in striking down the riots of 1984. By keeping it out of court, he hoped in particular to prevent the facts of what had actually happened at the time being unearthed, and the true extent of their involvement becoming public. These attempts to draw on religion in order to avoid criminal persecution met with heavy criticism because such a procedure was not intended to lead to fact-finding, compensation or rehabilitation. Despite the fact that some victims initially engaged in the process in the hope that this would finally bring to the fore the facts of the violent episode and provide explanations for what had happened, in the end it was unsuccessful. The victims felt there was no real mediation or dialogue and that what had really happened, the true degree of state and para-state violence and the extent of military involvement were not disclosed. Victims felt they had not been able to participate on an equal footing with the perpetrators. There was also an issue of corruption (Thufail 2010: 13). Many participants therefore refused to sign the Islah Charter, a contract to be signed by all participants to mark the successful conclusion of *islah*, because it was presented in a top-down manner and contained no apology or an explanation for the people who had disappeared, nor did it promise compensation or rehabilitation. The Charter merely called upon the state to pay compensation and rehabilitate the victims. Although the Charter had the legal form of a contract, no reference was made to any substantive law. Instead it was full of quotations from the Qur'an.

These very different processes of mediation for coming to terms in large-scale political disputes involving mass violence were alike insofar as they drew on transnationally transmitted notions of reconciliation from TRCs that foreground forgiving and repairing and re-establishing social relationships, and *islah*, a term commonly referring to a reform movement to return to *syariah* teachings and *syariah* law, but in the Indonesian context referring instead to the reparation of social relationships. Together these modes of mediation provided a specific Indonesian mixture of legal and religious discourse (Thufail 2010: 12). With this form of mediation, discourses of criminal law that imply 'investigation, clarification and court examination' (Thufail 2010: 9) were shunned, but as the example of the draft decision in the Tanjung Priok case shows, it was not completely devoid of recourse to law. Besides, even unsuccessful mediation had some consequences for the legal system. As Thufail (2010: 14) points out, despite the fact that mediation was at best only very partially successful, with the dialogues the civil society organizations brought the concept of 'violence victim' into a legal sphere.

American-Style Mediation

From the beginning of the twenty-first century, international organizations, especially from the USA and Australia, introduced a new type of mediation into Indonesia, directed at disputes that had a somewhat lower political profile. I shall refer to this type of mediation as American-style mediation. Its background was the utterly dysfunctional Indonesian court system (Pompe 2007). Some donor agencies and in particular the International Monetary Fund (IMF) began to help the Indonesian administration design programmes to improve the judiciary itself. Parallel to this, the mediation lobby that had little confidence in the improvement of the court system propagated mediation as an alternative mode of dispute management that was considered less susceptible to corruption. International and foreign donor agencies began offering training courses in mediation, often to a bewildered audience that wondered why they had to learn mediation at all. Was mediation not the hallmark of Indonesian society? Why call it 'alternative' dispute management? Was local mediation not the standard for which the state judiciary might provide alternative dispute management? To be sure, many Indonesians had had very bad experiences with perverted instances of mediation during Suharto's rule, when friends of the regime had been favoured and perpetrators of violence close to the regime had been systematically protected. Yet mediation has been a persistent mode of dispute management, especially in rural Indonesia, even though it is not quite as widespread and certainly not as effective as the romantic ideology wants it to be. Indeed, many villagers would prefer a well-functioning court system. The organizations that came to sell mediation in villages assumed that mediation was entirely new and simply taught the mediation techniques that were developed in the US or Australian contexts. This implied, among other things, an impartial mediator who for that reason could have no ties whatsoever with the parties. All village authorities were therefore disqualified to act as mediators. It also implied a procedure in which parties would come up front with their interests and objectives. Although the organizations were wrong in assuming that mediation was unknown, they were right in claiming that they introduced a new mode of dispute management, for this was indeed quite different from what Indonesians had been used to. The local procedures were premised on the idea that a mediator could only be trusted to be impartial if they knew the local situation well; had kinship relationships and a firm social position within the community; understood the social context of the conflict; and had a good reputation for listening. Unconnected outsiders were distrusted because their interest in acting as mediators could not be assessed. The goals and interests of parties would often not be discussed openly, but rather became known in a more oblique way. The members of international civil society organizations that came to introduce their new forms of mediation made no attempts to learn about local methods and institutions of mediation or to see how the techniques they wanted to introduce could be matched or adjusted to existing techniques. To the contrary, they had been taught to distrust local authorities and therefore often made it a point not to collaborate with local authorities who often were the main local mediators. During our fieldwork in West Sumatra in the early 2000s, in the beginning of the post-Suharto era, we met several groups that were sent out to teach mediation. Blissfully unaware of the rich mediation tradition that was already there, and of the reasons why it did not function so well, they did not even consider the possibility that such knowledge might be useful. They merely wondered why the type of mediation they propagated was met with uneasiness and sometimes even outright rejection. Most of these organizations disappeared as quickly as they came.

Some of the large international and bilateral organizations were more successful. Their training courses were quite popular among Indonesian lawyers, civil servants and members of advocacy NGOs, though the reasons for participation were not always in line with what the agencies intended. In the same pragmatic style by which they participated in training courses for good governance, democracy, human rights and so on, people took part in mediation training. Some participants were truly interested in learning new techniques; for others it looked good on their CV and was a welcome opportunity to travel, make contacts and earn some additional income from the daily allowances.

These imported forms of mediation were not entirely new in Indonesia. They had helped end high-level disputes between the Indonesian state and its neighbours in the past (Lee 2013: 191ff). They have been instrumental in mitigating the levels of violence in the conflict with Aceh. But for the rural population they were new and most people were highly sceptical about them. The situations in which they had been somewhat successful entailed conflicts between village populations and companies and a sustained involvement of civil society organizations. Dhiaulhaq et al. (2014) report that mediation in disputes over land and forests due to expanding oil palm and pulpwood plantations in Sumatra transformed the conflict so that the levels of violence were reduced and an agreement could be reached. This required the long-term involvement of civil society organizations that in turn were coached by university staff. Careful composition of the representatives of the village communities, trust-building among these and representatives of the company, and involving all relevant stakeholders were crucial for reaching an agreement. As civil society organizations often started out as advocates of local groups, they had to spend much energy on convincing all sides that they switched to the role of neutral mediators. The analysis of Dhiaulhaq et al. (2014: 6–7) is particularly valuable because they look beyond the agreement and pay attention to the problems of implementation. Reaching an agreement does not mean that it is actually implemented. The authors show that a new political constellation within village government (new village head and village council) and within the district (new district head) may overturn an agreement. This is done with a technique that is well known from traditional mediation: objecting to the agreement with the claim that they have not been involved has been a standard way of rejecting an inconvenient agreement. Their study suggests that merely having representatives of certain categories of villagers (men, women, youth, etc.) is not sufficient if not all political factions are involved in the mediation process.

This form of mediation seems to have been most successful in larger, politically sensitive conflicts, and when powerful, external parties and civil society organizations acting as representatives of village communities or as mediators were involved. There are indications that some of the international organizations involved in this transnational training have learned from such experiences and are now more careful to develop modes that are more in accord with local styles of mediation (Cremades 1998), but thus far I have not encountered examples of such adjusted modes of American-style mediation in dispute management among rural disputing parties in Indonesia. For the more classic intra-village or inter-village conflicts, this form of mediation seems to have had little impact. People rejected it for various reasons, for example because they felt there was too much direct confrontation and because the new mediators lacked authority in their eyes. They were used to more oblique and indirect ways of putting their interests and claims on the table and felt uncomfortable with the more direct style that was propagated in the courses.

'Traditional' Mediation

The field of mediation was also changing in the realm of what is called 'traditional' mediation.[11] What drove the changes depended on the specific character of political and social changes that were occurring within the region and changes at the national level. The fall of the Suharto regime in 1998 not only allowed more political freedom; it also opened the door to the construction of a decentralized state in which the regions had far greater fiscal and administrative autonomy than under the highly centralized New Order of Suharto. Decentralization meant very different things in different regions. Some regions, such as Aceh and Papua, negotiated a special position within the nation state in which they had control over a larger share of the natural resources found within their province. For West Sumatra, a province with relatively few natural resources beyond the fertile agricultural land, decentralization meant in the first place that the revenues that they could generate would not be sufficient and that the province would remain financially dependent on the national government. Decentralization also provided an opportunity to reorganize village government in which elements of customary government were reactivated.[12] For the purpose of mediation, three points are of importance. First, the decentralization policies generated a remarkable interest in village government, among ordinary villagers as well as urban elites from within and outside the province. The latter had lost virtually all interest during the Suharto regime when traditional villages had been split up into smaller administrative units. The reorganization of village government entailed a return to the *nagari*, the political organization that had been in place until 1983. The process required reconsideration of its government structure. Secondly, and as a result of the return to the *nagari*, what was seen as the traditional council of lineage elders, or *adat* council, was revitalized as the primary mediating body of dispute settlement. And third, control over land, especially village land, became more important because villages were required to generate resources of their own. This was new, because during the Suharto period villages had been fully funded by the national government. For these reasons the interest in village matters arose not merely out of identity nostalgia; it had solid material reasons as well.

These factors sparked renewed interest in village government not only among the rural population, but also among emigrants, often highly educated with jobs in the state administration, retired members of the armed forces or civil service, and senior men in business. Internet and cheap and frequent air connections between Jakarta and Padang and a good infrastructure within the province of West Sumatra allowed a degree of involvement that previously had been impossible. An active exchange of views developed among emigrants and the regional elites within West Sumatra about the role of *adat*. These were political and politicized debates about the kind of democracy that was to be established in villages, and about the appropriate balance between *adat*, the state and religion, with frequent references to Minangkabau identity. In addition to these political debates among urban elites, the position of lineage head, which had been a mere 'cultural' adornment under Suharto, once again obtained substantive content. Many lineages elected a high-profile emigrant as lineage head because of their good administrative skills and political connections. These emigrant heads of lineage began to take their task seriously and some even became members of the village body of dispute management. Electronic communication through e-mail and Facebook, and affordable and quick transport, allowed them to remain informed, communicate and travel to their home village when their presence was needed. This had a profound impact on how these traditional mediating bodies operated. The kind of issues that came before village justice had remained the same over the past century: the majority were about land claimed as lineage property by competing lineages, or land of which the legal status of lineage land or of personally acquired property was contested. More often than in the past, disputed land registration and certification was part of the problem, and with it accusations of embezzlement and corruption on the side of the registration office and other officials. In addition, under the Suharto regime, it had been common practice for parties to mobilize as many high-level officials as possible, preferably from among the police or armed forces, to support their case. At that time, such constellations of disputing parties would prevent the village council from getting involved. But, as we observed in a village, the new set of members of the village council that was elected after the reforms had fewer qualms to take on such issues, not least because they often had good connections within government. These new lineage heads were far more familiar with the bureaucratic and formal style of the state administration and courts than with mediation practices as they had been common in villages. And thus, despite the fact that they went out of their way to demonstrate that they were mediators and not judges, their formal style of mediating with a strong emphasis on documents (including the final decision) suggested differently. Hearings and production and evaluation of evidence strongly resembled that of court procedures. Formalization was not entirely new, but it seems to have intensified since the 1970s, when we began our studies of village justice in West Sumatra. It was most pronounced in the generation and evaluation of evidence with a strong emphasis on written evidence and a formal way of hearing witnesses. Acquiring and assessing evidence required intimate knowledge of what happens in villages on an everyday basis. Most *adat* councils had enough local members so this would not pose a serious problem. But in a village in which a majority of the *adat* council lived elsewhere, evidence formed a great challenge. Since they had to travel a long way to attend the meetings, the customary way of obstructing the work of the village council by not turning up at meetings put an enormous burden on the procedure, especially on the establishment of facts. There were few means to entice parties to cooperate. At lower levels of village justice, no-one was obliged to participate in mediation, but when a dispute reached the *adat* council, cooperation was obligatory. The traditional way of forcing obstructing parties into cooperation was by way of threatening exclusion from the *adat* community. This meant that such a person was ostracized, could not participate in *adat* ceremonies, was not invited to rituals and feast, and in the worst case had to leave the village. This could only be an *ultimum remedium* and worked only for those interested in remaining part of the *adat* community. However, with the new importance of *adat*, the threat of exclusion has become more meaningful than it had been in the previous decades. *Adat* councils also made use of the newly invented village *adat* security services to ensure cooperation of unwilling parties, but these had to manoeuvre carefully so as not to step into the jurisdiction of the police or local military commander. On the other hand, there was also far greater attention to the state legal system and the limits this put on the mediating efforts of the council. Emigrant lineage heads seem to be more aware of the jurisdictional limits of village councils and tend to be very careful not to step into the jurisdiction of the land registration office or the mayor. It is extremely difficult under such circumstances to come to a settlement to which both parties agree. We attended a case before an *adat* council's dispute management section with an unusually high number of emigrant members in which the formalized procedures were particularly visible.[13] After careful preparations by telephone and e-mail, the council finally assembled to bring the dispute to an end. However, the two-day meeting of the section was not successful because one of the parties systematically refused to cooperate, despite the pressure put upon them by the head of the village council, a former higher military officer. The party that refused to cooperate was also supported by a military kinsman, who was known for his violence. Although the issue of appropriate registration of the property under dispute was intensively discussed, the dispute management section considered the alleged wrongs committed by the registration office to be outside their jurisdiction. The case was adjourned in the vague hope that a solution might be concocted at a later stage.

Adat councils not only drew on procedures derived from the state legal system. They also took recourse to religion, mainly as a way to cool down the emotions that flare up during the hearings, and as a moral appeal to the disputing parties to cooperate and come to an agreement. This was a new development, related to the general trend towards a more prominent role of religion in public life. In the 1970s, when we did our first study of village justice in West Sumatra, there would be no reference to religion at all in disputes before the *adat* council, apart from a short ritual greeting at the beginning and the end of a meeting. If the emotions threatened to disrupt the procedures, or if one of the parties was too obstinate, members of the council would begin to recite *adat* proverbs. But the moral message was exactly the same as what is now expressed in religious discourse.

This case shows that a combination of decentralization policies and the simultaneous spread of information and telecommunication techniques put a new set of mediators on the stage, persons who would not have been elected as village or lineage authorities before because the distance would prevent them from attending to village business. These new mediators lived in the main urban centres but were able to maintain close communication with their home village and could go there any time. They had a more bureaucratic style than people having lived within a village all their lives, and lacked the intimate knowledge of village affairs that local traditional authorities have. And this style resembled that of court and administrative procedures. They were far more sensitive to the existence of a broad range of alternative modes of dispute management and of administrative jurisdictions than the lineage heads that were more traditional mediators as they spent their life within the villages. In line with national and global developments, they created a style of mediation that draws not only on local laws, but also on religion and the state legal system.

Some Conclusions

The field of mediation has, under different labels, broadened immensely in Indonesia, both in terms of neo-traditional dispute management and of transnationally imported forms of mediation of civil and religious provenance. Many of the new types of mediation were hybrids, combining characteristics derived from different legal orders. In these processes, actors often referred to several distinct legal and moral discourses such as religion, and the legal discourses of the state and *adat*. Some processes that were called mediation were no more than a mere shadow of mediation and clearly crossed its boundaries towards arbitration.

Like court procedures, mediation serves a great variety of purposes, interests and political constellations. Discourses and strategies pursued in concrete cases have to be understood in light of these factors. The examples of religious mediation discussed in this chapter show that powerful military officers proposed *islah* to show that they were willing to deal with past atrocities, but at the same time as a way to avoid the true events being disclosed. But above all they expected it would serve to evade criminal persecution. The mediation process was characterized by strong and one-sided pressure towards a decision that was detrimental to the victims, the reason why it eventually did not lead to an agreement. But it was successful for the perpetrators in so far as the unity among the victims was broken and that no criminal persecution has followed thus far. In cases that were not quite as politically sensitive, *islah* and its related religious discourses did serve to deal with disputes among persons of different faiths and to avoid incidences of violence and retaliation.

In the case of the conflicts between local communities and plantation companies, the purpose was to come to a long-term working relationship, for which an agreement was only a first step. Here, civil society organizations switched from advocating to mediation, a process that took intensive trust-building and careful crafting of the groups that represented the village in the mediation process. However, as became clear after the next elections, not all factions appeared to have been included in the decision-making. These factions obstructed implementation of the agreement, claiming not to have been involved in the process, which is, as has been pointed out above, a characteristic technique in local dispute management.

The motivation and drive for change in the field of mediation varied a great deal. I have argued that the changes and diversity have to be understood not only by considering the power relationships among the disputing parties and the mediators, but also by looking at the broader political and social context in which the old and new mediators operate. The changes in neo-traditional mediation occurring in rural West Sumatra were a result of three interrelated factors. First were the general political developments at the national level. Secondly, the simultaneous spread of information and telecommunication techniques, in combination with affordable transport, put a new set of mediators on the stage. It allowed successful migrants in urban centres to become active in mediation in their home village. Thirdly, there was a broad range of alternative modes of dispute management to which the new mediators were far more sensitive than before. In other regions, other modes of mediation and dispute management may have emerged due to different local responses to national political change. Any attempt to explain differences primarily by reference to national cultural characteristics is bound to fail. This does not mean that cultural differences do not play a role at all. The rejection of American-style mediation in village justice can to some extent be explained in cultural terms. But the social and political constellations in which mediation occurs are more important factors for the way in which mediation operates and for explaining why new hybrid forms of mediation emerge and how they work in practice. In the new forms of mediation in village justice discussed here, the mediators were keenly aware of the boundaries of mediation and demonstrated at great length that they remain within the boundaries of mediation. They operated under the assumption that the parties know that there are alternatives – courts, but also the administration and the armed forces if necessary. Depending on their perception of the chances they might have in each of these alternatives, parties opted for cooperation or for obstructing the attempts at mediation according to village justice.

While there was a general trend towards dispute management outside the courts, neo-traditional village mediation in West Sumatra acquired more features of adjudication and bureaucratic decision-making. This process was on its way before the Suharto regime fell but took up momentum after the reforms. Modern communication techniques and a heightened interest in *adat* institutions in their villages of origin due to Indonesia's constitutional decentralization allowed a new set of mediators to become active in village government and dispute management. The changes were due to the fact that more so-called 'traditional' mediators have been socialized in the state bureaucracy, with its paternalistic adjudicative mode of decision-making. On the other hand, the renewed interest in and importance of *adat* also gave new impulse to the threat to punish those who obstruct cooperation with social and ritual exclusion, something that had become quite obsolete. This did not prevent obstruction and was by no means a guarantee for successful mediation, but exclusion could no longer be dismissed as socially totally irrelevant. *Adat* as a discourse and a political factor is fully back on stage, but at the same time the mediators were keenly aware of the limits of *adat* and seem to be less willing to pass judgement on wrongful or unjust decisions by administrative authorities than the classical *adat* authorities. Moreover, religious discourse became a more prominent feature of *adat* mediation.

Finally, contrary to the standard ideology of mediation, the new types of mediation discussed in this chapter are deeply legal modes of dispute management. Some were operating in the shadow of the law, with legal issues always lurking in the background. Despite the fact that discourses often suggest otherwise, the cases show that legal issues, whether in terms of *adat* or religion or the state generally, are at the core of mediation, if not always explicitly.

Acknowledgements

I thank Carolin Hillemans, Karl Haerter, Günther Schlee and an anonymous reviewer for their thoughtful comments.

Keebet von Benda-Beckmann is Professor Emerita of Social and Legal Anthropology. She was head of the Project Group 'Legal Pluralism' at the Max Planck Institute for Social Anthropology in Halle, Germany. Her research in Indonesia and the Netherlands focuses on legal pluralism, social security, governance and the role of religion in disputing processes.

Notes

1. This term was first used for state and off-state activities of civil servants in the Moluccas. See Benda-Beckmann and Benda-Beckmann (1998), reprinted in Benda-Beckmann and Benda-Beckmann (2007: 205–34).
2. See Rahmadi (2010) and Simandjuntak, Suroto and Nurhayati (2014) on the Indonesian legislation concerning mediation.
3. But see Wall, Stark and Standifer (2001: 372) for regional differences within the US.
4. See in particular Abel (1982).
5. See Ali (2013: 231) for a distinction between mediation and conciliation in the context of Chinese mediation.
6. I rely for this section on the work of Fadjar Thufail (2010 and 2012).
7. In a situation in which disagreement about the appropriate tenet of faith is not subject to conflict within the religious community, referring to religion may have a mitigating effect on the conflicts. If religious discourse itself is a subject of deep contestation, such as is the case among Muslims in rural Morocco, religious discourse would not serve this mitigating effect. See Turner (2013: 59).
8. It was not until December 2015 that the International People's Tribunal 1965 set up in The Hague commenced its proceedings. And even then, the Indonesian government did not recognize the tribunal and refused to cooperate. See https://www.tribunal1965.org/en/final-report-of-the-ipt-1965/ (accessed 13 March 2020).
9. For reasons why the ad hoc human rights court had only limited success, see Thufail (2010: 14).
10. See Thufail (2010: 12) for the different connotations of the term in the Islamic world at large and the meaning it obtained in the specifically Indonesian post-reform context.
11. Similar developments occur elsewhere. For African neo-traditional modes of mediation, see Mutisi (2012). For Bougainville, see Larcom (2013).
12. For the specific reasons why reorganization of village government elicited so much enthusiasm in West Sumatra, see Benda-Beckmann and Benda-Beckmann (2013).
13. See Benda-Beckmann and Benda-Beckmann (2013: 333ff).

References

Abel, R. (ed.). 1982. *The Politics of Informal Justice*. New York: Academic Press.

Ali, S. 2013. 'The Jurisprudence of Responsive Mediation: An Empirical Examination of Chinese People's Mediation in Action', *Journal of Legal Pluralism* 45(2): 227–48.

Beardsley, K.C., et al. 2006. 'Mediation Style and Crisis Outcomes', *The Journal of Conflict Resolution* 50(1): 58–86.

Beber, B. 2010. 'International Mediation of Military Conflicts: Causes and Consequences', Ph.D. dissertation. Columbia University.

Benda-Beckmann, F. von, and K. von Benda-Beckmann. 1998. 'Where Structures Merge: State and Off-State Involvement in Rural Social Security on Ambon, Eastern Indonesia', in S. Pannell and F. v. Benda-Beckmann (eds), *Old World Places, New World Problems: Exploring Resource Management Issues in Eastern Indonesia*. Canberra: The Australian National University, Centre for Resource and Environmental Studies, CRES Publications, pp. 143–80.

———. 2007. *Social Security between Past and Future: Ambonese Networks of Care and Support.* Münster: LIT Verlag.

———. 2013. *Political and Legal Transformations of an Indonesian Polity: The Nagari from Colonization to Decentralization*. Cambridge: Cambridge University Press.

Bercovitch, J., and G. Schneider. 2000. 'Who Mediates? The Political Economy of International Conflict Management', *Journal of Peace Research* 37(2): 145–65.

Callister, R.R., and J.A. Wall Jr. 2004. 'Thai and US Community Mediation', *The Journal of Conflict Resolution* 48(4): 573–98.

Cremades, B.M. 1998. 'Overcoming the Clash of Legal Cultures: The Role of Interactive Arbitration', *Arbitration International* 14(2): 157–72.

Dhiaulhaq, A., et al. 2014. 'Transforming Conflict in Plantations through Mediation: Lessons and Experiences from Sumatera, Indonesia', *Forest Policy and Economics* (2014). Retrieved 13 March 2020 from http://dx.doi.org/10.1016/j.forpol.2014.01.003.

Engel, D.M. 1978. *Code and Custom in a Thai Provincial Court: The Interaction of Formal and Informal Systems of Justice*. Tucson: University of Arizona Press.

Engel, D.M., and J.S. Engel. 2010. *Tort, Custom, and Karma: Globalization and Legal Consciousness in Thailand*. Stanford, CA: Stanford University Press.

Girolamo, D. de. 2012. 'Seeking Negotiated Order through Mediation: A Manifestation of Legal Culture?', in D. Nelken (ed.), *Using Legal Culture*. London: Wildy, Simmonds and Hill, pp. 153–88.

Greig, J.M. 2001. 'Moments of Opportunity: Recognizing Conditions of Ripeness for International Mediation between Enduring Rivals', *The Journal of Conflict Resolution* 45(6): 691–718.

Gulliver, P.H. 1979. *Disputes and Negotiations: A Cross-Cultural Perspective*. New York: Academic Press.

Larcom, S. 2013. 'Taking Custom and Law Seriously: A Case of Legal Re-ordering in Kieta', *Journal of Legal Pluralism* 45(2): 190–208.

Lee, S.-M. 2013. 'Mediator Impartiality and Mediator Interest', Ph.D. dissertation. Kentucky: University of Kentucky, Political Science. Retrieved 4 May 2020 from http://uknowledge.uky.edu/cgi/viewcontent.cgi?article=1007&context=polysci_etds.

Merry, S.E. 1982. 'The Social Organization of Mediation in Nonindustrial Societies: Implication for Informal Community Justice in America', in R. Abel (ed.), *The Politics of Informal Justice*, vol. 2. New York: Academic Press, pp. 17–46.

Merry, S.E., and N. Milner (eds). 1993. *The Possibility of Popular Justice: A Case Study of Community Mediation in the United States*. Ann Arbor: University of Michigan Press.

Mutisi, M. (ed.). 2012. *Integrating Traditional and Modern Conflict Resolution: Experiences from Selected Cases in Eastern and the Horn of Africa*. Durban: African Centre for the Constructive Resolution of Disputes (ACCORD).

Pompe, S. 2007. 'The Probosutedjo Case and the Crisis in Indonesian Judicial Reform 2005–2007', unpublished paper.

Rahmadi, T. 2010. *Mediasi: penyelesaian sengketa melalui pendekatan mufakat*. Jakarta: Rajawali Pers.

Simandjuntak, M.E., V. Suroto and B. Resti Nurhayati. 2014. 'Indonesia', in C. Esplugues and S. Barona (eds), *Global Perspectives on ADR*. Cambridge: Intersentia, pp. 203–32.

Thufail, F.I. 2010. 'The Social Life of Reconciliation: Religion and the Struggle for Social Justice in Post-New Order Indonesia', *Max Planck Institute for Social Anthropology Working Paper* No. 127. Retrieved 4 May 2020 from http://www.eth.mpg.de/cms/de/publications/working_papers/wp0127.

———. 2012. 'When Peace Prevails on Kasih Hill: The Protestant Church and the Politics of *adat* in Minahasa', *Asian Ethnicity* 13(4): 359–71.

Turner, B. 2013. 'Religious Subtleties in Disputing: Spatiotemporal Inscriptions of Faith in the Nomosphere in Rural Morocco', in F. and K. von Benda-Beckmann, M. Ramstedt and B. Turner (eds), *Religion in Disputes: Pervasiveness of Religious Normativity in Disputing Processes*. New York: Palgrave, pp. 55–73.

Wall, J.A. Jr., J.B. Stark and R.L. Standifer. 2001. 'Mediation: A Current Review and Theory Development', *The Journal of Conflict Resolution* 45(3): 370–91.

Woolford, A., and R.S. Ratner. 2010. 'Disrupting the Informal–Formal Justice Complex: On the Transformative Potential of Civil Mediation, Restorative Justice and Reparations Politics', *Contemporary Justice Review* 13(1): 5–17.

Part III

Mediation and Arbitration in International Arenas

Chapter 8

Interstate Mediation and Arbitration

Concepts, Cases and Actors of Third Party Dispute Resolution (Seventeenth to Nineteenth Century)

Jakob Zollmann

Introduction

Throughout the nineteenth century, third party dispute resolution in case of controversies between two or more state governments was used with increasing intensity. From the seventeenth century, such third party involvement in interstate disputes was linked by European lawyers and philosophers alike to the hope of a durable and peaceable conflict resolution on a continental if not global scale. Evidently, there were predecessors of third party involvement: 'the method of settling controversies and disputes by means of arbitration seems to be one of immemorial antiquity . . . in practically every system of law' – as was also known to authors of the seventeenth century like Hugo Grotius.[1] This chapter sketches the historical practice of third party dispute resolution in public international law (differentiated as interstate 'mediation' and 'arbitration') as well as the peace movement and its (criticized) aspirations for pacification by 'juridification'. This continual 'juridification' of international relations was supposed to bring about (eternal) peace, as it would make wars superfluous in the future.

Several points are at issue. What are the historical-political conditions under which political actors choose to resort to conflict resolution by third parties instead of bilateral negotiations or military force? Who were the beneficiaries of interstate arbitration? How efficient was this 'tool' of international law? What role did the domestic relevance of an international controversy play in the decision to agree to third party dispute resolution? This touches upon a major problem under discussion in the discipline of International Relations: the condition(s) required for the possibility of non-military conflict solution between states.

Interstate Mediation and Arbitration: Wide Concepts

What did seventeenth-, eighteenth- and nineteenth-century European and American contemporaries understand by the terms interstate 'arbitration' and 'mediation'? Both terms encompassed some sort of third party dispute resolution; that is, disputes between states were resolved (or were attempted to be resolved) by additionally involving someone other than formal agents (e.g. diplomats) of the states having the dispute.[2] However, an analysis of the historical development of third party involvement in interstate dispute resolution shows a plurality of instruments used for this end. It is therefore important to underline that the meaning of 'arbitration' and 'mediation' as terms used in the written sources evolved over the period under review. It follows from this historical variety that it is impossible to clearly distinguish between, for example, 'pure' forms of 'arbitration' or 'mediation'. At times, 'the two institutions were intimately linked because, *inter alia*, the arbitrator was often obliged, before imposing his award upon the parties, to attempt to reconcile their differing points of view' (Verzijl 1976: 131, referring to fifteenth- and sixteenth-century documents). In addition, philosophers and other political thinkers enriched (or complicated) the debate about interstate third party dispute settlement, for instance with their concepts of international tribunals (without, however, always using the terms 'arbitration' or 'mediation'). Indeed 'the question of how to achieve a pacific order among potentially bellicose modern states was central to eighteenth-century political thought' (Grewal 2016: 624). Authors like William Penn (1693), Abbé de Saint-Pierre (1713), Immanuel Kant (1795) or William Ladd (1840) submitted proposals for future 'congresses' or 'courts of nations'. These schemes were informed by the liberal insight that sovereigns need to accept (for the greater good, i.e. peace) that they are bound by 'the law' – law to be employed by such 'courts of nations' in order to bindingly resolve interstate disputes (cf. Justenhoven 2006: 127–80; Gerhardt 1995). These early modern thinkers were also convinced that the steady global spread of commerce emanating from Europe would tame conflict between sovereigns (Kapossy et. al. 2017). In particular, Kant renewed political thought by locating 'peace at the culminating point of a progressive philosophy of history in the form of "a perfect civic union of mankind"' (Bernasconi 2011: 44).

At the same time, the preparation and conclusion of peace treaties by diplomats increasingly took on legalistic forms in language and content. Beginning as early as the seventeenth century, the diplomatic 'art of making peace' turned into a lawyer's skill that was henceforth an inseparable part of statesmanship

(*Staatskunst*) (cf. Bély 2007). With the growth of international law as an academic subject, several authors proposed their own concepts of third party dispute resolution with the purpose of securing peace. Legal authorities widely cited in eighteenth- and nineteenth-century Europe (who were still used as references prior to World War I by advocates of interstate arbitration to give credence to their cause [cf. Zollmann 2018b]), employed a variety of expressions and definitions, as the three references mentioned below indicate.

Among these 'classics of international law', several attempts to distinguish between mediators and arbitrators can be found. Samuel von Pufendorf (1632–94) explained in 1672: 'Mediators, as they are termed, who of their own accord interpose between contending parties and nations, either preparing for, or already waging war, and who endeavor by their authority, their arguments and their entreaties, to bring them to a peaceful settlement and a prudent application to law, are not strictly speaking Arbitrators' (Pufendorf [1672] 1711: 244). A few years later, the same author explicitly pointed to several cases of historic instances of 'mediations' (*Vermittelung*) between states when describing peace negotiations to end a (still) ongoing war.[3] For Pufendorf, the term *arbitri* (arbitrators) thus did not describe those who 'of their own accord interpose between contending parties', but those who were chosen by the parties themselves to decide on the controversy. He also underlined that *arbitri* had to use 'the laws' in their endeavours to end the controversy between the parties (Pufendorf [1672] 1711: 239).

Another 'classic' figure of international law, Johann Wolfgang Textor (1638–1701) dealt explicitly with the question of third party involvement in concluding peace. In 1680, Textor referred to two types, arbitrator and mediator, involved in dispute resolution – but he pointed to a distinction between private and public law: 'The part played in private affairs by an arbitrator, appointed by consent of all parties to arrange a friendly settlement of a dispute, is in public affairs played by a mediator'. Evidently, in both cases, the disputing parties (or combatants) had to give their consent for mediation/arbitration. As to the enforcement of the award of the mediator of peace, Textor clarified: 'It is merely a friendly office, and the award of a mediator has not the force of a judgment' (Textor [1680] 1916: cap. XX, p. 58; 228f.).

Emer de Vattel (1714–67) also wrote about 'mediation': the mediator 'ought to observe a strict impartiality; . . . but he ought not scrupulously to insist on rigid justice. He is a conciliator, and not a judge: his business is to procure peace; and he ought to induce him who has right on his side to relax something of his pretensions'. Vattel emphasized that 'mediation is a mode of conciliation much used' between European rulers. And, different from the examples given by Pufendorf, he mentioned mediation as a means to prevent states from waging war, not merely to end an ongoing war: 'The friendly powers . . . offer their mediation, and make overtures of peace and accommodation' (Vattel [1758] 1916: 223).

The history of eighteenth-century European international relations is indeed rife with episodes of mediations, and historians recount these occurrences more often as diplomatic manoeuvring than as neutral third party settlements. Considerations of law were wholly absent from the picture of, for instance, the French 'prime minister' Cardinal Fleury seeking 'to wean his state from British ties, starting with clever mediation between Britain and Spain at the Congress of Soissons (1728–1729)' and resulting in the 'union of interests between the two Bourbon crowns' [France and Spain] that kept 'Britain in near helpless isolation'. In short: 'mediation in the Anglo-Spanish war of 1727–29 served French ends' (Schumann 2016: 277, 279). More often than not, in these instances the 'art of making peace' was considered by contemporaries as the 'art of deceiving' and not being deceived.

Interstate arbitration, on the other hand, was barely used as a term of foreign policy practice during the eighteenth century, but as a (legal) dispute resolution mechanism it was not entirely forgotten by public international law writers. Vattel, clearly distinguishing it from mediation, dealt with questions of arbitration in an extra sub-chapter. Arbitrators, he argued, were also chosen by the disputing states to re-establish *or* to maintain peace, but with a higher degree of formality: 'When once the contending parties have entered into articles of arbitration, they are bound to abide by the sentence of the arbitrators: they have engaged to do this; and the faith of treaties should be religiously observed'. In order to prevent faulty awards that exceed the competences of the arbitrators, Vattel recommended listing precisely all claims and counter-arguments in the '*compromis*' of the parties. The arbitrator's award had to remain within these limits of the '*compromis*'. Vattel, an outspoken proponent of interstate arbitration, went so far as to argue: 'This wise precaution [of Swiss foreign policy 'to agree beforehand on the manner in which their disputes were to be submitted to arbitrators'] has not a little contributed to maintain the Helvetic republic in that flourishing state which secures her liberty, and renders her respectable throughout Europe' (Vattel [1758] 1916: § 329, 423–426).

Vattel's distinction between interstate mediation and arbitration procedures can be found also in the language of practitioners of international relations, diplomats and court councillors, to underline a certain element of one of these two 'alternatives'. While both involve the invitation to a third party ('a friend') to assist in the solution of the dispute between two state parties, only the arbitration award is *binding* upon the disputing state parties. To give but one example: in 1776, after centuries of constant dispute about the definition of the borderline between their respective possessions in South America according to the Treaty of Tordesillas (1494) and subsequent treaties the Kingdoms of Spain and Portugal requested the 'good office' of the governments of England and France, asking for assistance in finding a compromise. After a lengthy discussion on the procedure to be followed, one proposal read:

> that all questions relative to the Execution of the Treaty of Paris 1763 be decided at the Congress at Paris by the Plenipotentiaries of the Courts of Great Britain and France as Arbitrators, and not as Mediators; the Kings of Spain and Portugal abiding by decision of their Britannick and Most Christian Majesties, without any further doubts, reply or delay.[4]

It can only be summarized here that these attempts at arbitration came to naught and war broke out (again), only to be terminated in 1777 by the Treaty of San Idelfonso. It added a further legal text to the question of the Spanish-Portuguese borderline in South America and, indeed, by the 'eighteenth century, the quantity of [legal] material that had accumulated was such that contemporaries complained it was virtually impossible to handle'. Every new treaty or new legal commentary added more questions rather than answers, among them 'how to discern which sources and authorities were more trustworthy'. Experts were needed and some 'sustained that authors belonging to neutral parties were more reliable' (Herzog 2015: 29).

With the diplomats' usage of juridic terminology, as this proposal of 1776 exemplified, international law was turned into a tool of diplomacy, used for political ends. It appears that in the late eighteenth century, a conceptualization of interstate mediation became more and more accepted that located it still within the realm of classic diplomacy.[5] Arbitration, on the other hand, referred to the realm of (international) law, and the settlement was often considered binding, similar to a decision of a domestic court, precisely because the parties had – under international law – previously agreed to accept it as such. However, in the age of absolutism, as German international lawyer Georg F. von Martens lamented in 1788, the 'examples of offered and accepted arbitration have become increasingly rare' (Transl. in Grewe 2000: 313).

Yet it is important to underline that similar terms may have differing meanings at different times. As the above-quoted examples have shown, one should not be too surprised to find historic documents in which the terms mediation and arbitration were used interchangeably. Historical types and modes of conflict solution have changed markedly in the international arena, irrespective of whether they are considered from a procedural perspective, the appointment of mediators/arbitrators, or the norms that were relevant in an arbitration award. Differing modes of appointing a third party, the obligatory character of the settlement/award by those charged with finding a solution, or a specific procedure to be followed are mere examples to distinguish the two (Darby 1904: 796). It would be a superfluous task to attempt a non-ambiguous definition of the terms interstate 'arbitration' and 'mediation' (others also would include 'conciliation') based on contemporary usages (Grewe 2000: 519). Instead of trying to search for a clear-cut (legal) distinction between the two terms, it seems more apposite to underline that both, interstate 'mediation' and 'arbitration', as the terms are used in the twenty-first century, were historically connected.

The nineteenth century seems to have been an era particularly prone to the tenets of international third party involvement; this is at least what contemporaries assumed, claiming that never before was arbitration more often referred to (Tanquerey [1902] 1923: 1732). This was true not only with regard to the number of actual arbitration cases and arbitration treaties (this is discussed in the following sections), but also considering the academic and conceptual analysis of the subject.

Following earlier proposals such as Kant's or Jeremy Bentham's (1748–1832) for arbitration to settle differences between nations (Bentham 1927 [1789]), the American lawyer David Dudley Field (1805–94) included in his proposal for an international law code a general obligation of governments to arbitrate certain disputes with other states before a 'High Tribunal of Arbitration' (Field [1872] 1881: 415). The Moscow law professor and outspoken peace activist Leonid Kamarowsky (1846–1912) wrote an entire volume on *The International Tribunal* (1881). He admitted that it is a difficult task (*tâche*) of such a tribunal 'to develop among the peoples a sentiment of necessity to seek recourse by law' in case of interstate dispute. However, this was 'nothing impossible' in the future, even when it came to the question of *obligatory* arbitration between states. In order to encourage his readers to believe in this path of (legal) progress, Kamarowsky pointed to the 'centuries of struggles, hesitations, and errors' it took for the 'English constitution' to reach its 'état *actuel*' (Kamarowsky 1887: 317, 477). Ten years later, the French lawyer Michel Revon also wrote a voluminous book about *International Arbitration* (1892). After long considerations of the history of interstate arbitration, he left no doubt that in the future progress would inevitably lead all peace-loving and 'civilized' nations towards the recognition of obligatory arbitration for all disputes, that is, the rule of law on a global scale. After seeking historical sanction in Immanuel Kant's legal philosophy, Revon concluded – in unmistakable millennial optimism – with a shiny 'domestic analogy' (to use an anachronism): 'The rule of law succeeding the empire of force, nations subject to a superior rule just as individuals today, justice spanning all over the world, princes and peoples, states and individuals . . . in short, the law as absolute master of the universe, what more beautiful spectacle than that? This is the true universal monarchy!' (Revon 1892: 528).[6]

Less millenial, but dogmatically the period's most advanced monograph on the topic was *The Doctrine of Arbitration* (1914) by Vienna law professor Heinrich Lammasch (1853–1920), who remained a steadfast pacifist throughout World War I. In the decades prior to the war, peace advocates, many international lawyers and also some politicians considered interstate arbitration as an 'all-purpose method' to strengthen peace and cooperation between states, resulting – one day – in 'les États-Unis d'Europe' or even in a World Federation. This conviction was also based on numerous 'successful' arbitrations that had been executed in these decades.[7] The first Nobel Peace laureate Frédéric Passy showed himself just as convinced of this positive development as US Secretary of State Elihu Root, who in 1912 also received the Nobel Peace Prize for his support of interstate arbitration.

The Permanent Court of Arbitration (PCA) established by the 'Convention for the Pacific Settlement of International Disputes', concluded in 1899 during the first Hague Peace Conference (revised during the Second Peace Conference by the Convention of 18 October 1907), was the most prominent result of decades-old endeavours of a wide array of individuals and pressure groups related to international peace movements, academics and politicians, to install under international law one central juridical institution sanctioned by all states – even though the PCA was merely a list of arbitrators and a secretariat in The Hague.[8] Article 37 stated: 'International arbitration has for its object the settlement of disputes between States by Judges of their own choice and on the basis of respect for law. Recourse to arbitration implies an engagement to submit in good faith to the Award'. In 1900, seventeen signatory states had ratified the 1899-Convention, thus giving credence to their desire, repeated in the preamble of the 1907-Convention, 'of extending the empire of law and of strengthening the appreciation of international justice'.

Also under the Hague Convention, mediation remained a valid means of settling interstate disputes, as laid out in Articles 2 to 8 of the 1907 Convention. Article 6 stated: 'Good offices and mediation undertaken either at the request of the parties in dispute or on the initiative of Powers strangers to the dispute have exclusively the character of advice, and never have binding force'. Furthermore, states that were party to the Conventions of 1899 and/or 1907 were not obliged to employ the means provided by the PCA. According to Article 42 of the 1907 Convention, the institution of 'a special Tribunal' was a valid alternative to recourse to the PCA. Also, all these procedures were to be used by governments 'as far as circumstances allow'. Compulsory jurisdiction about some or all interstate controversies was rejected by a number of states and 'firm resistance by the German Empire finally killed the idea'.[9]

It was in this particular period of the history of third party interstate dispute resolution from the second half of the nineteenth century that a distinct and rigorous conceptualization of arbitration as a quasi-judicial process settled by 'judges' emerged, as opposed to mediation by a third party, which could function as a form of political negotiation between three parties without reference to (international) law. This development was in line with the emergence of modern international law (and international lawyers) as a distinct field of academic research (Koskenniemi 2001). In the writings of authors such as the few mentioned above, 'arbitration' was described as a rational and 'juridical' means of dispute settlement between states. It was conceived as an apolitical tool of progress towards peace, and as such not only a viable, but a better alternative to violent conflict solution or the emotionally driven intricacies of diplomacy. In their view, the complex disputes between governments could not be left to government officials, but must be submitted to neutral arbitrator(s) who were to determine facts and apply (international) law to those facts in order to bindingly resolve the dispute between these states.

Considering the steady increase of the use of 'arbitration' in the international arena throughout the nineteenth century and the great number of specific arbitration agreements, it comes as no surprise that the generic term 'interstate arbitration' described the undertakings of a wide array of arbitration commissions, single arbitrators, mixed tribunals and international 'courts'. A distinction between courts and arbitration bodies has been made in legal literature (cf. Brownlie 1990: chap. 30). However, given the above-described 'juridification' of interstate arbitration, it was already argued decades ago that 'the distinction between arbitral and judicial panels is not well grounded. In the international field, most arbitrators behave like judges' (Sohn 1961: 217). It is to be emphasized again that historically, a strict separation between the two types is not cognizable.[10] Irrespective of the denomination of a third party as arbitration tribunal or court, a number of elements can be identified that defined this institution at the end of the nineteenth century:

(1) Unlike during diplomatic negotiations, the decision process was not under the disputing parties' direct control, but given to a third party.
(2) By calling upon third persons or institutions that were entrusted with the decision of disputes between states, the parties recognized that, first, there was an *alternative* to violent conflict including retaliation, in case diplomacy had failed to render a solution; and, second, that the (way of) presentation of the *facts* upon which the dispute is based was decisive for the final decision, the award or settlement.
(3) The third party/arbitrator was not only attributed with qualities such as rationality, objectivity or neutrality, but was well versed in the (professional) interpretation of those norms previously recognized by both parties. This interpretation was of decisive relevance for the elucidation of the facts presented by both parties having a dispute. For reasons of legitimacy and 'fairness', it was to be ascertained that during the procedure in front of a third party tribunal both states were entitled to the same rights to present their facts and arguments.[11]
(4) Both parties agreed *previously* to accept the award about their dispute as *final and binding* upon them (this is the decisive difference from the diplomatic practice of mediation).[12]
(5) Parties were free to conclude agreements about third party dispute resolution about their potential *future* disagreements (anticipatory agreements).

Practices and Cases of Third Party Dispute Resolution

It must be added that not only contemporaries, but also historians have from time to time applied not the most stringent definitions when analysing third party conflict solutions between disputing states. The most surprising example might be the Jay Treaty of 1794 in which 'the British had acknowledged for the first time the territorial integrity of the United States as a sovereign country' and which avoided a war between the US and Great Britain (Paul 2018: 103). Given that US Chief Justice John Jay, a former secretary of foreign affairs, had agreed with the British on a three-member border-commission procedure in order to delimit the border between the USA and British North America along the 'Saint Croix River', this eighteenth-century treaty is often cited as the starting point of modern interstate arbitration.[13] However, when looking at the practical details of this "rebirth" (Grewe 2000: 517), it becomes evident that the disputed boundaries were negotiated by 'joint arbitral commissions' (Kolb 2013: 46), which consisted only of British and American members (Articles IV and V). There was no neutral third party involvement, but the third commissioner, as an umpire of either British or American nationality, was either agreed upon by the two commissioners appointed by their governments, or, if they disagreed, the umpire would be selected by lot. And yet the procedure has been described since the late nineteenth century in a manner resembling an invention of tradition as if it were an arbitration procedure (Lingens 2011). Wilhelm Grewe spoke of the 'success' of this 'arbitral tribunal' (Grewe 2000: 517), even though the commissioners (most of them trained lawyers) did not settle the boundary disputes and no award was issued by the commission. Yet the extensive use of legal arguments provided by both parties in their memoirs, as well as the provision of material evidence (maps and surveyor reports about the disputed area), pointed to the future practices of arbitration procedures, as they evolved over the course of the nineteenth century.[14] On the other hand, the promise of both governments to 'consider such decision [by the three commissioners] as final and conclusive' (Article V), was, as mentioned above, already used in previous treaties.

It should be noted that throughout the nineteenth century also, mediation remained a feasible diplomatic practice and a policy component to be included in international treaties. In 1801 during the Napoleonic Wars, for instance, Russia mediated a peace treaty between France and the Kingdom of Naples.[15] In 1856, in their arrangement of one of the most important peace treaties of the century, the Treaty of Paris (1856) ending the Crimean War, the Austrians chose to follow a policy of 'armed mediation' between Russia and its enemies Great Britain, France and the Ottoman Empire. 'Armed mediation', the Austrians let the Russians know, meant that Austria would 'fight [together with the British] if her mediation was refused' (Temperley 1932: 390). Article VIII of this mediated peace treaty then stipulated that if 'there should arise between Turkey [*la Sub-*

lime Porte] and any of the other signatories a difference endangering peace, these Powers, before resorting to forcible measures, should afford the other contracting parties the opportunity of preventing such an extremity by means of their mediation' (Phillipson 1916: 79). This was clearly a *discretionary* clause concerning the involvement of third parties, which, as the Austrian foreign minister Buol conceded privately, 'has hardly any practical value' (Temperley 1932: 413). As these examples of international practice indicate, 'mediation of inter-State disputes was undertaken primarily by States having a direct political interest in the dispute. The term mediation did not connote disinterestedness' (Jackson 1958: 512).

Over the course of the nineteenth century, a tendency among foreign policy makers became noticeable that favoured interstate arbitration over third party mediation, in particular when it came to disputes that were not (at least at first sight) related to political questions of war and peace. Agreements grew in numbers concerning the *obligatory* involvement of third parties and the previously agreed binding acceptance of their awards. According to a recent count 'beginning with the Anglo-American Jay Treaty of 1794, there were more than one thousand instances of arbitration agreements entered into by the time of World War I' (Harris 2016: 306). Not all initial agreements necessarily led to actual arbitration cases, but contemporaries counted 177 '*instances arbitrales*' during the period 1794 to 1900. Of course, given the above-mentioned difficulties to differentiate between arbitration and mediation, the classification of individual cases remains ambiguous. Other authors have identified more than 220 or even 537 instances of international arbitration for the long nineteenth century. Irrespective of the exact numbers, they exemplify the thriving practice of third party involvement in interstate disputes (La Fontaine 1997: xii; Riemens 2010: 80; Darby 1904: 769–917; see Grewe 2000: 519; Stuyt 1972).

In the following subsections, a few interstate arbitration cases will be analysed so as to elucidate the changing modes of parties agreeing to let a third party decide and to consent to abide by that third party's decision. By choosing this non-chronological approach, a number of conditions can be clarified that increasingly led political actors to the decision to refer a conflict between states to a self-chosen third party.

Four central questions shall be posed that shed light on the contemporary legal and political practices of interstate arbitration:

(1) Who were the actors in the arbitration bodies and what were their qualifications?
(2) Which subject areas, types or causes of interstate disputes were referred to third party arbitration – and which were not?
(3) Were there any specific beneficiaries of interstate arbitration cognizable? For example, can it be shown that small states in particular (those with-

out a powerful army) counted on this sort of conflict resolution in order to escape their asymmetry in a violent conflict situation?

(4) How relevant was public opinion for the initiation and the course of an arbitration procedure?

(1) Actors, Their Qualifications and Their Success in Ending the Dispute

Evidently, third parties who were requested to decide a dispute between states were expected to bear qualities such as rationality, objectivity and neutrality. The latter point increasingly (the failures of the Jay Treaty served as a historical warning) led the parties to require the arbitrator/third party institution to come from another country presumably not involved in the dispute. This stands in marked contrast to the finding that since the late eighteenth century the nomination by both parties of one's own nationals as arbitrators/judges had 'continued unabated across international courts' (Smith 2004: 11). The historical processes of choosing the decision-maker or establishing the parameters under which the decision-makers would render their award was more complicated than this summary observation about a 'judicial nationalism' implies. Indeed, there were mixed commissions comprised of the parties' nationals to the dispute, but other individuals or tribunals were available for disputing parties in search of a third party willing to decide the matter. In the early nineteenth century, parties most often requested other heads of state to be their arbitrators. Over the course of the century, more and more legal experts and/or other civil servants were employed to that end. This trend resulted in more multi-member tribunals comprising primarily or solely nationals of other states.

Who became members of arbitral tribunals? Who decided about this question? Who represented the parties – only one's own nationals, lawyers or experts of another profession? Given the development of the labour market for the legal profession and the development of specific legal curricula during the nineteenth century, it needs to be asked whether there was any form of 'professionalization' of the careers of 'international dispute experts' (Halpérin 2004: 172–93).

The question of who should decide on an interstate dispute and which qualifications should be required for this purpose was essential for the disputing parties, as it concerned in the end the recognition of an arbitrator/tribunal and thus the execution of the resulting award. In medieval Europe and at the beginning of the European concert of powers, it was the Pope, the emperor or other kings or princes who were at times asked by governments to render a decision on a certain point of dispute (Grewe 2000: 98). The above-mentioned Johann Wolfgang Textor quoted an instance where Louis XIV of France did not protest against the Pope as 'mediator himself, but against a minister of the mediator'; 'when a person has been carefully chosen, it is meant that no deputy shall be put in his place or carry out the mediation' (Textor [1680] 1916: 229).

In the eighteenth century, a tendency for the professionalization of third party 'peace-making' became cognizable, thus indicating the ambivalent relations between international law and diplomacy: diplomacy was more than the exchange of arguments between government representatives based on international law. For instance, the tendency to assign specialists in the drafting, negotiation and execution of international treaties was palpable in the British-American mixed commission set up according to the Jay Treaty of 1794 to clarify the border between the USA and British North America. The commission consisted not only of lawyers but also of land surveyors. Similar special commissions were employed later on all over the world to define and map (colonial) borders. The dispute between Portugal and the Netherlands over the border across the island of Timor based on numerous technical documents is an example at hand. It was decided in 1914 by the single arbitrator Charles E. Lardy (1847–1923), for three decades Swiss minister in Paris, *doctor iuris*, president of the Institut de droit international (1899–1902) and 'one of the most sought-after international arbiters by virtue of his reliability, impartiality and clear judgment' (Probst 1989: 63; see also Thévenaz 1968). Probably the most renowned arbitrator prior to World War I was Fyodor Fyodorovich Martens (1845–1909), a man who, throughout his career, prided himself on combining tasks at the university of Saint Petersburg and at Russia's Ministry of Foreign Affairs. Author of the first comprehensive textbook on *Contemporary International Law of Civilized Peoples* (2 volumes, 1882/83, French 1833) in the Russian language, Martens 'persistently defended Russia's legal interests abroad' and served as arbitrator in a number of high-profile cases (Mälksoo 2014: 819). Among the interstate disputes that he settled were the dispute between Great Britain and France over Newfoundland (1891); the dispute between the Netherlands and Great Britain over the English whaling ship *Costa Rica Packet* (1896); the dispute between Venezuela and Great Britain over the boundary of British Guiana (1899); and the Pious Fund Affair between Mexico and the United States (1902) on the monetary indemnification after expropriations. This was the first case determined by the Permanent Court of Arbitration in The Hague set up during the First Hague Conference.

These biographies of 'internationalists' show interstate arbitration becoming more and more an affair for a very small (and lavishly funded) legal elite with outstanding academic credentials. Once the political decision had been made to refer a dispute to third party settlement, the actors taking over 'the case' had to be professionals with claims to authority based on wide legal knowledge and argumentative competence (Grewe 2000: 520). Through the labours of these men (they were only men), 'law made historically specific relations of power seem natural and acceptable' (Koskenniemi 2019: 18).

The assumption that heads of state of countries considered neutral with regard to the dispute could be requested as arbitrators was not limited to the Pope. In 1830, the king of the Netherlands rendered an award regarding the American-

British border still under dispute since the Jay Treaty and settled only in 1842.[16] Thirty years later, in 1870/71, it was the German Emperor William I to whom the same parties submitted for arbitration the further clarification of their border.[17] In 1869, US President Ulysses Grant agreed to be the arbitrator for the Anglo-Portuguese dispute about the Island of Bulama off the coast of West Africa, but other government institutions of 'neutral' states like the Swiss Federal Council (*Bundesrat*, i.e. the government) were also requested to render an arbitration award.[18] A 'judicial nationalism' cannot be discerned from this policy of choosing an arbitrator.

Yet, the medieval tradition of governments to refer to the moral authority of the Catholic Church and to request the Pope for dispute settlement was continued well into the twentieth century (Grewe 2000: 199; Schneider 2003b; Duve 2013). In 1870, the offer of Pius IX to effectuate a mediation to prevent war between France and Prussia was to no avail. However, in 1885 Leo XIII rendered an arbitral award in the dispute between Spain and Germany about the Caroline Islands in the Pacific. Disputes about the limits of the spheres of influences (later called colonial borders) in the Congo region were referred to the Pope in 1890 by Great Britain and Portugal. Political and ecclesiastical borders were also disputed between Portugal and the Kingdom of Congo, who agreed in 1891 to request the Pope for mediation in case both parties could not agree on the issue. The government of Venezuela asked the Pope in 1894 to mediate in the border dispute with Great Britain, but the British government did not agree to this solution. One year later, Leo XIII adjourned his acceptance of the office of arbitrator in the border dispute between Haiti and the Dominican Republic. Only in 1920 did a treaty between both parties finally designate Pope Benedict XV to be their arbitrator.[19]

An answer to the question of how these institutions (heads of states, government bodies) reached their decision is not always easy to discern from the sources. The assumption that these men did indeed delegate the decision-making to other persons suggests itself. In 1885, for example, Pope Leo XIII charged a commission of Cardinals to prepare the award about the Caroline Islands after having received the memoranda containing the arguments of the Spanish and German governments. It is also passed down that the above-mentioned legal expert Charles Lardy prepared for the Swiss Federal Council an award that was requested by the governments of Colombia and Venezuela to settle a border dispute (Béhaine 1898; Probst 1989: 56).

The development described here for the nineteenth century points out a correlation between tendencies of juridification on the domestic and international scales, thus mirroring a social process by which 'expertise' gained a greater role and the self-description as 'professional' increasingly became a source of legitimacy (see Dingwall 2008). This can be recognized in the growing rules of procedures of interstate arbitration – and their 'relevance'. The actors involved in interstate arbitration cases in the decades prior to World War I, party representatives and arbitrators, oriented themselves towards national legal standards and thus adopted a legalistic discourse of interstate dispute resolution. One reason for this correlation (not to speak of an analogy) between tendencies of juridification and professionalization is to be found in those lawyers who worked interchangeably on domestic and international (court) cases (Lammasch 1924: 346).

The (historical) actors of interstate arbitration remind historians of international law today 'that the recourse to domestic constitutional analogies and the search for ways to tame sovereignty are not postmodern gifts to contemporary international lawyers'. These actors argued and operated with general principles of law, which led them to conclude that the differences between domestic and international law were small.[20] The correlation between domestic and international scales was based on the objective to set up limits to state sovereignty by constitutional *and* international law. This contemporaneousness and reciprocity presents itself as key to explaining (in the context of theories of modernization in the second part of the nineteenth century) the change of international law. The growth in procedural requirements was but one 'instrument' among others for that end of limiting sovereignty. Juridification, professionalization and institutionalization also meant academization of international law and its practice. Academic knowledge about international law became more relevant for national governments – also for presenting one's own 'case' before the arbitrator(s). In the end, intelligent and cognizable legal reasoning as the basis of an arbitration award that was in line with precedents was expected to increase the legitimacy of the award for the parties and the public at large. A subsequent question of what (if any) effect possible differing notions of international law due to different 'national schools' had on interstate arbitration procedures is even more difficult to answer for the nineteenth century. Prior to the twentieth century, few documents from the actual procedures have survived.[21]

It is noteworthy that since the early nineteenth century most arbitration awards were accepted and the arbitrators were thus overwhelmingly successful in ending the dispute. To explain the reasons for this success, one has to remember that the defeated parties accepted that they had previously agreed (*compromis*) to accept the award as final and binding and were thus not prepared to bear the political costs of noncompliance – the principle of *pacta sunt servanda* remained a 'necessary norm' also for interstate arbitration (Grimm 2015: 80). Resultingly, considerations of sustainability and non-recognition of the arbitration awards, once handed down, seemed to be of minor importance for the 'defeated' party. This can be described as a high degree of efficiency of historical third party conflict resolutions. This author knows of only one case in which one party to a dispute formally refused to accept an award: in 1911 the US government claimed an *excès de pouvoir* by the arbitrator in the Chamizal border dispute with Mexico which had been going on since the end of the US-Mexican war in 1848 – only in 1963 was the case finally resolved (Liss 1965; Sepúlveda 1983; Lamborn 1988).

(2) Types or Causes of Interstate Disputes Solved by Interstate Arbitration

Fyodor Martens, Tsarist Russia's most acclaimed international lawyer and one of the dominant councillors during both Hague Conferences, cautioned as early as 1882 against overloaded expectations and 'illusions' regarding the possibilities of interstate arbitration. He was not convinced of the millennial hopes that arbitration would be the definite answer to all political disputes between states. Having an 'ambivalent' attitude 'towards the Russian government', his experience as the legal counsel for the foreign office in Saint Petersburg led him to assume that also in the future states would be unwilling to submit all their international differences to arbitrators, especially in cases where recourse to law would not help in finding a solution (Mälksoo 2014: 819). Martens categorically stated: 'In all international difficulties where the political element predominates, arbitration is inapplicable'. Thus, he concluded that arbitration could only be employed in disputes of 'minor importance', especially those concerning legal questions and where the rights of the parties involved could be clearly established (Martens 1887: 154–55; Pustogarov 2000: 214; cf. Aust 2013: 169–70).

This distinction between disputes based on either 'law' or 'politics' – made by a man who knew both realms and who was a much-sought after arbitrator in subsequent decades – invites historical substantiation: which subject areas, types or causes of interstate disputes were referred to arbitration – and were the disputes of 'political' importance excluded from arbitration? And what constituted a 'political' dispute for contemporaries? In interstate arbitration, 'the issues at stake concerned mostly boundary questions, debt recovery, maritime seizure, territorial questions, private claims, mutual claims, claims after insurrection or civil war, claims made due to act of war, illegal arrest, and fisheries' (Riemens 2010: 80); one can add here the interpretation of treaties.

Territorial questions in particular, as affirmed by political science research into the period 1816 to 1945, were 'highly war prone compared to non-territorial disputes' (Senese and Vasquez 2005: 610). For areas 'where control of territory carries with it important security implications, state leaders should be very unlikely to allow the fate of strategically valuable territory to be decided by a third party ruling' (Allee and Huth 2006: 228). However, considering the period between 1814 (Treaty of Ghent between Great Britain and the US ending the war of 1812 and consenting to submit border disputes to arbitration) and 1900, contemporaries already recognized two fields of particular relevance for interstate arbitration: border questions and economic damages (Tanquerey [1902] 1923: 1732). It is apparent that numerous examples of early interstate arbitration fall into the first category, dealing with disputes about territory – not always located in 'faraway' colonies. The historical dimension of the consolidation of a claim to territory has been emphasized by researchers early on, and interstate tribunals had worked out this historical consolidation in their awards (Schwarzenberger 1957: 310–11).

Were those territories that became objects of a dispute and a subsequent arbitration procedure indeed *not* 'strategically valuable'? Were they of 'minor importance', to use Martens' expression, so state leaders would 'allow the[ir] fate . . . to be decided by a third party ruling'? In other words, was a 'political' dispute important and a 'legal' dispute of 'minor importance'? Legal scholars did not provide a conclusive answer based on precedents. From a European perspective, several of the disputed territories and borderlines were indeed in faraway places in America, Africa or somewhere in the sea.[22]

There are, however, examples that suggest that not all the resulting territorial disputes were considered to be of 'minor importance' by governments. In the early days of the Scramble for Africa, the Anglo-Portuguese dispute over Delagoa Bay (1875, Mozambique) was important to the British because the bay offered the shortest access from the South African Transvaal region to the sea. At the same time, this access was to be denied under all circumstances to the two independent Afrikaner Republics, polities more likely to be controlled successfully if the bay came under British rule, instead of the hitherto Portuguese colonial administration. Still, in 1875, the arbitrator, French president Marshal MacMahon, ruled in favour of the Portuguese and Great Britain abided by the award.[23]

The Anglo-Portuguese dispute about Matabeleland (modern-day Angola/Zambia) involved two competing colonial territorial concepts that contradicted each other. While the British aimed at a south–north connection from Cape to Cairo, the Portuguese hoped for an international recognition of their east–west connection from Mozambique to Angola along the Zambezi River. Only one party could hold the disputed upper Zambezi territories, and in 1890 Britain issued a threat of war ('the ultimatum') to Lisbon over Portugal's attempt to connect the colonies of Angola and Mozambique via the inland corridor. At this stage of affairs, something of a showdown between Britain and her oldest ally, arbitration was rejected by the British government. Portuguese troops withdrew from the territories. The government in Lisbon resigned and the country was swept by an 'incredible wave of Anglophobia' (Labourdette 2000: 535). However, the question of the border drawing itself was then referred to arbitration. This was, if one believes contemporary claims, also the result of the European peace movement that put pressure on both governments to come to an amicable solution (Revon 1892: 173). In 1905, the arbitration award was handed in by the king of Italy.

The second type of interstate dispute often solved by arbitration, the payment of damages for an alleged wrong, was equally deeply engrained in contemporary politics. The most famous case is probably the Alabama affair. The case involved numerous claims for damages by the US government against the

British government for the assistance given to the Confederate cause during the Civil War (1862–65). A treaty between the governments set up an arbitration tribunal in 1871 consisting of five (British, American, Swiss, Italian and Brazilian) arbitrators. They endorsed the American position in 1872, and Britain paid $15.5 million (considered a huge sum by contemporaries) to the US for damages done by warships built in Britain and sold to the Confederacy. The arbitrators, however, denied compensation for other than direct damage, a decision that was subjected to criticism. However, later awards, although more open to include indirect damages in their calculation of compensation, also abstained from using the required payments as a form of punishment or 'retaliation' (exemplary, punitive or vindictive damages).[24]

These cases suggest that governments also referred 'several highly political' or 'important' disputes to arbitration (Indlekofer 2013: 108). The characterization by Fyodor Martens, followed today by some historians, that 'international arbitration [was restricted] to causes of minor importance' (Lovrić-Pernak 2015: 74; cf. Grewe 2000: 519), thus remains incomplete and needs to be substantiated on a case-by-case basis. To be sure, there were cases of 'minor importance' rife with numerous (legal) technicalities that the diplomats wanted to rid themselves of. They happily handed these disputes over to the 'neutral' legal experts. Still, other cases, like those referred to above, had serious economic, territorial and/or political implications, depending on whether one party or the other party won – and yet the parties agreed to refer them for binding settlement to a third party.

(3) Beneficiaries of Interstate Arbitration

From the above-mentioned types of arbitration, a strong connection can be assumed between European expansion and the causes for disputes that gave rise to interstate arbitration procedures. Thus, British, US-American, French, Portuguese and most of all Latin American governments rank most prominently among those who resorted to interstate arbitration. In 1823, Chile and Peru 'signed the first treaty in modern times that expressly provided for the arbitration of disputes arising from that agreement'. Overall, and 'across the [nineteenth] century, the number of Latin American arbitration agreements and the number of countries involved dramatically exceeded those in Europe'.[25] Even though Germany was 'averse to international arbitration law as a matter of principle', it ratified the PCA Convention in 1900. Since 1889, Germany had been party to a number of interstate arbitration cases, also in a colonial context.[26] Contemporaries were eager to point out that interstate arbitration was a mode of guiding foreign policy that was common to 'all civilized nations', including extra-Europeean ones.[27]

'According to realist logic, an agreement to adjudicate the dispute is very unlikely when there is a significant imbalance of military power between two disputants' (Allee and Huth 2006: 228, 232). However, a correlation between the military capacity of the disputing parties and their consent to seek a legal solution to their disputes is yet to be established for the period prior to World War I. The question is, who were the beneficiaries of interstate arbitration? When did war become a ready threat in case of a dispute that could not be solved diplomatically? Around 1900, Great Powers with plenty of military capacity like Russia, Great Britain or the US favoured interstate arbitration. Their motives for this policy were more or less distinct.

Russia was falling behind in the arms race and was thus eager to argue for disarmament and peaceful conflict solution. Great Britain's government, faced with a formidable domestic peace movement, was willing to concede certain territorial disputes to be decided by third parties for which the waging of war seemed inopportune. Furthermore, arbitration seemed to offer legalistic means to protect the (commercial) interests of British citizens globally. It was thus a tool of (informal) empire to be used for one's own benefit against foreigners and foreign governments, in particular in Latin America. This did not preclude setbacks, as the lost arbitration cases against Portugal (Delagoa) and the US (Alabama) indicated. In line with the Monroe Doctrine, the US government could see arbitration as a positive means to limit European military engagements in the Americas while promoting and protecting its own interests in the region by employing international law. Resultantly, US and British governments were the most frequent participants in interstate arbitration. Their willingness to increasingly use arbitration was based on cultural commonality that made war, in case diplomacy had failed to solve a dispute between the two nations, seem a very distant likelihood (Grewe 2000: 523). The defeat of the Olney-Pauncefote Treaty of 1897 in the US Senate concerning a general arbitration agreement, also covering (nearly) all disputes in the future, shows, however, that even between these sister nations many politicians were unwilling to see any benefit in giving up state sovereignty to unknown third party arbitrators (Blake 1945; Campbell 1957; Blakeney 1979).

The example of Portugal shows that small states also profited from interstate arbitration. Given that her Iberian neighbour Spain lost almost her entire colonial empire in a war against the US in 1898 (Papal attempts at mediation remained fruitless), it becomes evident how improbable it seemed at the beginning of the age of imperialism that Portugal would remain a colonial power to such an extent. It becomes apparent, too, how successfully several Portuguese governments instrumentalized interstate arbitration in order to defend Portugal's colonial sovereignty in Africa and beyond. Military means and the possibility to exert economic pressure on her adversaries were not available to the poor and small state of four million inhabitants at the edge of Europe. The 'imbalance of military power' was decisive for Great Britain's success in 'the ultimatum' of 1890. However, the Anglo-Portuguese consent to seek a legal solution for their territorial disputes about Bulama Island, Delagoa Bay, or the Barotseland boundary was not influenced by the parties' 'imbalance of military power'. Instead, the

Portuguese government prepared her case diligently and professionally in order to convince the arbitrator(s).[28]

Finally, Latin American states showed their 'cultural affinity for arbitration in principle' (hundreds of agreements were concluded), but used it 'relatively rarely among themselves'. Famously, the Drago Doctrine (1902/07) sought to limit the use of Western political and military power in the collection of debts owed by Latin American states and, to the benefit of the debtors, 'sought to effectively require the use of arbitration in such circumstances' (Harris 2016: 316, fn 35; cf. Waibel 2011: 37).

(4) The Public Sphere and the Domestic Relevance of Interstate Arbitration Tribunals

Concerning the reasons for the above-mentioned mediation provision in the peace treaty of Paris (1856), Austria's foreign minister Count Buol assumed, this article 'seems only to have been inspired by the desire of the Principal Secretary of Great Britain [Lord Clarendon] to do something agreeable to the friends of peace who have addressed requests to the members of the Congress [in Paris]'.[29] Buol's assumption hints at the growing impact that the campaigns of the British peace movement had not only on political debate, but also on policy, as exemplified by treaty making. Over the next decades, in Great Britain such civil society pressure groups (to use anachronistic terms) grew in relevance for the decision-makers of Britain's foreign policy. Throughout Western Europe and North America too, peace societies were founded who argued, like Frederick Passy, president of the French Arbitration Society, that states should no longer be entitled to decide their disputes by the use of threats or actual force (see Passy 1896; Ceadel 2000; Laity 2002). On the other hand, as the defeat of the Olney-Pauncefote Treaty on general arbitration showed, in the age of nationalism, imperialism and jingoism, other pressure groups likewise emerged who argued to the contrary in favour of a 'forceful' foreign policy and refused to set any limits to state sovereignty by (juridical) third party dispute resolution. Rather than avoiding it, they wished for the success of their nation in the arms race (English 2006).

Thus, any international conflict had its domestic dimension. Beginning in the mid nineteenth century, decisions on foreign policy were not only based on internal negotiations between a few political actors. Rather, those politically responsible interacted with the public sphere. The pressure of 'the street' and through newspaper articles left its mark on foreign policy in Europe and beyond. Emotions like fear or enthusiasm for a certain cause, such as territory or national honour, began to play a more important role. As a result, questions of international conflicts and/or their solution by third parties were also influenced by the national – and a slowly growing transnational – public sphere, that is, movements, political parties or otherwise (Koller 2003; Bormann, Freiberger, Michel 2010).

Political scientists have pointed to cases in which political actors preferred interstate arbitration over direct bilateral negotiation about conflicts with other states. Politicians preferred 'legal dispute settlement in situations where they anticipate sizable domestic political costs should they attempt to settle a dispute through the making of bilateral, negotiated concessions'. In the past they were more likely to seek this 'cover' if the dispute was emotionally charged, for example in territorial conflicts, and if both governments were democratically elected. The accusation of having been too 'soft' during negotiations could cause losses during subsequent elections. Thus, these findings illustrate that 'the primary motivations for seeking the cover of an international legal ruling could be found in domestic politics' (Allee and Huth 2006: 219, 231).

However, given that in the era before World War I not all governments seeking third party legal dispute settlement were democratically elected, this explanation for the consent to arbitration is historically not conclusive. Therefore, historical research will have to analyse additional motives that explain why particular conflict situations were deemed domestically to be 'arbitrable' while others were not. To be sure, it is difficult to find structural arguments like the military and/or economic strength of both parties in relation to each other. The term 'national honour' was also a factor always readily available to rule out third party involvement. Decisions about the arbitrability of disputes were thus more likely to be made by politicians on a case-by-case basis, which also took public opinion into consideration. For instance, while Britain and Portugal had several colonial border disputes settled by arbitration, in the above-mentioned Matabeleland conflict with Portugal, British leaders were unwilling to arbitrate about the territory because, next to questions of national honour, the strategic value of the Cape-to-Cairo line was valued highly (at least in public opinion). On the other hand, the chances of winning the case with historical arguments against Portugal, who had had representatives in the territory since the eighteenth century, were considered low. While the Portuguese, eager to present their 'historical rights' hoped that the dispute about the upper Zambezi territory could be decided by a third party as in previous disputes, Lord Salisbury 'cut this hope short by refusing to consider outside mediation' (Nowell 1947: 16; cf. Ralston 1929: 228).

With the peace movement's rise in numbers and political influence in the last quarter of the nineteenth century, the relevance of public opinion for initiating third party arbitration needs to be taken into consideration. However, given the flood of publications, the warning that 'published opinion is not public opinion' also needs to be taken seriously. Indeed, the (trans-)nationally acting peace movement considered itself a significant player in international relations. Its protagonists never grew tired of emphasizing the almost utopian potential of interstate arbitration. But their actual influence on European and American foreign offices not always materialized in comparison to other pressure groups (see Cooper 1991: 371–72; Fabre 1993).

The public sphere remained relevant with regard to successful third party settlement of interstate disputes for another reason as well. As mentioned, during the nineteenth century in almost all arbitration cases the defeated party accepted the award as final and binding. This compliance was also a matter of (national) honour; the promise given by statesmen and diplomats was to be kept. This was what gentlemen could expect from each other, irrespective of the fact that there was no sanction. No enforcement of the award was possible (other than force – what was to be avoided by arbitration). In this respect, around 1900, several legal experts pointed to the increasing influence of public opinion in the international arena, the 'international community' and the 'moral sanction' the latter would effect towards those not complying with an arbitration award. Charles Richet assumed: 'All nations will hold such a rebelling nation as an outlaw'. Leonid Kamarowsky also referred to the '"moral prejudice" that states would impose upon themselves as a consequence of such rejection'.[30]

Critique of the Peace Movement and the Concept of Interstate Arbitration

The reference to different public spheres illustrates that the critique of interstate arbitration's promise to make wars superfluous cannot be disregarded in this history. Before World War I, the peace movement grew in numbers, if not in importance, but it also had adversaries. Jean-Louis Halpérin reminds us that 'many lawyers remained sceptical towards the idea of binding international rules and the concepts of an international law "above" the authority of sovereign States' (Halpérin 2014: 157). One of the greatest challenges for the peace movement in the age of nationalism and imperialism was the (in their consideration unfortunate) connection between 'patriotism and warlike spirit' (Revon 1892: 165). Even well-meaning reviewers cautioned: 'It may be true that nations would not always voluntarily submit their causes to arbitration, when their interests may have suffered by the wrongful acts of others, or their national pride been touched, and their claims for redress disputed' (Wilds 1872: 345).

Adherents of the peace movement and interstate arbitration were criticized for their alleged 'utopianism' by academics as well as politicians (Reuvers 1983; Buhr and Dietzsch 1984: 292). For example, one reviewer missed the insight into the limits of the concept of arbitration so eagerly lauded by peace advocate Charles Richet. He reminded his readers about 'the worthlessness of paper promises when opposed to interest and passion'. With an unmistakable sense of superiority, he spoke of self-deceit: 'You cannot arbitrate with a mad dog or a howling Dervish' (Robinson 1900: 716).

More relevant than attempts to ridicule the peace movement were efforts to label pacifists as unpatriotic enemies of the military. Well into the twentieth century, German officials remained averse to arbitration in international law, also because they associated mechanisms of international law with pacifism, which they rejected. At the end of the nineteenth century, the German refusal of any limitation to the right to wage war was already evident. In the authoritarian society of Imperial Germany, militaristic modes of thinking and acting dominated. German officialdom successfully created a readiness in the young generation for war and a mentality prone to war. The writings of Karl Freiherr von Stengel, Professor of Public Law, can serve as an apposite example. He was considered an ardent opponent of the peace movement and never took interstate arbitration seriously. Emperor William II appointed him the German delegate to the first Hague Peace Conference in 1899. Stengel's short but merciless critique of the conference and the 'peace propaganda' was opened by an epitaph from General Moltke the Older: 'Perpetual peace is a dream and not even a beautiful dream. War is an element of the divine order of the world'. No less convinced of his mission than his argumentative adversaries, Stengel explained the positive political, economic, societal and educational aspects of war. He negated proposals for an eternal peace through arbitration by reference to the 'fact' that the final execution of a treaty of disarmament or an arbitration award – due to lack of other institutions – could only be enforced by other states by means of war. Stengel's argument mirrored a widely held conviction in Germany about the necessity of rejecting pacifist thinking.[31]

Even though the American peace movement was politically much better connected – as proven by the outspoken advocates of peace and arbitration secretaries of state Elihu Root and William Jennings Bryan[32] – US participants of the Hague Conferences such as US Admiral A.T. Mahan also remained sceptical about the position that 'arbitration could be substituted for war in all cases'. Mahan summarized the argumentation of the proponents of interstate arbitration as not only replacing war by law, but 'that effectually law instead of diplomacy was the desired end, for in diplomacy, in international negotiation, force underlies every contention as a final arbiter'. However, he pointed to 'necessities which transcend law' (Mahan 1911: 135). Moreover, for Mahan, the existing provisions of international law were not able to clarify those questions which diplomacy and war could solve, because international law would not allow for an intervention in the domestic affairs of a state. It seemed self-explicatory that Mahan referred to the US intervention in Spanish Cuba in 1898.[33]

Conclusions

'War appears to be as old as mankind, but peace is a modern invention.' This often-quoted piece of wisdom from nineteenth-century jurist Sir Henry Maine[34] implies notions of 'progress' (*modern*) and the necessity of man-made 'efforts' (*invention*) in order to reach peace. The Kantian belief in the moral imperative of peace may not have convinced the statesmen conducting the nineteenth-century

Concert of Europe, but the question of how peace may be achieved as a product of human reason was not only answered by the philosopher with reference to the law. The advocates of peace, the academics and politicians who believed in the 'Empire of Law', were convinced that only once a stable legal situation was created between states, only once organizations and institutions capable of guiding interstate relations were to replace the natural state of man (i.e. continuous preparation for war due to a lack of trust between states), would peace prevail. These men (and increasingly women) tirelessly referred to the history of peace-inducing institutions such as mediation and arbitration tribunals as a nucleus of future developments, in order to underline the feasibility and practicability of their ideas (Darby 1904: viii). They also worked on turning these past experiences of interstate dispute settlement into a solid ideological foundation for the establishment of a 'Permanent Court of Arbitration', a wish that came true in 1899. However, lauded with much fanfare, this institution was not a means to curb state sovereignty, and it was never intended as such by the national delegates. Most of them rejected compulsory arbitration and they ensured that the PCA's service, even in its 'Golden Age' before World War I (Indlekofer 2013: 4), was to be used only 'as far as circumstances allow', that is, the processes of dispute settlement remained purely political if the actors wished it to be so. International law as the product of philosophical concepts and diplomatic practice was in this respect less concerned with consistency. Irrespective of the restrictive application of arbitration to certain cases of dispute, such as territory or financial damages, the growing number of arbitration cases and treaties attests to the undeniable ability of this legal instrument to efficiently and convincingly settle interstate disputes once parties had agreed to go forward with this process.

This points to a development towards more juridified non-military conflict resolution between states that went beyond non-binding mediation. Due to the focus on domestic legal standards, there was a marked professionalization in terms of personnel and institutions of arbitration tribunals within the period investigated. This professionalization also applies to the procedural modalities of arbitration as well as the reasoning behind the awards. The impact of the public sphere – and especially of the peace movement – on the juridification and professionalization of interstate arbitration was nominal, although the self-perceptions of those involved did not view it as such. To the advocates of interstate arbitration, this concrete tool of legal craftsmanship seemed to be the beacon of practicality of international law. They considered arbitration as the appropriate tool for the mission to enable world peace through law (Hippler and Vec 2015). This included the colonial mission of bringing non-European peoples into the orbit of 'civilization' in order to make the *ius gentium europaeum* applicable globally. However, for their critics, international law and its institutions seemed inapposite to lead these 'humanitarian' missions to the end. These doubts were not based on scepticism about the European expansion and the means used for it (Stuchtey 2010). Rather, it was a critique of the faith in progress, a disapproval of the hope for crafting a world society that would lead to 'eternal peace' due to legal institutions like arbitration (Le Bon [1895] 2011: 82). Indeed, it seems tragic – if measured on the hopes connected to this institution – that the climax of the number of interstate arbitration cases was related not to peacekeeping but to claims settlement following World War I (Zollmann 2018a).

Acknowledgements

Grants from the Deutsche Forschungsgemeinschaft for researching and writing this chapter are gratefully acknowledged.

Jakob Zollmann has taught at the University of Namibia and the Free University Berlin, and was Visiting Fellow at the German Historical Institutes in Paris, London and Washington DC. He is a researcher at the Center for Global Constitutionalism of the WZB Berlin Social Science Center. His research focuses on the history of international law and the history of colonial Africa. He has published *Koloniale Herrschaft und ihre Grenzen: Die Kolonialpolizei in Deutsch-Südwestafrika* (Vandenhoek & Ruprecht, 2010) and *Naulila 1914: World War I in Angola and International Law* (Nomos, 2016).

Notes

1. Page (1919: sec. 2526); see Grotius ([1625/1631] 2005: 1123), Book II cpt. XXIII: Of the Dubious Causes of War, VIII; Ager (1996).
2. Interestingly, the *Oxford International Encyclopaedia of Legal History* (Katz 2009) does not contain an entry for 'arbitration'; however, see Lammasch (1924); Riemens (2010).
3. Pufendorf ([1684] 1695: 525, cap. VI § 17, on Anglo-Dutch peace negotiations mediated by Sweden leading to the Treaty of Breda [1667]; p. 644, cap. IX § 8, on Danish-Swedish peace negotiations mediated by the emperor and the kings of France and Poland leading to the Peace of Stettin [1560]).
4. TNA SP 89/81: 149, Walpole to Lord Weymouth, Lisbon, 16 March 1776. SP 78/298.
5. Cf. Drocourt and Schnakenbourg (2016); Kamarowsky (1887: 85f) regrets that 'science' and 'diplomacy' often fail to distinguish between mediation, *bon office* and arbitration.
6. My translation from the original: 'Le règne du droit succédant à l'empire de la force, les nations soumises à une règle supérieure comme aujourd'hui les individus, la justice s'étendant sur tout le monde, princes et peuples, États et particuliers . . . bref le droit maître absolu de l'univers, quel plus beau spectacle que celui-là? Voilà la vrai monarchie universelle!'. Cf. Grewal (2016: 626): 'The domestic analogy asserts a fundamental parallel between individuals and states, and hence between interpersonal and international relations'.
7. Revon (1892: 532); cf. Pasture (2015: 62–88), Schmale (2000: 100–101), Lammasch (1914, 1927: sp. 1528), Kaufmann (1927), Ralston (1929).
8. Dülffer (1981), Baumgart (1987: 137), Rosenne (2001), Schneider (2003a).
9. Kolb (2013: 41); see Hudson (1933: 441), Myers (1914).

10. See Kolb (2013: 45), Simmons (1999). A French author of the seventeenth century spoke of the 'juge arbitre' (Fontaine [1693] 1927: 654–55).
11. Franck (1995: 337): in the procedural practice of the International Court of Justice, parties have 'freedom to introduce, more or less, whatever evidence they may consider appropriate to prove their cases'.
12. See Kamarowsky (1887: 86): 'the mediator only hands out advice . . . the parties are always free to accept or to decline [it]'; Verzijl (1976: 131).
13. See Kolb (2013: 40); Justenhoven (2006: 189); Kamarowsky (1887: 169).
14. NARA RG 76 Entry 7 DoS, Jay Treaty Art. V, vol. 1, British Agent's first argument 1797, 'Reply to the first three parts': 351–52. 'Charles Morris: Observations on the Western Limits', 20 April 1789; cf. Combs (1970: 137 ss).
15. Phillipson (1916: 81–93) listing 'some instances' of mediation during the long nineteenth century; Leggiere (2016: 297).
16. Cf. TNA FO 352 Stratford Canning Papers, American-British border (Arbitration by the King of the Netherlands) 1830; Kamarowsky (1887: 169).
17. Cf. TNA CO 700/Canada 125/1, North-West American Water Boundary (San Juan). The case of the Government of Her Britannic Majesty submitted to the arbitration and award of H.M. the Emperor of Germany, in accordance with Article 34 of the Treaty between Great Britain and the USA, 1871–72.
18. Gent and Shannon (2010); Grewe (2000: 520); Probst (1989: 55–56 mentions four cases).
19. Brouillet (1979), Garrett (1985), Dupuy (1980), Blet (1982), D'Onorio (1989), Jankowiak (2003).
20. Galindo (2012: 96); see also Steinberg and Zasloff (2006: 67), Brunkhorst (2012: 193).
21. Cf. Becker Lorca (2015); for the problems German lawyers had with the Franco- and Anglo-German Mixed Arbitral Tribunals in the 1920s, see Nörr (1988: 102).
22. Cf., *Report of International Arbitral Awards (RIAA)*, e.g., NL-Venezuela 1865 (Aves), Oranje-GB 1870 (Vaal), GB-Nicaragua 1881 (Moskito Coast), GB-Portugal 1870 (Bulama), SAR-Griquas 1871, GB-Portugal 1875 (Delagoa), Argentina-Paraguay Boundary 1878, GB-SAR 1885, Germany-Spain 1885 (Karolinen), Germany-GB 1889 (Lamu), Fr-NL (Guyana) 1891, GB-Venezuela 1899 (Guyana), Fr-Brasil 1900 (Guyana), Brasil-GB 1904 (Guyana), GB-Portugal 1905 (Barotse), Germany-GB 1911 (Walvisbay), USA-Mexico 1911 (Chamizal), Portugal-NL 1914 (Timor), USA-NL 1928 (Palmas), Fr.-Mexiko 1931 (Clipperton).
23. Great Britain v. Portugal (1875), in *RIAA* (vol. 28: 157–62); cf. Bjorge (2014: 156).
24. Grewe (2000: 518); Cook (1975), Balch (1900), Ralston (1910: § 369): 'While there is little doubt that in many cases the idea of punishment has influenced the amount of the award, yet we are not prepared to state that any commission has accepted the view that it possessed the power to grant anything save compensation'.
25. Latin American states 'were parties to over 250 agreements to arbitrate specific cases, well over a third of the global total. Of these 75 were boundary disputes and 161 were cases involving property or commercial claims, over half of the world wide total' Harris (2016: 309); La Fontaine (1927: viii), the above-mentioned caveats regarding the classification as 'arbitration' apply.
26. Petersson (2009: 96); cf. Carl (2012), Schlichtmann (2003: 384), Ralston (1929: 232); *RIAA*: Germany vs. UK relating to Lamu Island, 1889 (vol. 28: 237–48); Germany vs. UK, USA reg. Samoan Claims, 1902 (v. IX: 15–27); Germany vs. Venezuela (Mixed Claims Commission) 1903 (v. X: 363–476); Germany, France, UK vs. Japan reg. real

estate tax, 1905 (v. XI: 51–58); Germany vs. France reg. consular jurisdiction (Casablanca deserters), 1909 (v. XI: 126–31); Germany vs. UK reg. Walfish Bay, 1911 (v. XI: 263–308).
27. Tanquerey ([1902] 1923: 1732); statistical overview in La Fontaine (1997: xiii).
28. On the hope of smaller nations to gain standing in the international order by making reference to international law, see, e.g., Phyzzenzides (1896).
29. Buol and Hübner to Emperor, 4 April 1856, quoted in Temperley (1932: 413).
30. Quoted and translated in Lovrić-Pernak (2015: 73–74).
31. Von Stengel (1899), English translation in Mazower (2012: 77); cf. von Stengel (1909), Hueck (2004), Schönemann-Behrens (2011: 209).
32. Bryan 'regarded himself a Tolstoyan' (True 1995: 40).
33. 'The ground of domestic bad government, however extreme, is not one for an international court; exactly as the ground of good government does not constitute the legal justification of the presence of Great Britain in Egypt or of the United States in the Philippines' (Mahan 1911: 135).
34. Quoted in Bernasconi (2011: 44) referring to Howard (2000: 1).

References

Archival Sources

The National Archives – London-Kew (TNA)

TNA CO 700/Canada 125/1, North-West American Water Boundary (San Juan). The case of the Government of Her Britannic Majesty submitted to the arbitration and award of H.M. the Emperor of Germany, in accordance with Article 34 of the Treaty between Great Britain and the USA, 1871–2.

TNA FO 352 Stratford Canning Papers, American-British border (Arbitration by the King of the Netherlands) 1830.

TNA SP 89/81: 149, Walpole to Lord Weymouth, Lisbon, 16.3.1776.

National Archives and Record Administration – Washington DC (NARA)

NARA RG 76 Entry 7 DoS, Jay Treaty Art. V, vol. 1, British Agent's first argument 1797, 'Reply to the first three parts': 351f. 'Charles Morris: Observations on the western limits', 20.4.1789.

Published Sources

Ager, S.L. 1996. *Interstate Arbitrations in the Greek World, 337–90 B.C.* Berkeley, CA: University of California Press.

Allee, T.L., and P.K. Huth. 2006. 'Legitimizing Dispute Settlement: International Legal Ruling as Domestic Political Cover', *American Political Science Review* 100(2): 219–34.

Aust, M. 2013. 'Das Zarenreich in der Völkerrechtsgeschichte 1870–1914', in M. Aust (ed.), *Globalisierung imperial und sozialistisch: Russland und die Sowjetunion in der Globalgeschichte 1851–1991*. Frankfurt am Main: Campus, pp. 166–80.

Balch, T.W. 1900. *The Alabama Arbitration*. Philadelphia: Allen, Lane & Scott.

Baumgart, W. 1987. *Vom Europäischen Konzert zum Völkerbund: Friedensschlüsse und Friedenssicherung von Wien bis Versailles*. Darmstadt: Wissenschaftliche Buchgesellschaft.

Becker Lorca, A. 2015. *Mestizo International Law: A Global Intellectual History 1842–1933*. New York: Cambridge University Press.

Béhaine, E.L. de. 1898. *Léon XIII et le prince de Bismarck*. Paris: Lethielleux.

Bély, L. 2007. *L'art de la paix en Europe: Naissance de la diplomatie moderne, XVIe–XVIIIe siècle.* Paris: Presses Universitaires de France.
Bentham, J. 1927 [1789]. *Plan for a Universal and Perpetual Peace [The Principles of International Law. Essay 4].* London: Sweet and Maxwell.
Bernasconi, R. 2011. 'Perpetual Peace and the Invention of Total War', in N. Eckstrand and C. Yates (eds), *Philosophy and the Return of Violence: Studies from this Widening Gyre.* London: The Continuum International Publishing Group.
Bjorge, E. 2014. *The Evolutionary Interpretation of Treaties.* Oxford: Oxford University Press.
Blake, N.M. 1945. 'The Olney-Pauncefote Treaty of 1897', *American Historical Review* 50(2): 228–43.
Blakeney, M. 1979. 'The Olney-Pauncefote Treaty of 1897: The Failure of Anglo-American General Arbitration', *Anglo-American Law Review* 8: 175–90.
Blet, P. 1982. *Histoire de la représentation diplomatique du Saint-Siège: Des origines à l'aube du XIX siècle.* Vatican City: Archivio Vaticano.
Bormann, P., T. Freiberger and J. Michel (eds). 2010. *Angst in den internationalen Beziehungen.* Göttingen: V&R unipress.
Brouillet, A. 1979. 'La médiation du Saint-Siège dans le différend entre l'Argentine et le Chili sur la zone australe', *Annuaire français de droit international* 25: 49–76.
Brownlie, I. 1990. *Principles of Public International Law.* New York: Oxford University Press.
Brunkhorst, H. 2012. 'The Co-evolution of Cosmopolitan and National Statehood: Preliminary Theoretical Considerations on the Historical Evolution of Constitutionalism', *Cooperation and Conflict* 47: 176–99.
Buhr, M., and S. Dietzsch (eds). 1984. *Nachwort zu: Kant, Immanuel. Zum Ewigen Frieden. Mit Texten zur Rezeption 1796–1800.* Leipzig: Reclam.
Campbell, C.S. 1957. *Anglo-American Understanding 1898–1903.* Baltimore, MD: Johns Hopkins Press.
Carl, M.I. 2012. *Zwischen staatlicher Souveränität und Völkerrechtsgemeinschaft: Deutschlands Haltung und Beitrag zur Entstehung des Ständigen Internationalen Gerichtshofs.* Baden-Baden: Nomos.
Ceadel, M. 2000. *Semi-Detached Idealists: The British Peace Movement and International Relations, 1854–1945.* Oxford: Oxford University Press.
Combs, J.A. 1970. *The Jay Treaty: Political Battleground of the Founding Fathers.* Berkeley: University of California Press.
Convention for the Pacific Settlement of International Disputes 1899/1907. Retrieved 4 January 2017 from https://pca-cpa.org/wp-content/uploads/sites/175/2016/01/1907-Convention-for-the-Pacific-Settlement-of-International-Disputes.pdf.
Cooper, S.E. 1991. 'Pacifism in France, 1889–1914: International Peace as Human Right', *French Historical Studies* 17: 359–86.
Cook, A. 1975. *The Alabama Claims.* Ithaca, NY: Cornell University Press.
Darby, W.E. 1904. *International Arbitration: International Tribunals,* 4th ed. London: Dent.
Dingwall, R. 2008. *Essays on Professions.* Aldershot: Ashgate.
D'Onorio, J.-B. 1989. *Le Saint-Siège dans les relations internationales.* Paris: Ed. du Cerfs-Cujas.
Drocourt, N., and É. Schnakenbourg (eds). 2016. *Thémis en diplomatie: Le droit et les arguments juridiques dans les relations internationales.* Rennes: Presses Universitaire de Rennes.
Dülffer, J. 1981. *Regeln gegen den Krieg: Die Haager Friedenskonferenzen 1899 und 1907 in der internationalen Politik.* Frankfurt am Main: Ullstein.
Dupuy, A. 1980. *La diplomatie du Saint-Siège.* Paris: Téqui.
Duve, T. 2013. 'Treaty of Tordesillas', *Max Planck Encyclopedia of Public International Law* No. 21. http://opil.ouplaw.com/view/10.1093/law:epil/9780199231690/law-9780199231690-e2088?rskey=KSxoTo&result=1&prd=EPIL.

English, J. 2006. 'Empire Day in Britain, 1904–1958', *Historical Journal* 49: 247–76.
Fabre, R. 1993. 'Un exemple de pacifisme juridique: Théodore Ruyssen et le mouvement "la paix par le droit" (1884–1950)', *Vingtième Siècle. Revue d'histoire* 39: 38–54.
Field, D.D. 1872. *Outline of an International Code*. New York: Diossy & Company, Law Publishers. [Trans. Albéric Rolin, *Projet d'un code international: Proposé aux diplomates, aux hommes d'État, et aux jurisconsultes du droit international* (Paris, 1881).]
Fontaine, J. de la. [1693] 1927. 'Le juge arbitre, l'hospitalier, et le solitaire', in J. de la Fontaine, *Fables*. Paris.
Franck, T.M. 1995. *Fairness in International Law and Institutions*. Oxford: Clarendon Press.
Galindo, G.R.B. 2012. 'Force Field: On History and Theory of International Law', *Rechtsgeschichte* 20: 86–103.
Garrett, J.L. 1985. 'The Beagle Channel Dispute: Confrontation and Negotiation in the Southern Cone', *Journal of Interamerican Studies and World Affairs* 27: 81–109.
Gent, S.E., and M. Shannon. 2010. 'The Effectiveness of International Arbitration and Adjudication: Getting into a Bind', *Journal of Politics* 72: 366–80.
Gerhardt, V. 1995. *Immanuel Kants Entwurf 'Zum ewigen Frieden': Eine Theorie der Politik*. Darmstadt: Wissenschaftliche Buchgesellschaft.
Grewal, D.S. 2016. 'The Domestic Analogy Revisited: Hobbes on International Order', *The Yale Law Journal* 125(3): 618–80.
Grewe, W. 2000 [1984]. *The Epochs of International Law*. Translated and Revised by Michael Byers. Berlin: de Gruyter.
Grimm, D. 2015. *Sovereignty: The Origin and Future of a Political and Legal Concept*. New York: Columbia University Press.
Grotius, H. 2005. *The Rights of War and Peace*, ed. and introduction by R. Tuck [1625/1631]. Indianapolis: Liberty Fund.
Halpérin, J.-L. 2004. *Histoire des droits en Europe*. Paris: Flammarion.
———. 2014. *Five Legal Revolutions since the 17th Century: An Analysis of a Global Legal History*. Cham: Springer International Publishing.
Harris, S. 2016. 'The Global Construction of International Law in the 19th Century: The Case of Arbitration', *Journal of World History* 27(2): 303–25.
Herzog, T. 2015. *Frontiers of Possession. Spain and Portugal in Europe and the Americas*. Cambridge, MA: Harvard University Press.
Hippler, T., and M. Vec (eds). 2015. *Paradoxes of Peace in Nineteenth Century Europe*. Oxford: Oxford University Press.
Howard, M. 2000. *The Invention of Peace: Reflections on War and International Order*. New Haven, CT: Yale University Press.
Hudson, M.O. 1933. 'The Permanent Court of Arbitration', *American Journal of International Law* 27: 440–60.
Hueck, I. 2004. 'Peace, Security and International Organisations: The German International Lawyers and the Hague Conferences', in R. Lesaffer (ed.), *Peace Treaties and International Law in European History: From the Late Middle Ages to World War One*. Cambridge: Cambridge University Press, pp. 254–69.
Indlekofer, M. 2013. *International Arbitration and the Permanent Court of Arbitration*. Alphen: Kluwer.
Jackson, E. 1958. 'Mediation and Conciliation in International Law', *UNESCO. International Social Science Bulletin: Techniques of Mediation and Conciliation* 10(4): 508–43.
Jankowiak, F. 2003. 'Arbitrage du Pape', *Dictionnaire Historique de la Papauté*. Paris: Fayard, pp. 132–35.
Justenhoven, H.-G. 2006. *Internationale Schiedsgerichtsbarkeit: Ethische Norm und Rechtswirklichkeit*. Stuttgart: Kohlhammer.

Kamarowsky, L. 1887. *Le tribunal international*, trans. S. Westman. Paris: G. Pedone-Lauriel.
Kapossy, B., I. Stone Nakhimovsky and R. Whatmore (eds). 2017. *Commerce and Peace in the Enlightenment*. Cambridge: Cambridge University Press.
Katz, S.N. (ed.). 2009. *Oxford International Encyclopedia of Legal History*, 6 vols. Oxford: Oxford University Press.
Kaufmann, P. 1927. *Die Fortbildung der internationalen Schiedsgerichtsbarkeit seit dem Weltkrieg besonders durch den Locarno-Pakt*. Leipzig: R. Noske.
Kolb, R. 2013. *The International Court of Justice*. Oxford: Hart.
Koller, C. 2003. 'Die Ehre der Nation: Überlegungen zu einem Kernelement der politischen Kultur im 19. Jahrhundert', *Saeculum. Jahrbuch für Universalgeschichte* 54: 87–122.
Koskenniemi, M. 2001. *The Gentle Civilizer of Nations: The Rise and Fall of International Law 1870–1960*. Cambridge: Cambridge University Press.
———. 2019. 'Imagining the Rule of Law: Rereading the Grotian "Tradition"', *The European Journal of International Law* 30(1): 17–52.
Labourdette, J.-F. 2000. *L'histoire de Portugal*. Paris: Fayard.
La Fontaine, H. 1997. *Pasicrisie internationale 1794–1900: Histoire documentaire des arbitrages internationaux*, preface P.M. Eisemann. The Hague: Martinus Nijhoff Publishers. [First published in Berne: Stämpfli, 1902.]
Laity, P. 2002. *The British Peace Movement 1870–1914*. Oxford: Oxford University Press.
Lamborn, A.C. 1988. *Statecraft, Domestic Politics, and Foreign Policy Making: The El Chamizal Dispute*. Boulder, CO: Westview Press.
Lammasch, H. 1914. *Die Lehre von der Schiedsgerichtsbarkeit in ihrem ganzen Umfang* (Handbuch des Völkerrechts, vol. 5). Stuttgart: Kohlhammer.
———. 1924. 'Friedliche Schlichtung von Staatsstreitigkeiten', in J. Hatschek and K. Strupp (eds), *Wörterbuch des Völkerrechts*, vol. 1. Berlin: de Gruyter, pp. 346–349.
———. 1927. 'Internationale Schiedsgerichtsbarkeit', in *Staatslexikon der Görresgesellschaft*, vol. 5. Freiburg: Herder.
Le Bon, G. [1895] 2011. *Psychologie der Massen*. Berlin: Vergangenheitsverlag.
Leggiere, M. 2016. 'Napoleon's Quest: Great Britain versus France III', in J. Lacey (ed.), *Great Strategic Rivalries: From the Classical World to the Cold War*. Oxford: Oxford University Press, pp. 289–319.
Lingens, K. 2011. 'Der Jay-Vertrag (1794) als Geburtsstunde der modernen internationalen Schiedsgerichtsbarkeit?', in M. Vec and S. Dauchy (eds), *Les conflits entre peuples. De la résolution libre à la résolution imposée*, Baden-Baden: Nomos, pp. 65–82.
Liss, S.B. 1965. *A Century of Disagreement: The Chamizal Conflict 1864–1964*. Washington, DC: University Press of Washington DC.
Lovrić-Pernak, K. 2015. 'Aim: Peace – Sanction: War. International Arbitration and the Problem of Enforcement', in T. Hippler and M. Vec (eds), *Paradoxes of Peace in Nineteenth Century Europe*. Oxford: Oxford University Press, pp. 62–74.
Mahan, A.T. 1911. 'Diplomacy and Arbitration', *North American Review* 194(668): 124–35.
Mälksoo, L. 2014. 'F.F. Martens and His Time: When Russia Was an Integral Part of the European Tradition of International Law', *European Journal of International Law* 25(3): 811–29.
Martens, F. de. 1882. *Современное международное право цивилизованных народов*. Saint Petersburg: Benke.
———. 1887. *Traité de droit international traduit du russe par Alfred Lèo*, vol. 3. Paris: Maresq Aine.
Mazower, M. 2012. *Governing the World: The History of an Idea*. London: Allen Lane.
Myers, D.P. 1914. 'The Origins of the Hague Arbitral Courts', *American Journal of International Law* 8: 769–801.

Nörr, K.W. 1988. *Zwischen den Mühlsteinen: Eine Privatrechtsgeschichte der Weimarer Republik.* Tübingen: Mohr Siebeck.
Nowell, C.E. 1947. 'Portugal and the Partition of Africa', *Journal of Modern History* 19(1): 1–17.
Page, W.H. 1919. *The Law of Contracts.* Cincinnati, OH: W.H. Anderson.
Passy, F. 1896. 'Peace Movement in Europe', *American Journal of Sociology* 2: 1–12.
Pasture, P. 2015. *Imagining European Unity since 1000 AD.* New York: Palgrave Macmillan.
Paul, J.R. 2018. *Without Precedent: Chief Justice John Marshall and His Times.* New York: Riverhead.
Petersson, N.P. 2009. *Anarchie und Weltrecht: Das Deutsche Reich und die Institutionen der Weltwirtschaft 1890–1930.* Göttingen: Vandenhoeck & Ruprecht.
Phillipson, C. 1916. *Termination of War and Treaties of Peace.* New York: E.P. Dutton & Company.
Phyzzenzides, N. 1896. *L'arbitrage international et l'établissement d'un empire grec.* Paris: J. Goemaere.
Probst, R. 1989. *'Good Offices' in the Light of Swiss International Practice and Experience.* Dordrecht: Martinus Nijhoff.
Pufendorf, S. v. 1672. *De Jure Naturae et Gentium: Libri Octo.* Londini Scanorum. [1711. *Acht Bücher vom Natur- und Völcker-Rechte*, vol. 2 (Frankfurt am Main: Knoche).]
———. [1684] 1695 *Einleitung zu der Historie der vornehmsten Reiche und Staaten, so itziger Zeit in Europa sich befinden.* Frankfurt am Main: Knoche.
———. 1909. *Weltstaat und Friedensproblem.* Berlin: Reichl et Co.
Pustogarov, V.V. 2000. *Our Martens: F.F. Martens, International Lawyer and Architect of Peace. Edited and Translated from the Russian, with an Introduction by W.E. Buttler.* The Hague: Kluwer. [Russ. 1993].
Ralston, J.H. 1910. *International Arbitral Law and Procedure.* Boston, MA: Pub. for the International School of Peace, Ginn and Company.
———. 1929. *International Arbitration from Athens to Locarno.* Stanford, CA: Stanford University Press.
Reports of International Arbitral Awards (RIAA). Recueil des sentences arbitrales. http://legal.un.org/riaa/.
Reuvers, H.-Bert. 1983. *Philosophie des Friedens gegen friedlose Wirklichkeit: 'Gerechter' Krieg und 'Ewiger' Friede im Zeitalter der bürgerlichen Revolution.* Cologne: Pahl-Rugenstein.
Revon, M. 1892. *L'arbitrage international: Son passé, son présent, son avenir.* Paris: A. Rousseau.
Riemens, M.J. 2010. 'History of Arbitration of Disputes', in N.J. Young (ed.), *The Oxford International Encyclopedia of Peace.* Oxford: Oxford University Press, pp. 79–81.
Robinson, E. Van Dyke. 1900. 'Review of "Les Guerres et la paix. Etude sur l'arbitrage international" by Charles Richet, Paris 1899', *Political Science Quarterly* 15: 715–19.
Rosenne, S. 2001. *The Hague Peace Conferences of 1899 and 1907 and International Arbitration: Report and Documents.* The Hague: T.M.C. Asser Press.
Schlichtmann, K. 2003. 'Japan, Germany and the Idea of the Hague Peace Conferences', *Journal of Peace Research* 40(4): 377–94.
Schmale, W. 2000. *Geschichte Europas.* Vienna: Böhlau.
Schneider, P. 2003a. *Internationale Gerichtsbarkeit als Instrument friedlicher Streitbeilegung: Von einer empirisch fundierten Theorie zu einem innovativen Konzept.* Baden-Baden: Nomos.
Schneider, U. 2003b. 'Tordesillas 1494: Der Beginn einer globalen Weltsicht', *Saeculum. Jahrbuch für Universalgeschichte* 54: 39–62.
Schönemann-Behrens, P. 2011. *Alfred H. Fried: Friedensaktivist – Nobelpreisträger.* Zürich: Römerhof Verlag.

Schumann, M. 2016. 'A Contest for Trade and Empire: England versus France II', in J. Lacey (ed.), *Great Strategic Rivalries: From the Classical World to the Cold War*. Oxford: Oxford University Press, pp. 267–88.
Schwarzenberger, G. 1957. 'Title to Territory: Response to a Challenge', *American Journal of International Law* 51(2): 308–24.
Senese, P.D., and J.A. Vasquez. 2005. 'Assessing the Steps to War', *British Journal of Political Science* 35: 607–33.
Sepúlveda, C. 1983. *La frontera norte de México, historia, conflictos, 1762–1982*. Mexico City: Editorial Porrúa.
Simmons, B.A. 1999. 'See You in "Court"? The Appeal to Quasi-Judicial Legal Processes in the Settlement of Territorial Disputes', in P. Diehl (ed.), *A Road Map to War*. Nashville: Vanderbilt University Press, pp. 205–37.
Smith, A.M. 2004. '"Judicial Nationalism" in International Law: National Identity and Judicial Autonomy at the ICJ', *Bepress Legal Series Paper* no. 428: 1–55.
Sohn, L. 1961. 'The Role of International Institutions as Conflict Adjusting Agencies', *Chicago Law Review* 28: 205–57.
Steinberg, R.H., and J.M. Zasloff. 2006. 'Power and International Law', *American Journal of International Law* 100: 64–87.
Stengel, K. v. 1899. *Der ewige Friede*. Munich: C. Haushalter.
Stuchtey, B. 2010. *Die europäische Expansion und ihre Feinde: Kolonialismuskritik vom 18. bis in das 20. Jahrhundert*. Munich: Oldenbourg.
Stuyt, A.M. 1972. *Survey of International Arbitrations 1794–1970*. Leiden: Sijthoff.
Tanquerey, A. [1902] 1923. 'Arbitrage', in *Dictionnaire de Théologie Catholique*, vol. I 2. Paris: Letouzey et Ané, pp. 1730–37.
Temperley, H. 1932. 'The Treaty of Paris of 1856 and Its Execution', *Journal of Modern History* 4: 387–414.
Textor, J.W. 1680. *Synopsis Iuris Gentium*, ed. L. von Bar. Basileae: Bertschius. [Trans. John Pawley Bate, in James Brown Scott (ed.), *The Classics of International Law*, vol. 2 (Washington DC, 1916)].
Thévenaz, H. 1968. *La contribution de Charles-Edouard Lardy à l'arbitrage international*. Geneva.
True, M. 1995. *An Energy Field More Intense Than War: The Nonviolent Tradition and American Literature*. Syracuse, NY: Syracuse University Press.
Vattel, E. de. 1758. *Le droit des gens: Ou principes de la loi naturelle, appliqués à la conduite et aux affaires des nations et des souverains*, vol. 2 [Trans. Charles Fenwick, in James Brown Scott (ed.), *The Classics of International Law*, vol. 4 (Washington DC, 1916)].
Verzijl, J.H.W. 1976. *International Law in Historical Perspective, Part VIII: Inter-State Disputes and their Settlement*. Leiden: A.W. Sijthoff International Publishing Company.
Waibel, M. 2011. *Sovereign Defaults before International Courts and Tribunals*. Cambridge: Cambridge University Press.
Wilds, H.P. 1872. 'Field's International Code', *American Law Register* 20(6), New Series Vol. 11: 337–46.
Zollmann, J. 2018a. 'Reparations, Claims for Damages, and the Delivery of Justice: Germany and the Mixed Arbitral Tribunals (1919–1933)', in D. Deroussin (ed.), *La Grande Guerre et son droit*. Paris: L.G.D.J., pp. 379–94.
———. 2018b. 'Théorie et pratique de l'arbitrage international avant la Première Guerre mondiale', in R. Fabre et al. (eds), *Les défenseurs de la paix, 1899–1917*. Rennes: PUR, pp. 111–26.

Chapter 9

International Mediation and the Problem of Insincere Bargaining

Nathan Danneman and Kyle Beardsley

Introduction

We know empirically that relatively few instances of negotiations lead to settlements, which is puzzling because one might assume that moving to the negotiating table is endogenous to reaching a settlement (DeRouen and Möller 2013). That is, a naive observer would expect that disputants would move to the table if and when they expected to be able to strike a conflict-terminating bargain. Even more puzzling is the fact that many of the factors that have been shown to influence bargaining onset are not the same factors that have been shown to influence bargaining outcomes (Greig 2005). What explains the disjuncture between the willingness to bargain and the ability to strike bargains? Are failed efforts at conflict bargaining merely the result of mistakes or misperceptions by disputants, or are there strategic dynamics in place that prompt them to bargain but not reach an agreement?

One observation that allows us to begin answering these questions is that disputants can use the time during negotiations, especially those that occur in the context of a ceasefire, to increase their fighting capacity and overall bargaining position. Disputants thus may move for negotiations with no intention of bargaining. Colloquially, they may bargain in bad faith. Disputants have incentives to bargain deviously, initiating a lengthy round of bargaining with no intention of settling. Rather, they are stalling in hopes of returning to conflict on a substantially improved footing in the future. This generates a possible commitment problem for bargainers: they cannot credibly commit to striking a bargain, given that they may become substantially stronger while bargaining proceeds. Anticipating the possibility of this commitment problem to bind, opponents fear moving to the table, even when there is little uncertainty in the current bargaining environment.

In light of this problem of insincere bargaining, we argue that third parties can help ameliorate this situation by imposing costs – which might take the form of policies meant to punish one side or bolster its adversary – on disputants who move to the table only to reject reasonable offers. These third parties, if capable and willing, can reassure the disputants enough to reach the bargaining table, and then to strike bargains once there. Third parties accomplish this by enforcing the tacit agreement to bargain in good faith.

In what follows, we first provide an overview of the state of research that considers mediation in the context of rational bargaining to illustrate how mediation's role in addressing the problem of insincere bargaining is important to consider and has been overlooked in many studies. We then consider how mediators can address the problem of insincere bargaining and advance a testable implication. We examine this hypothesis using cross-national data from Greig and Regan (2008) on intrastate conflict (including civil wars) from 1944 to 1999 and find preliminary evidence consistent with the expectation that mediation can and does reduce the problem of insincere bargaining. The quantitative study provides a useful starting point for further case-specific analysis of the roles that third parties can play in assuaging concerns that conflict parties have about the sincerity of their opponents in seeking a settlement.

Mediation and Bargaining

One of the most common forms of conflict management is mediation, which is the consensual, non-violent and non-binding involvement of a third party in conflict management and resolution processes. A widely cited definition of mediation states that it is 'a reactive process of conflict management whereby parties seek the assistance of, or accept an offer of help from an individual, group, or organization to change their behaviour, settle their conflict, or resolve their problem without resorting to physical force or invoking the authority of the law' (Bercovitch and Houston 1996: 13). Essentially, mediation involves diplomatic engagement with both or multiple sides of a dispute (distinguishing it from third party consultations) and includes the consent of the involved parties (distinguishing it from various forms of coercive interventions) but without any binding legal authority (distinguishing it from arbitration and adjudication) and without the deployment of armed force (distinguishing it from peacekeeping).

The existing literature on mediation is rich and well developed (Wallensteen and Svensson 2014; Wilkenfeld, Beardsley and Quinn 2019). For reasons of space, we do not attempt to summarize the entirety of the extant contributions but rather focus on those that consider mediation in the context of rational bargaining because the problem of bargaining in bad faith arises from simply relaxing one of the assumptions made in many bargaining models of war – that bargaining does not have meaningful temporal length.

Bargaining models of war have become a dominant means of understanding conflict onset, conduct and termination (Reiter 2003). Even before rational bargaining models of war became en vogue in much of the international relations literature, Jacob Bercovitch's contingency approach to understanding when mediation is most effective in bringing about peace and the related discourse about ripeness in international bargaining well anticipated many of the expectations that have emerged from more recent studies that are explicitly couched in terms of rational bargaining (Bercovitch, Anagnoson and Wille 1991; Bercovitch and Langley 1993; Bercovitch and Jackson 2001; Bercovitch and Gartner 2006). According to the ripeness framework, conflict proceeds in stages, some of which are more amenable to resolution than others. Work by I. William Zartman, Jacob Bercovitch and other scholars has found that those periods of conflict associated with a mutually hurting stalemate are especially amenable to, or ripe for, successful conflict management by third parties.[1] The concept of ripeness comports well with an understanding of conflict as a bargaining process in which actors find a wider range of settlement possibilities more attractive than conflict when the costs of conflict increase.

Bargaining models of war have been used to show how uncertainty, audience costs for concessions, and commitment problems can lead to conflict bargaining failure. Seen from a rationalist perspective, mediation must alter one or more of these dynamics to affect the prospects for peace. Recent studies have examined how third parties can ameliorate each type of bargaining failure.

One way that third parties can help resolve barriers to efficient bargaining is through manipulating the relative benefits of conflict and peace. Mediation with leverage functions by increasing the costs of non-agreement and thereby expanding the set of mutually acceptable alternatives. Mediators often have bargaining power – the ability to exploit economic, political or military dependencies, or the ability to promise closer economic, political or military ties – vis-à-vis the combatants and wield that bargaining power to structure the incentives and induce the actors into agreement. That is, third parties can use inducements – 'carrots and sticks' – to incentivize the disputants to reach an agreement (Reid 2017). Svensson (2007b) finds that mediators can use leverage effectively to help resolve civil wars, especially when used in conjunction with lighter forms of mediation. Favretto (2009) takes up this question by examining how powerful third parties affect bargaining by inserting themselves into conflicts. In so doing, Favretto is able to study how a third party's proposal power and threat of intervention affect what bargain is struck. She finds that biased third parties can more credibly claim that they will intervene on the side of their protégé, thus ensuring it a preferable settlement. Some existing empirical evidence finds that mediation tactics that use leverage fare best in resolving international disputes or in enabling formal agreements to be reached.[2] Smith and Stam (2003), in constructing a theoretical model of mediation and peacekeeping, posit that altering the material costs and benefits of the combatants is the only means by which third parties can increase the prospects of peaceful settlement. Sisk (2008) similarly argues that 'power mediation' – mediation with leverage – is often the only way for third parties to resolve civil wars. Moreover, Zartman and Touval (1985: 40) write, 'Leverage is the ticket to mediation – third parties are only accepted as mediators if they are likely to produce an agreement or help the parties out of a predicament, and for this they usually need leverage'.[3]

Related to third party involvement with leverage, Walter (2002) addresses how third parties can help disputants overcome issues of commitment, focusing on the post-settlement, implementation phase of conflict resolution. Third parties can help ameliorate post-conflict vulnerabilities that intrastate conflict actors typically face by agreeing to monitor and enforce the implementation phase of agreements. Although Walter is primarily talking about peacekeeping, mediators often promise the types of protection that peacekeeping entails. Similarly, Svensson (2007a) finds that mediators often prove essential to helping reduce the vulnerabilities that governments face in making concessions to rebel groups.

Other studies, however, consider ways in which lighter forms of mediation can reduce the barriers to efficient bargaining. Without leverage, mediators are primarily tasked with enabling the actors to find a single agreement within the set of alternatives that are mutually preferable to conflict.[4] Mediators might do this through making proposals that bridge an actor's interests, reduce the costs of an agreement, logroll issues, expand the pie, address compensation between the actors or help them save face. The key is that the mediator is able to allow the actors to achieve some agreement that is mutually acceptable without actually changing the incentives to find a resolution. The third party does not introduce external incentives for peace and instead focuses on bringing together and integrating the existing political incentives in play to reach a deal. Rauchhaus (2006) finds that lighter forms of mediation actually tend to perform better than heavy-handed involvement (mediation with leverage).

In this vein, some work has considered ways in which mediators can improve the information environment and allow the disputants to more efficiently hone in on agreements that are mutually preferable to conflict. One such area of research comes from some of the literature on bias, which explores whether third parties could help disputants resolve uncertainty by relaying information between disputants and/or by providing outside information. Kydd (2003, 2006) and Rauchhaus (2006) show formally that mediators can credibly convey some signals of resolve and trustworthiness depending on their levels of partiality. Savun (2008) empirically shows that biased mediators tend to fare better in reducing uncertainty and facilitating an agreement, in support of Kydd (2003). It is also worth noting that, although there are disagreements over whether being biased towards *a particular adversary* affords the mediator greater informational potential, a general tenor of consensus has emerged that being biased *towards peace* inhibits the third party from providing credible information. When mediators desire peace above all else, the actors will dismiss the mediator's pleas to make a deal as cheap talk meant only to reach an agreement, without the interests of the combatants in mind (Smith and Stam 2003).

Also related to lighter forms of mediation, third parties can additionally provide political cover when disputants face high domestic audience costs for unpopular, though potentially prudent, concessions. When locked into a conflict because of domestic pressure, leaders might turn to a third party to help sell their constituents on a more concessionary tack. The need to 'save face' can refer to similar situations in which a leader encounters costs from backing down and needs to concede without losing support at home (Druckman 1973; Pruitt 1981b; Rubin 1981; Carter 1984).[5] Within the bargaining framework, effective provision of political cover entails that leaders would face fewer costs for conceding and would then be able to find more alternatives mutually preferable to conflict. Even though the potential to blame a third party for concessions is weaker for mediation than arbitration, mediators can additionally provide needed domestic political cover through informing the domestic audiences about the merits of the concessions. The third party can signal to the domestic public that the agreed outcome was nominally fair. General citizens might be uncertain of whether a deal is in their interest and look to an expert third party's approval of terms that are prudent for both sides.[6] By receiving inside information about a peace process, the third parties will be more informed than the domestic audiences and can signal to them – for example by supporting a proposed peace plan – that any resulting concessions are in the interest of both parties. According to Pruitt (1981b: 208), this is why it is important for mediators to 'sponsor concession exchanges'. Beardsley and Lo (2013b) have shown empirically that mediation can improve the ability for challengers to make minor concessions when doing so is likely to be politically costly.

While the recent literature has identified how a mediator might attenuate bargaining problems, this does not mean that mediators are always effective in doing so. A number of studies have identified hindrances to third party effectiveness. One concern is over whether mediators can be expected to perform the basic function of providing information and reducing uncertainty. Smith and Stam (2003) raise the concern of cheap talk, in which many mediators are so concerned with peace that they cannot credibly convey information that would be used to convince a belligerent to back down. More fundamentally, Fey and Ramsay (2010) argue that it is not likely that mediators will even have access to information that the disputants do not already have in the first place.

Providing nuance to the question of mediation efficacy, Beardsley (2008, 2011, 2013) has identified a trade-off between short- and long-term effectiveness. Werner and Yuen (2005) also demonstrate that agreements which followed substantial third party pressure are less stable than agreements reached more 'naturally'. Quinn et al. (2013) find similar patterns of mediated outcomes in intrastate ethnic conflicts.[7] The general logic of this trade-off is that mediation, especially when the mediator relies on leverage, can facilitate the ability for the combatants to recognize mutually preferable agreements, give political cover for concessions, provide incentives that expand the set of mutually preferable alternatives, and offer post-conflict security guarantees. Relevant to the long run, the involvement of an intermediary can introduce artificial incentives for peace that do not persist and interfere with the ability for the actors to fully understand each other.

At the same time, we must be careful not to make the wrong inferences from 'negative' cases in which mediation does not help foster conflict resolution because of the inherent difficulty in examining the impact of mediation when it is not randomly assigned to cases. The set of crises that experience mediation is likely to be very different, in terms of the *ex ante* likelihood of mediation success, than the set of crises that did not experience mediation or experienced mediation of another type. For example, if mediators generally intervene in intractable situations, the conflicts that never experience mediation are likely to be more amenable to successful peace-making. Without accounting for the non-random selection of mediation as a type of treatment for conflict, causal inference of the impact of mediation is difficult because we must separate the effects of mediation on the conflict outcome from the effects of the contextual factors that are correlated with both mediation incidence and effectiveness. If actors only prefer mediation to negotiations when the barriers to successful resolution are high, then mediation is predisposed to higher failure rates, and will appear to have less positive impact than it really does. This would be a form of endogeneity bias or selection effects.

Scott Sigmund Gartner has shown that it is crucially important to distinguish between selection effects – the part of the relationship between mediation and peaceful outcomes that can be explained by the types of cases that experience mediation – and process effects – the part of the relationship that is actually attributable to the involvement of the third party (Gartner and Bercovitch 2006; Gartner 2011, 2013). Increasingly, scholars have used rational bargaining frameworks to study the selection processes behind mediation incidence and, in so doing, allow us to better understand the baseline against which we should compare mediation outcomes.[8] These studies also help us understand and address the related problem of selection bias, discussed later, which is likely to plague analyses of datasets that only include mediated cases.

Insincere Negotiations

While the existing literature has helped us understand how mediation relates to a number of barriers to efficient bargaining, an important piece is missing. Neither the overall bargaining nor mediation literatures have adequately considered the implications for insincere motivations for peace processes. Many of the bargaining models of war assume that bargaining occurs with no meaningful elapse of time, while much of the mediation literature assumes that mediators are trying to assist negotiators who are bargaining in good faith. This section develops an understanding of why bargaining in bad faith is a potentially powerful explanation for negotiation failure and how mediation can ameliorate the problem.

Like all theories, rational bargaining models make simplifying assumptions in order to get traction on a particular strategic dynamic. Although these assumptions are necessary for certain applications, they also obscure interesting bargaining dynamics. A common assumption across nearly all studies of conflict bargaining in political science is that the exchange of offers during bargaining happens instantly. This assumption is not usually stated as such; rather, scholars simply assert that a bargain is crafted, conveyed, and that a response is formed, all with no change to any conflict-relevant parameters.

Both parts of this assumption, that bargaining is instant and that conflict-relevant parameters do not change during bargaining, are false. In reality, developing and communicating offers can be extremely time-consuming. For example, the negotiations leading to the 2015 Iran nuclear deal lasted over two years. The fact that bargaining often takes a substantial amount of time means that the assumption that conflict-relevant parameters remain fixed during bargaining is also false. For example, during the 1994–95 round of bargaining between the LTTE and the Sri Lankan government, the rebels ferried heavy weaponry into their areas of operation from India, including advanced surface-to-air missiles. This is reported to have dramatically increased their fighting power when the LTTE broke off these insincere negotiations.

Once we relax these assumptions, we begin to understand how disputants may have incentives to bargain insincerely – that is, to bargain in order to gain power and then return to conflict, with no intention of settling. A limited amount of literature has examined these 'devious' disputants. Ikle (1964), in an important early work, points out that negotiations can be used to divide a good, but they can also be used for their 'side effects'. One side effect that Ikle notes is the ability for negotiations to be used as a stalling tactic, allowing disputants to rest, rearm and become better prepared for an anticipated return to conflict. Richmond (1998) coined the term 'devious disputants' to refer to those who undertake bargaining with their adversaries with no intention of striking a bargain.

Two factors allow for insincere negotiations to transpire: the difficulty of monitoring one's opponent during ceasefires, and the observational equivalence of hard bargaining and stalling. Without these, the disputant at risk of being taken advantage of would simply walk away from negotiations when it realized its adversary did not intend to settle. We briefly examine why both conditions are often present and thus why the problem of insincere bargaining is widespread.

The monitoring of ceasefire agreements is a difficulty that is well studied. Walter (2002) notes that, after a rebel group and a government have agreed on how to divide a country and its leadership, they are stuck with the difficult task of implementing that agreement. Often, this means transitioning from a period of ceasefire to one of demilitarization and shared responsibility for security and governance. Walter argues that monitoring whether or not the opponent is abiding by a ceasefire is difficult because violations are easy to carry out in secret, and because sides are unlikely to permit each other access to their areas of operations. Furthermore, actions that bolster a state's resolve by communicating the value of the good in dispute are not usually thought of as violations at all. Walter argues that ceasefire monitoring is so difficult for disputants that they will often need the assistance of outside parties to help with monitoring and verification.

Monitoring a ceasefire that precedes or co-occurs with active bargaining is no less difficult. Actors are unlikely to be able to observe whether their opponent is taking steps to increase its power during the ceasefire, both because the task is inherently difficult, and because of the lack of proximity to the other side's forces.

The problem of adjudicating between hard bargaining and stalling is similarly rampant. Hard bargaining over a zero-sum good and stalling are observationally equivalent. This observational equivalence comes from the fact that disputants bargaining under uncertainty can use delay as a way to demonstrate their resolve. Admati and Perry (1987) show that bargainers can avoid making or accepting offers in order to signal the relative strength of their bargaining position, while Cramton (1992) demonstrates a similar dynamic in games that feature two-sided uncertainty. Given the zero-sum, high-stakes nature of conflict bargaining, we should expect disputants to use this and other tactics to try to maximize their share of the disputed good. The fact that stalling is useful to sincere bargainers makes disputants unable to discriminate between opponents who are holding out for a better offer and those who are merely stalling in a bid to gain strength during the lull in fighting.

Bargaining with insincere motivations is not just a problem for bilateral bargaining but could especially apply to the involvement of third party conflict managers. Richmond (1998) delineates a bundle of assets that often accompany instances of mediation that disputants may attempt to attain in spite of having no desire to settle. Mediation, aside from offering a chance at settling a dispute, allows disputants to regroup, reorganize, search out allies, gain recognition and legitimacy for their side, save face and defer making costly concessions.[9]

Richmond (1998) considers how mediation might sometimes be used as a stalling tactic, but he does not consider how some forms of mediation, specifically those that bring substantial leverage to bear on the bargaining process, can actually provide a critical solution to the problem of bargaining in bad faith. Danneman (2013) shows formally that mediators can use leverage to reduce the problem of insincere bargaining. His model establishes a novel role for third party actors who want to help arrest conflicts: enforcing the tacit agreement to bargain.

Mediators might impose costs on bad faith negotiators via a number of means. The mediators might threaten to withdraw material support, akin to Gerald Ford's threat to 'reassess' the provision of military aid from the USA to Israel when negotiations for a second Sinai disengagement agreement had stalled (Stein 1999: 176). The mediators might also threaten to withdraw less tangible diplomatic support that could affect the geostrategic positioning of the adversaries, akin to Jimmy Carter's threats to Anwar Sadat at Camp David – that Egypt would be less secure in preventing the Soviet Union and radical Arabs from gaining a foothold in the region without staunch US support – as Sadat's delegation prepared to leave prior to the conclusion of a peace agreement (Carter 1982: 392). Moreover, mediators might publicly blame an intransigent party, akin to James Baker's threats to 'leave the dead cat on the doorstep' of the parties most responsible for scuttling the Madrid peace process (Baker III 1999: 188).

Being seen as willing and able to impose costs on disputants who agree to bargain but then fail to make or accept reasonable proposals helps disputants strike more bargains. The mechanism at work has two components. Foremost, third parties help make suspicious states come to the table – a necessary condition for reaching a settlement. In the absence of a third party, there are a wide range of circumstances under which a suspicious state would prefer to fight rather than making an offer. Secondly, the threat of costs imposed by a third party pushes potentially insincere negotiators to accept a wider envelope of offers. This function of mediation comports with the classic 'sticks and carrots' view of what a mediator does (Touval and Zartman 1985a; Schrodt and Gerner 2004; Reid 2017). However, in this context the stick does not help disputants overcome an empty bargaining range created by uncertainty; rather, the stick helps an ascendant disputant commit to an otherwise unacceptably small division of a good. Stated differently, third parties help disputants tie their hands (Fearon 1997).

The core proposition advanced in this chapter is that mediators whom disputants expect to impose greater costs for intransigence are more likely to assuage concerns over insincere bargaining than are mediators whom disputants expect to impose lesser costs for intransigence. We capture the concept of perceived or expected costs imposed for intransigence by measuring a potential mediator's ability to impose costs, and its willingness to do so. The combination of these factors, we argue, captures expected costs for intransigence. More directly, we expect that strong and interested mediators are more likely to generate successful instances of mediation than their less powerful and less interested counterparts.

Empirical Analysis

Inference in the Study of Mediation Outcomes

We test the expectations using quantitative data of conflict and peace processes. It is important to note that the expected patterns of behaviour could be consistent with observationally equivalent claims that stronger and more willing third parties are the types that can better leverage the disputants to reach short-term agreements sooner rather than later – more by enticement than by resolving the potential for insincere bargaining considered here. We recognize this issue and do not disagree with the potential for these types of mediators to have other effects on the likelihood for settlement beyond reducing the manipulation of the bargaining process. We therefore offer caution in concluding too much from the following test. While the findings are consistent with the preceding logic, without further tests – and further process tracing of key cases – that can distinguish our mechanism from other mechanisms, the findings remain suggestive.

There are several potential threats to inference that must be accounted for when using observational data on conflict mediation. Foremost, mediator characteristics, such as strength and interest, may be correlated with factors that make mediation more or less likely to be successful. For instance, mediators are known to be active in cases that are less likely to be resolved, such as those with high levels of violence (Gartner and Bercovitch 2006; Gartner 2011). This threat to inference arising from confounding can be ameliorated by accounting for likely confounding covariates in a regression framework.

More troubling than simple confounding is the fact that mediators, by definition, are only present in a conflict if both the mediator in question and both parties to the dispute want mediation to occur. This opens any analysis of mediation efficacy to the possibility that unobservable or unmeasured factors may influence the process of mediation onset and the process that leads to mediation outcomes. Importantly, these unobserved or unmeasured factors could be related to why mediators intervene, or they could be related to why disputants accept mediation, or both. In the language of econometrics, there could be selection bias present due to unobservable factors related to mediator or disputant motivations.

A potential driver of selection bias is the prior belief each disputant has related to its opponent being able to reap a large power shift during bargaining. This unobservable factor would cause mediation to be less likely to begin, and more likely to fail once begun. Consequently, an analysis of what factors make mediation more or less effective that only looks at the set of mediation cases would tend to misestimate the actual effect of this problem of power shifts during bargaining. A careful empirical examination will need to begin by being wary of the threat of selection bias (Heckman 1979). We thus use a Heckman probit (also known as a censored probit) model to simultaneously estimate the occurrence of mediation and the characteristics that shape whether it is effective.

An additional threat to inference is that instances of mediation are not randomly assigned with respect to a conflict's history. Conflicts that attract offers of mediation tend to attract several of them in close succession, while those that attract few offers in a given period are likely to continue to be unmediated in the future (Greig and Regan 2008). We account for the temporal effects of mediation offers on subsequent offers by including the time since last mediation offer by any party, its square, and its cube (Carter and Signorino 2010). Finally, conflicts almost certainly exhibit conflict-specific characteristics that make assuming independence across observations untenable. We employ bootstrapped standard errors to generate accurate estimates of uncertainty in the models presented below.

Concepts and Measures

This chapter tests the proposition that mediators who are stronger and more interested are more successful in their efforts to foster settlements than weaker, less interested ones. Testing this hypothesis requires measurements for three concepts: mediator interest, mediator strength, and mediation success. As a scope condition, we only consider the characteristics of third party states so that the observations are comparable – the leverage and interests that states have are not easily comparable to the leverage and interests that non-state third parties might have.[10]

In terms of interests, why might a third party state be particularly interested in generating a peaceful solution to a civil war? To address this, we draw on two literatures. Civil wars are problematic for nearby states for a whole host of security reasons. Foremost, civil wars cause civil wars in nearby states (e.g. Buhaug and Gleditsch 2008). Civil wars are massively destructive to a state, and threaten the tenure of those in power. As such, concerns about their spread should motivate nearby states to take an active interest. Secondly, civil wars depress the economies of nearby states, causing a loss of domestic support and financing (Murdoch and Sandler 2004). Danneman and Ritter (2013) show that civil war in neighbouring states prompts leaders to take pre-emptive, repressive action in hopes of quelling future dissent. However, this repression may risk increasing domestic tensions. Civil wars also generate massive public health externalities that hurt nearby states (Ghobarah, Huth and Russett 2003). Finally, civil wars create refugee flows that inflame security and distributional concerns in nearby states (Salehyan and Gleditsch 2006). Overall, security concerns likely prompt states to be particularly concerned with ending civil wars.

A second factor that might motivate a state to take costly action to end a civil war is money. Civil wars are not only caused by dismal economic performance, they cause it as well (Ghobarah, Huth and Russett 2003). A precipitous drop in imports and exports from a major trading partner due to civil war is likely to have adverse effects on nearby countries. Although economic actors in some sectors may be able to shift their trading profiles, others will not. Furthermore, even those who can trade elsewhere will find the change costly. In sum, then, economic interests are likely to cause states to be concerned with ending civil wars.

In addition to these 'hard' or realist factors, liberal factors may generate interest in resolving a civil war as well. Adler and Barnett (1998) argue that security communities can form regionally, and that states therein take each other's security very seriously. These actors are often initially driven by small gains from cooperation, but eventually these relationships develop to the point where nations feel a sense of kinship and responsibility to each other. Similarly, Crescenzi et al. (2011) find empirically that democracies feel normative pressure to assist one another through the provision of conflict mediation services, and also find that mediation is more likely to come from nearby states.

Importantly, the security, economic and communal factors that generate interest in civil war termination are all intimately tied to geography. Civil wars cluster tightly in space (Buhaug and Gleditsch 2008). The economic externalities associated with conflict and refugees flow outwards from a conflict's centre. Refugees rarely have the capacity to get further away from a conflict than across a single border (Salehyan and Gleditsch 2006); communicable disease usually does not outpace them. Trade between nations is very strongly predicted by geographic proximity, so much so that baseline models of trade draw their name from physical models of gravity, in which distance is a key component. Finally, the sense of community among nations is often related to relationships based in common language, ethnicity and economic interest, all of which are highly correlated with proximity.

Not every proximate nation will be equally interested in resolving a given conflict. However, we expect geographic distance to capture most of these drives, and serve as a reasonable proxy for how important any given state feels it is to quell civil conflict in another state. Generally, this measurement strategy is similar to the one employed by Danneman and Ritter (2013) in that both use a general variable to capture the influence of several potential direct causes.

Measuring a state's capacity to inflict costs for intransigence is similarly complicated. States exert pressure on one another in a host of ways, though not every way is equally available to all states. Foremost, states may use military pressure or coercion to get disputants to make and accept reasonable bargains. Favretto (2009) shows convincingly that military coercion can be used, when credible, to generate agreement. Coercion can be in the form of direct military action,[11] threats to withdraw military support, or threats against the diplomats themselves.[12]

States can also pressure other actors economically. Promises to increase aid upon agreement, or withhold it in response to intransigence, are common. For example, in 1979 the United States promised, and has delivered, a flow of continued economic and development aid to Egypt contingent upon its signing the 1979 treaty with Israel. This aid is non-trivial: it amounts to around $1.3 billion annually (US Department of State 2012) and its threatened withdrawal in response to recent political violence in Egypt caused widespread concern in Egypt. Trade restrictions can also serve as a source of leverage, as can sanctions (Tsebelis 1990).

The mechanism through which a mediator employs leverage is unimportant to the theory of intra-bargaining commitment. The theory merely stipulates that the ability to use leverage, in combination with incentives to do so, is crucial. Thus, like the use of distance to account for the multiple potential causes of interest, we use a state's major power status as a proxy for its generalized ability to impose costs.

As alluded to above, closeness is likely a noisy measure of interest, and major power status is likely a noisy measure of leverage. Insofar as the noise in these measures is merely noise, and is uncorrelated with other concepts, this noise serves to make the tests of the hypothesis presented here more conservative by causing attenuation bias.

The final concept to be operationalized is mediation success. In terms of the theory being tested here, mediation success is a short-term concept that deals with the extent to which mediators are able to help disputants reach settlements. This concept is intentionally narrow; it is not meant to include the durability of settlements, how the disputants view the fairness of settlements, or any other facet of agreements. From the point of view of the intra-bargaining commitment theory, an instance of mediation is successful if a settlement is reached, and unsuccessful if, instead of reaching some agreement, the disputants return to violent conflict.

We use Bercovitch's coding of settlement from the International Conflict Management (ICM) dataset. Specifically, we create a variable that takes on a value of 1 if a full or partial settlement is reached, and 0 otherwise. This variable measures the concept of short-term bargaining success, and thus mirrors the concept described in the theory nicely. Understanding short-term bargaining success is also important for practical and humanitarian reasons. On the pragmatic side, questions about settlement duration and settlement enforcement are all moot unless disputants can agree to a settlement in the first place. On the humanitarian side, settlements, even short-lived ones, can still afford time for aid workers to assist with refugee relocation, dispersing food aid and providing medical assistance to soldiers and bystanders (Touval 1995).

Data and Model

We analyse a dataset of potential and actual third party mediation efforts. To construct this dataset, we began with the Greig and Regan (2008) potential intervenor-conflict-year dataset. This dataset has an observation for every potential state mediator, for every civil conflict, in every year that that conflict persisted. Thus, an observation in that dataset is, for example, Germany-Surinam Guerrilla Insurgency-1993. As in, during 1993 the Surinam Guerrilla Insurgency (a civil war) was ongoing, and Germany was a state in the system, and thus could have offered to mediate. We then add data on mediation outcomes from the ICM dataset (Bercovitch 2000). We chose to keep all observations when there are multiple instances of mediation in a single intervenor-year.

As mentioned above, we utilize a censored probit model to account for the possibility of selection bias. In the dataset, there are 173,017 potential or actual intervenor-years. Of these, 241 experience a mediation effort. We use Bercovitch's coding of mediation success, in which each mediation instance leads to a full or partial settlement, or is coded as being unsuccessful. Of the 241 mediation efforts, 108 reach some degree of settlement.

The first equation in the selection model estimates the probability of mediation occurrence. We analyse all potential intervenors, rather than just each conflict-year, in order to account for both supply- and demand-side unobservables that may generate selection bias. We model mediation onset as a function of both dispute and potential mediator factors. Dispute-specific variables include the duration of the dispute to date, in years; the log of the number of battle deaths in the dispute to date; the sum of previous mediation efforts in the dispute; and the number of years since the last mediation effort (and its square and cube), to account for duration dependence. As mediator-specific characteristics, we include historic ties to the country in conflict; major power status; the distance from the potential intervenor to the conflict; and the interaction between distance and major power status. The data on mediation onsets, mediator characteristics and historic ties come from Greig and Regan (2008). The distance between potential intervenors and the civil war state is taken from the C-Shapes R package, and utilizes the inter-border distances between states (Weidmann and Gleditsch 2010).[13] Summary statistics are presented in Table 9.1.

Table 9.1 Summary statistics

Variable	Min	Mean	Max
Log Battle Deaths	0	6.9	12.8
Major Power	0	.0.4	1
Closeness	0	1.0	9.4
Closeness*MP	0	0	9.4
Historic Ties	0	0.01	1
Sum of Previous Acceptances	0	0.01	5
Dispute Duration	1	7	52
Mediation Efforts	241		
Mediation Successes	108		

Summary statistics for variables used in the regression model.
Source: Data are from Greig and Regan (2008) and Bercovitch (2000). Values are shown for the minimum, mean and maximum of the variables.

In the outcome equation, we predict the probability of any settlement, whether partial or full under the Bercovitch codings, being reached. The argument predicts that interested, capable mediators should generate a higher probability of mediation success. As such, we include closeness, major power status and the interaction of these two variables. Since the relationship between the probability of mediation success and mediator characteristics may vary by level of costs of conflict, we control for the log of cumulative battle deaths. Following Achen (1986), we limit the amount of miscellaneous control variables in the outcome equation, as doing so may worsen the estimate of the treatment effect. Furthermore, few standard controls are likely to correlate with the specific mediator characteristics examined here (power and distance) *and* mediation acceptance. As a final rationale for utilizing a minimal set of controls in the outcome equation, there are only 241 uncensored observations, making the use of more than four covariates in the outcome equation questionable. Finally, we bootstrap the standard errors on conflict, as censored probit models generate poor estimates of uncertainty, and because the errors are likely to be correlated within conflicts (Brandt and Schneider n.d.).

Table 9.2 reports the results of the bootstrap estimation of the censored probit model.[14] Analysing the degree of support for the hypothesis requires generating predicted probabilities of mediation success for both types of mediators, and comparing them directly. Figure 9.1 depicts the predicted probability of mediation success across the range of closeness, for both major powers and non-major powers, with the log of battle deaths held at its mean. The graphic makes it clear that major power mediators in close proximity to civil wars are highly effective mediators, generating settlements in a predicted 98 per cent of mediation efforts. Meanwhile, mediators who are not major powers, and who are far from the disputants they are serving, are much less effective, generating settlements in a predicted 6 per cent of mediation efforts. This difference is highly statistically significant ($p < 0.001$).

We additionally perform a number of robustness checks, not shown. The first set of robustness checks, along with the basis expansion model, demonstrates that the exact specification of the selection stage does not influence the results in the outcome stage. The second set of robustness checks demonstrates that the results of the model are unaffected by limiting the analysis to observations that conform more closely to the theoretical model's implied scope conditions.

Conclusions

We have argued that mediators can address an overlooked barrier to efficient bargaining – that disputants often have incentives to use negotiations insincerely as a stalling tactic in order to improve their negotiating position. Third parties, when they are willing and able to punish bad faith bargaining, can reduce the potential

Table 9.2 Selection model results

Variable	Coefficient	95% CI
Mediation Outcome		
Log Battle Deaths	-0.07	(-0.16, 0.02)
Closeness	0.08	(0.02, 0.15)
Major Power	0.13	(-0.60, 0.83)
Closeness*MP	0.24	(0.03, 0.60)
Constant	-1.31	(-2.46, -0.06)
Mediation Onset		
Time	-0.20	(-0.28, -0.15)
$Time^2$	0.007	(0.003, 0.016)
$Time^3$	-0.00005	(-0.0002, -0.00001)
Closeness	0.16	(0.14, 0.17)
Major Power	1.33	(1.17, 1.50)
Closeness*MP	-0.15	(-0.22, -0.09)
Historic Link	0.53	(0.35, 0.70)
Duration	0.06	(0.03, 0.12)
$Duration^2$	-0.002	(-0.004, -0.0007)
Sum(Acceptances)	0.59	(0.50, 0.67)
ln(Battle Deaths)	-0.007	(-0.03, 0.02)
Constant	-3.25	(-3.48, -3.03)
rho	0.48	(0.21, 0.72)

Censored probit results. N = 173,017 with 1,000 bootstrapped samples.
Source: Data are from Greig and Regan (2008) and Bercovitch (2000). Note the highly statistically significant positive correlation between the selection and outcome equations, rho. This result means that the selection model setup is necessary.

gains that ascendant (potentially devious) disputants might have to prolong talks. Results from a quantitative analysis of conflict management events are consistent with this argument; mediators who are powerful and proximate to the disputants do quite well in securing peace agreements with few instances of failed talks.[15] These findings are robust to concerns about selection bias and time dependency.

This theory of intra-bargaining commitment dynamics implies that some of what we know about conflict mediation onset is right, but for the wrong reasons. In studies of mediation outcomes, it is common (and important) to account for the non-random assignment of mediation to conflicts. Studies that use this empirical strategy have often noted that mediation 'goes to the hard cases'. That is, disputants and mediators opt into mediation when conflict-level characteristics do not favour resolution (see especially Gartner and Bercovitch

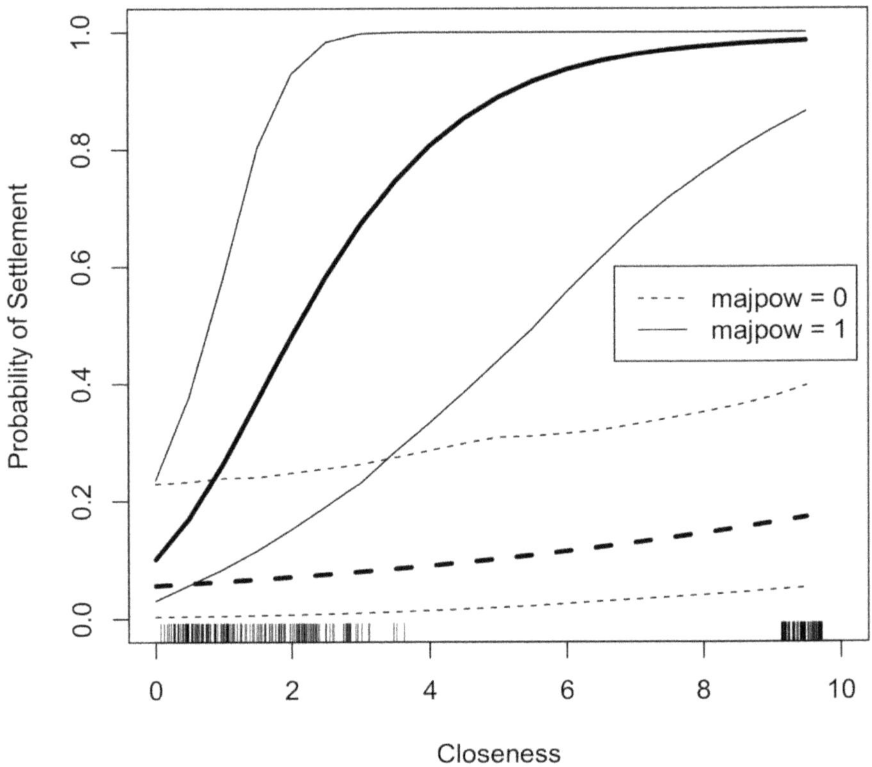

Figure 9.1 Estimated probability of mediation success: bootstrapped estimates. Figure created by the authors.

Note: Predicted probability of settlement across the range of closeness, for both major powers and non-major powers. Bold lines denote estimates; lighter lines indicate 95% confidence intervals. The rug along the x-axis depicts jittered observed instances of closeness. This graphic displays strong support for the hypothesis that close, major power mediators are much more successful than far-flung, non-major power mediators.

2006). However, this finding may be driven by its contrapositive. The theory put forward here shows that mediation can be useful to disputants who fear intra-bargaining commitment problems across a wide range of situations. However, bilateral talks are only feasible under more favourable conditions, when concerns about commitment are less pressing. Thus, it may not be the case that mediation goes to difficult cases, but rather that bilateral negotiation does not happen in difficult cases.

The theory set out above also helps make sense of a poorly explained empirical regularity: great powers rarely seek the assistance of mediators. For instance, in the domain of enduring rivalries, Greig (2005) finds that major powers are significantly less likely to utilize mediation. He explains the infrequent use of mediation by great powers as being the result of great powers disdaining intervention in their affairs. The theory of intra-bargaining commitment dynamics provides a parsimonious, rationalist account for why strong states are rarely offered mediation, and why they prefer not to use it when it is offered. Third parties can only serve as efficacious enforcers of the tacit agreement to bargain if they are willing and able to impose meaningful costs on the disputants for breaking their commitment. It is unlikely that small states would have this capability with respect to major powers. Other major powers might have sufficient enforcement power, but using it against a fellow major power would require a large amount of coercion. This may be untenable because of the possibility of provocation, or because doing so would be unpalatable to the domestic audience of the potential intervenor or the major power in the dispute.

Nathan Danneman is Principal Data Scientist at Data Machines. He received his PhD in political science at Emory University in 2013. He works on a wide variety of data science problems with social science applications.

Kyle Beardsley is Professor of Political Science at Duke University. He is co-director of the International Crisis Behaviour Data Project. His research interests focus on questions related to the role of third parties in shaping conflict dynamics, the pervasiveness of gender power imbalances in security institutions, the diffusion of armed conflict across space, and the impact of nuclear weapons on international crisis behaviour.

Notes

1. See especially Bercovitch (1997), Bercovitch and Langley (1993), Greig (2001), Haas (1991), Modelski (1964), Mooradian and Druckman (1999), Northedge and Donelan (1971), Ott (1972), Pruitt (1981a), Regan and Stam (2000), Rubin (1991), Touval and Zartman (1985b), Young (1967) and Zartman (1985). Kleiboer (1994) provides a provocative critique of the ripeness framework.
2. For studies on the relationship between leverage and general conflict resolution, see Beardsley (2011), Bercovitch (1986), Bercovitch, Anagnoson and Wille (1991), Bercovitch and Houston (1996), Carnevale (1986), Reid (2017), and Schrodt and Gerner (2004). For similar analyses of formal agreements, see Beardsley et al. (2006), Quinn et al. (2006), Svensson (2007b), and Wilkenfeld et al. (2003, 2005).
3. Also see Touval (1994).
4. Carnevale (1986) and Kressel (1972) use 'integration' to refer to the same type of third party involvement.
5. Note that saving face can be used more broadly to also include the social-psychological costs, e.g. embarrassment, of conceding or the fear of looking weak to an opponent. In this regard, see Pruitt and Johnson (1970), Touval (1982); Ott (1972) and Young (1972).
6. In a similar vein, Chapman and Reiter (2004) and Chapman (2007) have found that security institutions such as the UN Security Council provide credible signals to domestic audiences about the prudence of foreign policy actions.

7. Other work has similarly considered how third parties can interfere with the combatant incentives to fully resolve their conflicts. See, for example, Greig and Diehl (2005), Svensson (2009), Zartman and Touval (2007) and Gurses, Rost and McLeod (2008).
8. See, for example, Beardsley (2010), Beardsley and Lo (2013a), Bercovitch and Jackson (2001), Böhmelt (2009), Crescenzi et al. (2011), Greig (2005), Greig and Diehl (2006), Greig and Regan (2008), Hensel (2001), Melin (2011), Melin and Svensson (2009), Mitchell (2002), Mitchell, Kadera and Crescenzi (2008), Shannon (2009), and Terris and Maoz (2005).
9. Beardsley (2009) uses the presence of devious disputants to help explain the prevalence of low-capacity mediators.
10. Future research might consider how other types of third parties such as international organizations and private citizens would compare to state actors in their potential leverage and interests.
11. E.g. the US in the Balkans.
12. E.g. Quaddhafi with N. and S. Yemeni diplomats in 1972.
13. We take the log of this variable, and reverse code it into a variable called 'closeness', which takes its minimum for states on opposite sides of the globe, and its maximum for contiguous states.
14. The selection stage estimates are perhaps surprising at first. However, the results from this first stage should not be given too much credence as there is undoubtedly a large amount of selection bias present in those first-stage estimates. That is, mediation onset is a result of offers and acceptances, and to estimate unbiased coefficients for mediation onset, one would have to include a selection stage prior to this. The purpose of the first stage of this model is not to accurately estimate these coefficients, but to account for a portion of the variation in mediation onsets in order to estimate the degree of correlation in the errors between this stage and the outcome equation.
15. As mentioned above, these findings might also confirm observationally equivalent claims about these types of mediators, so we present the results as suggestive.

References

Achen, C.H. 1986. *The Statistical Analysis of Quasi-Experiments.* Berkeley: University of California Press.

Adler, E., and M. Barnett. 1998. 'A Framework for the Study of Security Communities', in E. Adler and M. Barnett (eds), *Security Communities.* Cambridge: Cambridge University Press, pp. 29–66.

Admati, A.R., and M. Perry. 1987. 'Strategic Delay in Bargaining', *The Review of Economic Studies* 54(3): 345–64.

Baker III, J.A. 1999. 'The Road to Madrid', in C.A. Crocker, F.O. Hampson and P. Aall (eds), *Herding Cats: Multiparty Mediation in a Complex World.* Washington, DC: United States Institute of Peace, pp. 183–206.

Beardsley, K. 2008. 'Agreement without Peace? International Mediation and Time Inconsistency Problems', *American Journal of Political Science* 52(4): 723–40.

———. 2009. 'Intervention without Leverage: Explaining the Prevalence of Weak Mediators', *International Interactions* 35: 27.

———. 2010. 'Pain, Pressure, and Political Cover: Explaining Mediation Incidence', *Journal of Peace Research* 47(4): 395–406.

———. 2011. *The Mediation Dilemma.* Ithaca, NY: Cornell University Press.

———. 2013. 'Using the Right Tool for the Job: Mediator Leverage and Conflict Resolution', *Penn State Journal of Law and International Affairs* 2(1): 57–65.

Beardsley, K., and N. Lo. 2013a. 'Democratic Communities and Third-Party Conflict Management', *Conflict Management and Peace Science* 30(1): 76–93.

———. 2013b. 'Third-Party Conflict Management and the Willingness to Make Concessions', *Journal of Conflict Resolution* 58(2): 363–92.

Beardsley, K., D. Quinn, B. Biswas and J. Wilkenfeld. 2006. 'Mediation Style and Crisis Outcomes', *Journal of Conflict Resolution* 50(1): 58–86.

Bercovitch, J. 1986. 'International Mediation: A Study of Incidence, Strategies, and Conditions of Successful Outcomes', *Cooperation and Conflict* 21(3): 155–68.

———. 1997. 'Mediation in International Conflict: An Overview of Theory, a Review of Practice', in I.W. Zartman and J.L. Rasmussen (eds), *Peacemaking in International Conflict: Methods and Techniques*. Washington, DC: United States Institute of Peace, pp. 125–53.

———. 2000. *International Conflict Mediation, 1945–1999*. 2000 Codebook. Retrieved 27 March 2020 from http://www.arts.canterbury.ac.nz/bercovitch/databases.shtml.

Bercovitch, J., J.T. Anagnoson and D.L. Wille. 1991. 'Some Conceptual Issues and Empirical Trends in the Study of Successful Mediation in International Relations', *Journal of Peace Research* 28(1): 7–17.

Bercovitch, J., and S.S. Gartner. 2006. 'Is There Method in the Madness of Mediation? Some Lessons for Mediators from Quantitative Studies of Mediation', *International Interactions* 32: 329–54.

Bercovitch, J., and A. Houston. 1996. 'The Study of International Mediation: Theoretical Issues and Empirical Evidence', in J. Bercovitch (ed.), *Resolving International Conflicts: The Theory and Practice of Mediation*. Boulder, CO: Lynne Rienner, pp. 11–35.

Bercovitch, J., and R. Jackson. 2001. 'Negotiation or Mediation? An Exploration of Factors Affecting the Choice of Conflict Management in International Conflict', *Negotiation Journal* 17(1): 59–77.

Bercovitch, J., and J. Langley. 1993. 'The Nature of the Dispute and the Effectiveness of International Mediation', *Journal of Conflict Resolution* 37(4): 670–91.

Böhmelt, T. 2009. 'International Mediation and Social Networks: The Importance of Indirect Ties', *International Interactions* 35(3): 298–319.

Brandt, P., and C. Schneider. N.d. 'So the Reviewer Told You to Use a Selection Model? Selection Models and the Study of International Relations', Working Paper.

Buhaug, H., and K.S. Gleditsch. 2008. 'Contagion or Confusion? Why Conflicts Cluster in Space', *International Studies Quarterly* 52: 215–33.

Carnevale, P.J.D. 1986. 'Strategic Choice in Mediation', *Negotiation Journal* 2(1): 41–56.

Carter, D.B., and C.S. Signorino. 2010. 'Back to the Future: Modelling Time Dependence in Binary Data', *Political Analysis* 18(3): 271–92.

Carter, J. 1982. *Keeping Faith: Memoirs of a President*. New York: Bantam Books.

———. 1984. *Negotiation: The Alternative to Hostility*. Macon, GA: Mercer University Press.

Chapman, T.L. 2007. 'International Security Institutions, Domestic Politics, and Institutional Legitimacy', *Journal of Conflict Resolution* 51(1): 134–66.

Chapman, T.L., and D. Reiter. 2004. 'The United Nations Security Council and the Rally 'Round the Flag Effect', *Journal of Conflict Resolution* 48(6): 886–909.

Cramton, P. 1992. 'Strategic Delay in Bargaining with Two-Sided Uncertainty', *Review of Economic Studies* 59: 205–25.

Crescenzi, M.J.C., K.M. Kadera, S.M. Mitchell and C.L. Thyne. 2011. 'A Supply Side Theory of Mediation', *International Studies Quarterly* 55(4): 1069–94.

Danneman, N. 2013. 'Committing to Bargain: How Mediation Contributes to the Onset and Success of Peace Talks', Ph.D. dissertation. Atlanta: Emory University.
Danneman, N., and E. Ritter. 2013. 'Contagious Rebellion and Preemptive Repression', *Journal of Conflict Resolution.* https://doi.org/10.1177/0022002712468720.
DeRouen, K., and F. Möller. 2013. 'The Short-Term Effects of Mediation on Low-Intensity Civil Wars', *Negotiation Journal* 29(4): 413–38.
Druckman, D. 1973. *Human Factors in International Negotiations: Social-Psychological Aspects of International Conflict.* London: Sage Publications.
Favretto, K. 2009. 'Should Peacemakers Take Sides? Major Power Mediation, Coercion, and Bias', *American Political Science Review* 103(2): 248–63.
Fearon, J.D. 1997. 'Signalling Foreign Policy Interests', *Journal of Conflict Resolution* 41(1): 68–90.
Fey, M., and K.W. Ramsay. 2010. 'When Is Shuttle Diplomacy Worth the Commute? Information Sharing through Mediation', *World Politics* 62(4): 529–60.
Gartner, S.S. 2011. 'Signs of Trouble: Regional Organization Mediation and Civil War Agreement Durability', *Journal of Politics* 73(2): 380–90.
———. 2013. 'Deceptive Results: Why Mediation Appears to Fail but Actually Succeeds', *Penn State Journal of Law and International Affairs* 2(1): 27–37.
Gartner, S.S., and J. Bercovitch. 2006. 'Overcoming Obstacles to Peace: The Contribution of Mediation to Short-Lived Conflict Settlements', *International Studies Quarterly* 50(4): 819–40.
Ghobarah, H., P. Huth and B.M. Russett. 2003. 'Civil Wars Kill and Maim People Long after the Shooting Stops', *American Political Science Review* 97: 189–202.
Greig, J.M. 2001. 'Moments of Opportunity: Recognizing Conditions of Ripeness for International Mediation between Enduring Rivals', *Journal of Conflict Resolution* 45(6): 691–718.
———. 2005. 'Stepping into the Fray: When Do Mediators Mediate?', *American Journal of Political Science* 49(2): 249–66.
Greig, J.M., and P.F. Diehl. 2005. 'The Peacekeeping-Peacemaking Dilemma', *International Studies Quarterly* 49: 621–45.
———. 2006. 'Softening Up: Making Conflicts More Amenable to Diplomacy', *International Interactions* 32: 355–84.
Greig, J.M., and P.M. Regan. 2008. 'When Do They Say Yes? An Analysis of the Willingness to Offer and Accept Mediation in Civil Wars', *International Studies Quarterly* 52(4): 759–82.
Gurses, M., N. Rost, and P. McLeod. 2008. 'Mediating Civil War Settlements and the Duration of Peace', *International Interactions* 34(2): 129–55.
Haas, R. 1991. 'Ripeness, De-Escalation, and Arms Control', in L. Kriesberg and S.J. Thorson (eds), *Timing the De-Escalation of International Conflicts.* Syracuse, NY: Syracuse University Press, pp. 83–96.
Heckman, J. 1979. 'Sample Selection Bias as a Specification Error', *Econometrica* 47: 153–61.
Hensel, P. 2001. 'Contentious Issues and World Politics: The Management of Territorial Claims in the Americas, 1816–1992', *International Studies Quarterly* 45(1): 81–109.
Ikle, F.C. 1964. *How Nations Negotiate.* New York: Harper & Brothers.
Kleiboer, M. 1994. 'Ripeness of Conflict: A Fruitful Notion?', *Journal of Peace Research* 31: 109–16.
Kressel, K. 1972. *Labor Mediation: An Exploratory Survey.* New York: Association of Labor Mediation Agencies.
Kydd, A. 2003. 'Which Side Are You On? Bias, Credibility and Mediation', *American Journal of Political Science* 47(4): 597–611.

Kydd, A.H. 2006. 'When Can Mediators Build Trust?', *American Political Science Review* 100(3): 449–62.

Melin, M.M. 2011. 'The Impact of State Relationships on If, When, and How Conflict Management Occurs', *International Studies Quarterly* 55(3): 691–715.

Melin, M.M., and I. Svensson. 2009. 'Incentives for Talking: Accepting Mediation in International and Civil Wars', *International Interactions* 35(3): 249–71.

Mitchell, S.M. 2002. 'A Kantian System? Democracy and Third-Party Conflict Resolution', *American Journal of Political Science* 46(4): 749–59.

Mitchell, S.M., K.M. Kadera and M.J. Crescenzi. 2008. 'Practicing Democratic Community Norms: Third Party Conflict Management and Successful Settlements', in J. Bercovitch and S.S. Gartner (eds), *International Conflict Mediation: New Approaches and Findings*. New York: Routledge.

Modelski, G. 1964. 'International Settlement of Internal Wars', in J.N. Rosenau (ed.), *International Aspects of Civil Strife*. Princeton, NJ: Princeton University Press.

Mooradian, M., and D. Druckman. 1999. 'Hurting Stalemate or Mediation? The Conflict over Nagorno-Karabakh, 1990–95', *Journal of Peace Research* 36(6): 709–27.

Murdoch, J., and T. Sandler. 2004. 'Civil War and Economic Growth: Spatial Dispersion', *American Journal of Political Science* 48: 138–51.

Northedge, F.S., and M. Donelan. 1971. *International Disputes: The Political Aspects*. London: Europa Publications.

Ott, M.C. 1972. 'Mediation as a Method of Conflict Resolution: Two Cases', *International Organization* 26: 595–618.

Pruitt, D.G. 1981a. 'Kissinger as a Traditional Mediator with Power', in J.Z. Rubin (ed.), *Dynamics of Third Party Intervention: Kissinger in the Middle East*. New York: Praeger, pp. 136–47.

———. 1981b. *Negotiation Behavior*. New York: Academic Press.

Pruitt, D.G., and D.G. Johnson. 1970. 'Mediation as an Aid to Face Saving in Negotiation', *Journal of Personality and Social Psychology* 14(3): 239–46.

Quinn, D., J. Wilkenfeld, P. Eralp, V. Asal and T. McLauchlin. 2013. 'Crisis Managers but Not Conflict Resolvers: Mediating Ethnic Intrastate Conflict in Africa', *Conflict Management and Peace Science* 30(4): 387–406.

Quinn, D., J. Wilkenfeld, K. Smarick and V. Asal. 2006. 'Power Play: Mediation in Symmetric and Asymmetric International Crises', *International Interactions* 32(4): 441–70.

Rauchhaus, R. 2006. 'Asymmetric Information, Mediation and Conflict Management', *World Politics* 58(2): 207–41.

Regan, P.M., and A.C. Stam. 2000. 'In the Nick of Time: Conflict Management, Mediation Timing, and the Duration of Interstate Disputes', *International Studies Quarterly* 44: 239–60.

Reid, L. 2017. 'Finding a Peace that Lasts: Mediator Leverage and the Durable Resolution of Civil Wars', *Journal of Conflict Resolution* 61(7): 1401–31.

Reiter, D. 2003. 'Exploring the Bargaining Model of War', *Perspectives on Politics* 1(1): 27–43.

Richmond, O. 1998. 'Devious Objectives and the Disputants' View of International Mediation: A Theoretical Framework', *Journal of Peace Research* 35: 707–22.

Rubin, J.Z. 1981. 'Introduction', in J.Z. Rubin (ed.), *Dynamics of Third Party Intervention: Kissinger in the Middle East*. New York: Praeger, pp. 3–43.

———. 1991. 'The Timing of Ripeness and the Ripeness of Timing', in L. Kriesberg and S.J. Thorson (eds), *Timing the De-escalation of International Conflicts*. Syracuse, NY: Syracuse University Press, pp. 237–46.

Salehyan, I., and K.S. Gleditsch. 2006. 'Refugees and the Spread of Civil War', *International Organization* 60(2): 335–66.
Savun, B. 2008. 'Information, Bias, and Mediation Success', *International Studies Quarterly* 52(1): 25–47.
Schrodt, P.A., and D.J. Gerner. 2004. 'An Event Data Analysis of Third-Party Mediation in the Middle East and Balkans', *Journal of Conflict Resolution* 48(3): 310–30.
Shannon, M. 2009. 'Preventing War and Providing Peace? International Organizations and the Management of Territorial Disputes', *Conflict Management and Peace Science* 26(2): 144–63.
Sisk, T.D. 2008. *International Mediation in Civil Wars: Bargaining with Bullets*. New York: Routledge.
Smith, A., and A. Stam. 2003. 'Mediation and Peacekeeping in a Random Walk Model of Civil and Interstate War', *International Studies Review* 5(4): 115–35.
Stein, K.W. 1999. *Heroic Diplomacy: Sadat, Kissinger, Carter, Begin, and the Quest for Arab-Israeli Peace*. New York: Routledge.
Svensson, I. 2007a. 'Bargaining, Bias and Peace Brokers: How Rebels Commit to Peace', *Journal of Peace Research* 44(2): 177–94.
———. 2007b. 'Mediation with Muscles or Minds? Exploring Power Mediators and Pure Mediators in Civil Wars', *International Negotiation* 12: 229–48.
———. 2009. 'Who Brings which Peace? Neutral versus Biased Mediation and Institutional Peace Arrangements in Civil Wars', *Journal of Conflict Resolution* 53(3): 446–69.
Terris, L.G., and Z. Maoz. 2005. 'Rational Mediation: A Theory and a Test', *Journal of Peace Research* 42(5): 563–83.
Touval, S. 1982. *The Peace Brokers: Mediation in the Arab-Israeli Conflict, 1948–1979*. Princeton, NJ: Princeton University Press.
———. 1994. 'Why the UN Fails', *Foreign Affairs* 73(5): 44–57. https://www.foreignaffairs.com/articles/1994-09-01/why-un-fails-it-cannot-mediate.
———. 1995. 'Ethical Dilemmas in International Mediation', *Negotiation Journal* 11(4): 333– 37.
Touval, S., and I.W. Zartman. 1985a. *International Mediation in Theory and Practice*. Boulder, CO: Westview Press.
———. 1985b. 'Introduction: Mediation in Theory', in S. Touval and I.W. Zartman (eds), *International Mediation in Theory and Practice*. Boulder, CO: Westview Press, pp. 7–18.
Tsebelis, G. 1990. 'Are Sanctions Effective?', *Journal of Conflict Resolution* 34(1): 3–28.
US Department of State. 2012. 'US Relation with Egypt', Technical Report.
Wallensteen, P., and I. Svensson. 2014. 'Talking Peace: International Mediation in Armed Conflicts', *Journal of Peace Research* 51(2): 315–27.
Walter, B.F. 2002. *Committing to Peace: The Successful Settlement of Civil Wars*. Princeton, NJ: Princeton University Press.
Weidmann, N.B., and K.S. Gleditsch. 2010. 'Mapping and Measuring Country Shapes', *The R Journal* 2: 18–24.
Werner, S., and A. Yuen. 2005. 'Making and Keeping Peace', *International Organization* 59(2): 261–92.
Wilkenfeld, J., K. Beardsley and D. Quinn. 2019. *Handbook on Mediating International Crises*. Northampton, MA: Edward Elgar Publishing.
Wilkenfeld, J., K. Young, V. Asal and D. Quinn. 2003. 'Mediating International Crises: Crossnational and Experimental Perspectives', *Journal of Conflict Resolution* 47(3): 279–301.

Wilkenfeld, J., K.J. Young, D.M. Quinn and V. Asal. 2005. *Mediating International Crises.* New York: Routledge.

Young, O.R. 1967. *The Intermediaries: Third Parties in International Crises.* Princeton, NJ: Princeton University Press.

———. 1972. 'Intermediaries: Additional Thoughts on Third Parties', *Journal of Conflict Resolution* 16(1): 51–65.

Zartman, I.W. 1985. *Ripe for Resolution: Conflict and Intervention in Africa.* Oxford: Oxford University Press.

Zartman, I.W., and S. Touval. 1985. 'International Mediation: Conflict Resolution and Power Politics', *Journal of Social Issues* 41(2): 27–45.

———. 2007. 'International Mediation', in C.A. Crocker, F.O. Hampson and P.R. Aall (eds), *Leashing the Dogs of War.* Washington, DC: United States Institute of Peace, pp. 437–54.

Chapter 10

The International Court of Justice and Mediation

Pierre d'Argent

As is well known, the International Court of Justice (ICJ) is the 'principal judicial organ of the United Nations' (UN Charter, Art. 92; Rosenne 2006: 2012; Zimmermann et al. 2012: 1808). It is entrusted with a dual jurisdiction: under its contentious jurisdiction, the Court entertains disputes between states which are party to its Statute (jurisdiction *ratione personae*),[1] provided that both claimant and defendant have consented to its jurisdiction as far as the subject matter of the dispute is concerned (jurisdiction *ratione materiae*);[2] under its advisory jurisdiction, the Court 'may' (ICJ Statute, Art. 65) respond to 'legal questions' (UN Charter, Art. 96) submitted to it by UN organs or specialized agencies, provided that the conditions specified in Article 96 of the UN Charter are met.[3] The Court is a body of fifteen judges, each elected for a (renewable) term of nine years by the UN General Assembly and the Security Council (ICJ Statute, Art. 2–4). Disputing states may appoint *ad hoc* judges to sit on a case if they do not have a national as Member of the Court (ICJ Statute, Art. 31), a possibility reminiscent of international arbitration.

In international relations, mediation has been codified by the Hague Conventions of 1899 and 1907[4] and it is mentioned in Article 33 of the UN Charter among several means available to states in order to comply with their obligation to settle disputes peacefully. Without going into too much detail, mediation is a procedure under which a third party is entrusted by the opposing parties with the task of trying to find an agreeable solution to their dispute. As opposed to good offices where the third party is only tasked with trying to bring the parties together again, mediation goes a step further as the mediator is entitled to suggest to the parties some settlement.

At first hand, neither the contentious jurisdiction of the ICJ nor its advisory jurisdiction has much to do with the institution of mediation as traditionally understood in international relations and law. Differences between adjudication and mediation are indeed numerous and important, despite the fact that both institutions are, under international law, based on the consent of disputing states and involve a third party:

- While the mediator only proposes to the parties a settlement that they always remain free to decline or to depart from, a court of justice imposes a solution on them in the form of a binding judgement.
- While the settlement suggested by the mediator may depart from existing legal rules and principles, and even suggest new ones, a judgement is presumed to simply 'apply' pre-existing norms to a factual situation, so that – so goes the fiction – the decision of the judge is nothing more than the embodiment of those norms, as if the judge was just charged with finding out what those legal norms already required. The binding character of the judgement derives from the binding character of the legal norms it applies.
- Throughout a mediation, parties remain in control of the entire process: not only must they both consent to the intervention of the mediator, but they may also put an end to the mission of the mediator, or replace it; moreover, each of them is free to reject the mediator's suggestions, while they can both agree on a settlement different from the one suggested by the mediator. The control left by adjudication to the parties is much more limited: if it is true that consent plays a fundamental role in international adjudication and that jurisdiction depends on it, once consent is given and the Court has jurisdiction, the substantive content of the judgement is the result of the will of the majority of the Court, and not of the parties. During the proceedings, the parties remain free to settle out of court and to request that the case be discontinued, thus preventing the Court from exercising its jurisdiction and powers. It is also true that the parties could agree to disagree with the Court, so as to disregard the operative part of the judgement and replace it with a different outcome (provided no peremptory norm is at stake). But in both situations, disagreement between the parties does not affect the responsibilities and powers of the Court, while it is the agreement of the parties that gives to mediation its authority and usefulness.

Despite those important differences, the ICJ entertains some connection with mediation, at least in four respects in relation to its contentious jurisdiction.

Firstly, the very fact that resorting to the ICJ might be a possibility under a treaty, or under converging optional clauses, will usually favour amicable settlement between the parties. Secondly, and even if causality is not always easy to establish, the rather high rate of discontinuance among the cases that have been duly submitted to the Court testifies to the encouraging effect it has on non-judicial settlement between parties. Thirdly, the very procedure before the Court aims at bringing the parties closer together and reducing the dispute to its essential elements. Fourthly, the operative parts of judgements are sometimes drafted in such a way as to establish some equilibrium between the parties. As far as the advisory jurisdiction of the Court is concerned, it might also be possible to conceive its outcome in the form of non-binding opinions as facilitators of mediation.

Of course, all those elements detailed below do not make the ICJ a mediator. Despite the fact that judicial settlement (be it domestic or international) always simplifies reality as it focuses on only some aspects of it – a reduction which is even more present in ICJ proceedings because its *ratione materiae* jurisdiction is strictly limited by the disputing parties' consent[5] – it is nevertheless possible to identify what could be called some 'mediating effects' of the ICJ in international relations. By this, one refers to the appeasing and conciliatory effect that a judicial procedure might have, despite being by nature contentious and adversarial. This effect is not inherent in the judicial process, but it is submitted that it is most often a goal either explicitly or unconsciously pursued by most international judges individually, and by the collective bodies they form when sitting together on the bench.[6] Because international courts (and tribunals), and the ICJ in particular,[7] are tasked with the duty to settle disputes, their specific added value is to help opposing parties to get over the dispute, turn the page and resume friendly and cooperative relations. This being said, it would be rather foolish to try to develop an overall 'theory' of those effects from the elements identified here: this contribution has no theoretical pretention whatsoever and only aims at bringing the reader's attention to some dynamic aspects of a reality that are very often hidden or buried in the practice of a small group of highly qualified professionals who sometimes do not even notice them. The difficulty of developing a 'theory' – whatever that word might mean – results from the fact that, from their inception and notably during the 1899 and 1907 Hague Peace Conferences, the categories of mediation and judicial settlement have been envisaged, at least in international law, as being distinctively different, despite being complementary or alternative means for the peaceful settlement of international disputes. However, what this contribution aims to show – rather than to demonstrate – is that choosing adjudication from the menu of available peaceful means for the settlement of international disputes never entirely excludes mediation from a substantive point of view; in other words, that the separation between adjudication and mediation might be less clear-cut and more blurred than those categories suggest when they are idealized as distinct processes, and separately envisaged.

When Potential Judicial Process Facilitates Direct Settlement

The very fact that ICJ jurisdiction (or arbitration) is provided for under the compromissory clause of a treaty or through converging optional clauses tends to favour amicable settlement between the parties, or, at least, has an impact on the conduct of their negotiation. This reality is difficult to document since diplomatic negotiations are usually confidential, but experience tells us that it is not the same thing to negotiate a settlement when jurisdiction is looming large, and when it is not. If parties know that failure to agree may result in any one of them triggering a judicial procedure, they both may prefer to stay in control of the process and compromise in order to reach an agreeable outcome. Conversely, the possibility of a judicial settlement may lead one or both parties not to make the extra effort to reach an agreed settlement. This is because disputing parties know that failing to agree is not the end of the matter, while they may find it difficult to compromise if the dispute is highly sensitive for their respective public opinions. Be that as it may, conducting genuine negotiations is usually a prerequisite for the establishment of jurisdiction *ratione voluntatis*. Indeed, consent to jurisdiction being very often conditioned upon prior negotiations, the existence of a basis of jurisdiction between the parties will require that negotiations take place first if any of them intends to eventually rely on that jurisdictional ground in the future.[8] Of course, direct negotiations between the parties do not amount to mediation. However, as no mediation can be established without the consent of both parties, the judicial requirement of prior negotiations may lead them to agree on mediation.

Discontinuance

Even when the ICJ is duly seized of a dispute and has jurisdiction over it, parties are always free to settle their dispute out of court and terminate the proceedings at any moment by consent (ICJ Rules, Art. 88–89). The Court orders the discontinuance of the case and may be asked to specifically indicate that the parties found an agreeable settlement.

It is quite telling that about a third of all the cases submitted to the ICJ so far have been discontinued,[9] which testifies that negotiations very often continue after proceedings have been initiated and while the case is pending. As the Court's purpose is to decide over existing disputes, there is no need for it to exercise its jurisdiction when parties have managed to put an end to their quarrel by themselves. One is therefore led to think that the very existence of ICJ proceedings is an incentive to the parties to compromise and that, in some ways, the ICJ very often plays the role of a silent mediator. The reasons for states to continue negotiations while the case is pending and to request discontinuance are different from case to case, but they most often relate to the desire of the defendant state to avoid public scrutiny and possible condemnation of its allegedly wrongful acts.

For instance, the *Ecuador v. Columbia* herbicide spraying case was discontinued at the request of Columbia just before the oral hearings were supposed to take place,[10] after the parties agreed on a settlement that gave Ecuador almost everything it could have hoped for from a judgement. Such a favourable result was reached after Columbia lost its maritime delimitation case against Nicaragua,[11] which probably led Columbia to prefer an out-of-court settlement to a possible second blow at the ICJ.

Similarly, one can recall the discontinuance of the case introduced by Iran against the USA concerning the shooting down, in July 1988, of Iranian flight 655 by the USS *Vincennes*. Proceedings were instituted in May 1989 and an agreement was reached between the two states on 9 February 1996.[12] The Court speedily ordered the discontinuance of the case.[13] It is worth noting that under the agreement reached, Iran agreed to allocate the compensation sums received from the USA to the families of the victims without discriminating between men and women.[14] It is doubtful that such a result could have been ordered by the ICJ, as the case was based on diplomatic protection, a mechanism under which the injured state endorses the claims of its nationals but actually vindicates its own right to reparation. Had the Court ordered the USA to pay compensation to Iran, it would not have had the power to indicate that the sums to be paid had to directly benefit the heirs of the victims, men and women equally.[15]

Short of requesting that the case be discontinued, the parties may also request that, pending their negotiations, the opening of the oral proceedings be postponed *sine die*. Such a request is usually in anticipation of an agreement leading to discontinuance, as was the case in the *Iran v. USA* case. It may also be requested in other circumstances.[16]

The Virtues of Procedure

The very fact of bringing a case to the ICJ has both a transformative and reductive effect on the dispute between the parties. The transformative nature of judicial process is common to domestic or international proceedings: when submitting claims to a court of law, parties must switch language; they must use legal terms and grammar to articulate their claims. This process of legal 'dressing up' is often conducted by skilled lawyers. Despite their experience and imagination, talented professionals who want to protect their reputation will, however, not be ready to make simply any type of claim and will duly inform their clients that some of their political grievances will require legal adjustments in order to sound credible. In other words, while legal argumentation can be very imaginative, there are limits to such imagination. Hence, the very fact of switching from a political/diplomatic setting and discourse to a legal setting will have an effect on the discourse and its rationality. Changing from politics to law[17] is transformative of the dispute, and since that change results from instituting proceedings in a court of law, the ICJ may again be seen as a silent mediator between the parties, by asking them to phrase their dispute using the language of the law. Usually, this has the virtue of 'tuning down' claims.

Parties will not only be called to phrase their dispute, but also to exchange legal arguments about it. Usually, in addition to the Application, there are two rounds of written pleadings exchanged between the parties (memorial, counter-memorial, reply, and rejoinder; ICJ Rules, Art. 46), and two rounds of oral pleadings. The purpose of these numerous exchanges is to bring to light the quintessence of the dispute. And throughout these exchanges, parties will very often (but, of course, not always) get closer together on certain issues: some arguments will be rephrased or even dropped, some claims will be abandoned. The ICJ always recalls in the opening part of its judgements (called in French '*les qualités*') the procedural history of the case and quotes from the Application, the various written submissions and the oral pleadings, what each party successively requested from the Court. This may sound boring to the reader, but it is actually of paramount importance since the Court is only called to settle the dispute as it stands at the end of the written and oral procedure. The final submissions read in Court at the end of the oral hearings by the respective agents of the parties recall the points that *remain* in dispute; only those points call for a judgement by the Court. Recalling in the '*qualités*' what was requested initially in the Application, then later in the various briefs and, finally, in the final submissions, allows us to compare the various stages of the procedure and to see how, and to what extent, that procedure has had a reductive effect on the dispute, as it does in many cases. Comparing the dispute as it stood at the beginning of the procedure and as it stands at the end of it, that is, when the Court takes the case under deliberation, helps us to understand that the ICJ, through its lengthy procedure which works like a filter or a bottleneck, has some 'mediating effect' (within the meaning used above) on the dispute.

Balanced Operative Parts

Operative parts of judgements are their conclusive binding parts and contain the decision of the Court about the final submissions of the parties. They follow the reasons that precede it and which seem to naturally and inescapably lead to them. Of course, the operative part of a judgement is the apparent logical outcome of the reasoning that precedes it, but it is always in substance the expression of a choice, made by the majority of the Court, between various legal outcomes, such choice being justified by the legal reasons given.

Operative parts are quintessentially judicial and therefore very much alien to the very notion of mediation: they are a decision imposed on the parties, irrespective of their agreement to such an outcome. Yet, by the apparent equilibrium they sometimes very visibly strike between the parties, operative parts of ICJ judgements may contain some mediating effect, by providing for a result which both parties can accept. This may give the impression that the Court is in the business of pronouncing judgements of Salomon, rather than judgements that are strictly and solidly grounded in existing positive law, knowing that it is prevented from ruling *ex aequo et bono* except when the parties have specifically agreed thereto.[18] It would certainly be wrong to consider that the ICJ is not concerned with the acceptance of its rulings by both parties, and that therefore it has a natural tendency to judge in such a way as to really put an end to the dispute between the parties. However, it would also be wrong to ignore that, when the law requires a clear and inescapable outcome, the Court has not shied away from such pronouncement. In the case law of the Court, two cases are at point in order to illustrate both the Salomon's and the 'hard law' approaches.

In the recent *Peru v. Chile* case, the ICJ drew a maritime boundary between the two parties that can be considered as some middle ground between their respective positions.[19] This is not surprising when it comes to maritime delimitation, but the reasoning of the Court in this specific case is rather intriguing. Creating an equal form of mild discontent on both sides, the maritime delimitation drawn by the Court has however the advantage of offering them an outcome that both can accept and live with.

The 'hard law' approach is, for instance, to be found in the *Cameroon v. Nigeria* case, in which the Court ordered Nigeria to 'expeditiously and without condition . . . withdraw its administration and its military and police forces from'[20] the Bakassi peninsula, which it illegally occupied. The implementation of the Court's judgement was less expeditious than it should have been, as it took a few years and the mediation of the UN Secretary General, but Nigeria finally complied and Cameroon recovered its sovereignty over that part of its territory. Cameroon was similarly ordered to depart from the smaller parts of territory that were found by the Court to lie on the Nigerian side of the border it was called to draw.

The sort of equilibrium between the parties to be found in operative parts of ICJ judgements is all the more striking when the Court declares that the defendant is responsible for some wrongful acts and, at the same time, formulates statements of non-violations on the part of the same state on account of other alleged breaches. For instance, in the *Genocide* case, the Court found that Serbia did not commit three alleged wrongful acts (committing genocide, conspiring to commit genocide, being complicit in genocide), while it declared that it was responsible for three other breaches (breach of the duties to prevent genocide, to cooperate with ICTY, to comply with the provisional measures previously ordered by the Court).[21] It is difficult not to consider that the kind of aesthetic parallelism between statements of breaches and declarations of non-violation was envisaged by the Court as the expression of some balance that had to be struck between the parties. The declarations of non-violations are all the more interesting (or intriguing) that they were not requested by Serbia in its final submissions, which were simply phrased as a request to reject Bosnia's claims. I have expressed elsewhere some reservations about the practice of inserting declarations of non-violations in operative parts of judgements (d'Argent 2013), but one has to recognize that it is now well established in the case law of the Court and that it undoubtedly participates in the mediating effect that the Court is keen to give to its decisions.

Advisory Opinions

As the name indicates, advisory opinions of the ICJ are not binding. They are 'not a form of judicial recourse for states but the means by which the General Assembly and the Security Council, as well as other organs of the United Nations and bodies specifically empowered to do so by the General Assembly in accordance with Article 96, paragraph 2, of the Charter, may obtain the Court's opinion in order to assist them in their activities'.[22] Moreover, because the opinion 'is given not to states but to the organ which has requested it' (ibid.), it is *a priori* difficult to see how it could have some mediating effect between states. However, such an effect can be found in some specific circumstances.

For instance, two important mediating elements can be found in the opinion of the Court delivered on 9 July 2004 regarding the *Legal Consequences of the Construction of a Wall in the Occupied Palestinian Territory*.

The first element is that the Court decided to address the legal consequences resulting from the construction of the wall 'in the Occupied Palestinian Territory', therefore refusing to address those consequences in relation to the parts of the complex built or planned to be built 'on the territory of Israel itself'.[23] The latter territory was found to be the one not included in the 'Occupied Palestinian Territory', understood as the territory situated on the east of the Green Line. In other words, by affirming that there existed a 'territory of Israel itself', the ICJ implicitly rejected the most extreme views according to which Israel is an occupying power even west of the Green Line and could not have a valid title on any part of the historical territory of Palestine at the time of the Mandate. One can even consider that the Court thereby potentially limited *ratione loci* the exercise of the right of the Palestinian people to self-determination to the West Bank and East Jerusalem (and the Gaza Strip, but the Court did not need to pronounce itself in that regard). Such reading of the opinion could serve as an authorized neutral legal ground in peace negotiations.

The second element relates to the finding of the Court according to which 'Israel is under an obligation to make reparation for all damage caused by the construction of the wall in the Occupied Palestinian Territory, including in and around East Jerusalem'.[24] Remarkably, this finding is justified by a reasoning which clearly establishes that Israel has an 'obligation to make reparation for the damage caused to all the natural or legal persons concerned', that is, that the individual victims of the construction of the wall have a right to reparation for the damages resulting from it (d'Argent 2006). Taking stock of that finding, the UN General Assembly established in Vienna a 'register of damage'[25] where all Palestinian injured by the building of the wall can document their damages. It remains to be seen what use will be made of this collection of proofs, but if ever the issue of reparation is discussed as part of a global peace deal, no doubt such a mechanism could facilitate the negotiations by providing for some neutrally collected facts. The combined decisions of the ICJ and the General Assembly could therefore be seen as having, in that respect, some mediating effect.

Concluding Remarks

As recalled at the beginning of this chapter, this quick overview of the possible interplays between the International Court of Justice and mediation does not call for extensive theoretical debates. As a matter of principle, it is certain that a judicial organ is tasked with other responsibilities than those usually associated with mediation. Moreover, it must be kept in mind that the *ratione materiae* jurisdiction of the ICJ only exists in so far and to the extent that both disputing states have consented to it. In other words, the Court will very often only know one aspect of a much larger dispute. The *Bosnia v. Serbia* case about the Genocide Convention is a case at hand: while a war was ongoing between the parties where all sorts of crimes were committed, the Court's jurisdiction was limited to alleged breaches of the Genocide Convention. Likewise, the *Georgia v. Russia* case was brought under the Convention on the Elimination of All Forms of Racial Discrimination, whereas the two states were at war during the summer of 2008. It is perhaps difficult, when the jurisdictional scope is so narrow, to envisage any mediating effect that may result from the ICJ's intervention. Yet, as argued above, it is possible to discern such effect to a certain extent and in various ways. Of course, this remains far from being comparable to an all-encompassing and thorough mediation. However, the positive contribution of the ICJ – not only through its decisions but also because of its sheer existence – to the settlement of international disputes should not be underestimated.

Pierre d'Argent is full professor at the University of Louvain and guest professor at the University of Leiden. While on leave from the university between 2009 and 2011, he served the International Court of Justice (ICJ) as First Secretary. A Member of the Institute of International Law, he is the author of numerous articles, an award-winning book, a Massive Open Online Course (MOOC) on www.edx.org and courses at the Hague Academy of International Law and the United Nations Audiovisual Library of International Law. He is a Member of the Brussels Bar, special counsel to Foley Hoag LLP, and argues international law cases before international tribunals and domestic courts.

Notes

1. UN Charter, Art. 92; ICJ Statute, Art. 34–35. On *ratione personae* jurisdiction, see ICJ, *Application of the Convention on the Prevention and Punishment of the Crime of Genocide (Bosnia and Herzegovina v. Serbia and Montenegro)*, 26 February 2007, *ICJ Reports* (2007: para. 102, p. 85).
2. ICJ Statute, Art. 36. On *ratione materiae* jurisdiction and the paramount importance of consent, see ICJ, *Armed Activities on the Territory of the Congo (New Application: 2002) (Democratic Republic of the Congo v. Rwanda)*, 3 February 2006, *ICJ Reports* (2006: 6).
3. See ICJ, *Legality of the Use by a State of Nuclear Weapons in Armed Conflict (WHO Request)*, advisory opinion 8 July 1996, *ICJ Reports* (1996: 66).
4. See www.pca-cpa.org. Legal literature on the pacific settlement of disputes is vast. Among many textbooks, see Merrills (2011: 384). The second chapter addresses mediation.
5. For instance, when addressing the alleged violations of the Genocide Convention in *Bosnia and Herzegovina v. Serbia and Montenegro* on the basis of the compromissory clause contained in that treaty, the Court was without jurisdiction to address all the other crimes or breaches of international law committed during that conflict: see note 3 at p. 175, para. 319.
6. This assertion is impossible to document academically and it is only based on the personal experience of the author from informal conversations with judges.
7. Since the foundation of the Permanent Court of International Justice, it has been debated whether the PCIJ and its follower, the ICJ, were any different from arbitral tribunals, apart from their specific institutional features. This chapter does not intend to address that issue; but see Forlati (2014: 235).
8. ICJ, *Application of the International Convention on the Elimination of All Forms of Racial Discrimination (Georgia v. Russian Federation)*, 1 April 2011, *ICJ Reports* (2011: 70 at paras. 134–35, p. 126).
9. See the list of cases available on the ICJ website: www.icj-cij.org.
10. ICJ, *Aerial Herbicide Spraying (Ecuador v. Columbia)*, Order of 13 September 2013.
11. ICJ, *Territorial and Maritime Dispute (Nicaragua v. Colombia)*, Judgement of 19 November 2012, *ICJ Reports* (2012: 624).
12. Settlement Agreement, 9 February 1996, available on the ICJ website: https://www.icj-cij.org/files/case-related/79/11131.pdf.
13. ICJ, *Aerial Incident of 3 July 1988 (Islamic Republic of Iran v. United States of America)*, Order of 22 February 1996, *ICJ Reports* (1996: 9).
14. Settlement Agreement, 9 February 1996, Annex 2.
15. See, however, ICJ, *Ahmadou Sadio Diallo (Republic of Guinea v. Democratic Republic of the Congo)*, Compensation, Judgement of 19 June 2012, *ICJ Reports* (2012: para. 57, p. 344): 'The Court recalls that the sum awarded to Guinea in the exercise of diplomatic protection of Mr. Diallo is intended to provide reparation for the latter's injury'.
16. See *Questions Relating to the Seizure and Detention of Certain Documents and Data (Timor-Leste v. Australia)*, Press release of 5 September 2014 informing that the Court decided to grant the parties' request to postpone the oral proceedings due to open on 17 September 2014, referring to Art. 54 of the ICJ Rules. The case was finally discontinued and removed from the list at the request of Timor-Leste (see Order of 11 June 2015).
17. I do not ignore that law, in itself, is also always a political enterprise: see Koskenniemi (1990).
18. ICJ Statute, Art. 38, para. 2. So far, parties have never agreed to that effect. It might seem absolutely normal that a court of law must decide cases by applying law, rather than some

form of equity of its own finding. However, paragraph 2 of Article 38 is interesting because it stands in sharp contrast to paragraph 1, which lists the 'sources' of international law applicable by the Court to settle disputes. By stating that the Court is prevented from deciding *ex aequo et bono* except when parties specifically agree, paragraph 2 of Article 38 reinforces paragraph 1 and directs the Court to resist the temptation of resorting to natural law – a crucial point to convince states to establish a permanent Court and to accept its jurisdiction.

19. ICJ, *Maritime Dispute (Peru v. Chile)*, 27 January 2014.
20. ICJ, *Land and Maritime Boundary between Cameroon and Nigeria (Cameroon v. Nigeria: Equatorial Guinea Intervening)*, 10 October 2002, *ICJ Reports* (2002: 457, para. 325, V (A)).
21. ICJ, *Application of the Convention on the Prevention and Punishment of the Crime of Genocide (Bosnia and Herzegovina v. Serbia and Montenegro)*, 26 February 2007, *ICJ Reports* (2007: para. 471, p. 273)
22. ICJ, *Accordance with International Law of the Unilateral Declaration of Independence in Respect of Kosovo*, Advisory opinion, 22 July 2010, *ICJ Reports* (2010: 417, para. 33).
23. ICJ, *Legal Consequences of the Construction of a Wall in the Occupied Palestinian Territory*, Advisory opinion, 9 July 2004, *ICJ Reports* (2004: para. 67, p. 164).
24. Ibid.: para. 163, (3), C), p. 202.
25. A/RES/ES-10/17, 24 January 2007; see www.unrod.org and Williams (2010).

References

d'Argent, P. 2006. 'Compliance, Cessation, Reparation and Restitution in the Wall Advisory Opinion', in P.-M. Dupuy, B. Fassbender, M.N. Shaw and K.-P. Sommermann (eds), *Völkerrecht als Wertordnung – Common Values in International Law, Festschrift für/Essays in Honour of Christian Tomuschat*. Kehl am Rhein: N.P. Engel Verlag, pp. 463–77.

———. 2013. 'Les déclarations de non-violation du droit international dans les arrêts de la Cour internationale de Justice', in M. Kamga and M. Mbengue (eds), *Mélanges en hommage au Juge R. Ranjeva*. Paris: Éditions A. Pedone, pp. 471–81.

Forlati, S. 2014. *The International Court of Justice: An Arbitral Tribunal or a Judicial Body?* Cham: Springer.

Koskenniemi, M. 1990. 'The Politics of International Law', *European Journal of International Law* 1: 4–32.

Merrills, J.G. 2011. *International Dispute Settlement*, 5th edn. Cambridge: Cambridge University Press.

Rosenne, S. 2006. *The Law and Practice of the International Court, 1920–2005*, 4 vols. Leiden: Brill.

Williams, R.C. 2010. 'United Nations Register of Damage (UNRoD) Rules and Regulations Governing the Registration of Claims – Introductory Note', *International Legal Materials* 49(2): 620–28.

Zimmermann, A., K. Oellers-Frahm, C. Tomuschat and C.J. Tams (eds). 2012. *The Statute of the International Court of Justice: A Commentary*, 2nd edn. Oxford: Oxford University Press.

Conclusion

Karl Härter, Carolin Hillemanns and Günther Schlee

The contributions to this volume represent a variety of disciplines and approaches and explore a great diversity of cases, actors, spaces and periods of conflict regulation. Pulling all this together in the form of a conclusion at first glance does not appear to be an easy task. But a number of general conclusions as to conceptualizing mediation and related practices of conflict regulation clearly emerge:

- In historical, anthropological and international settings, meaning the times, places and situations that historians, anthropologists and students of international relations and international law typically deal with, mediation is closely entangled with other modes of 'alternative' conflict regulation and, thus, can hardly be studied as an isolable practice of dispute settlement only. Procedures and practices of mediation, arbitration and adjudication are often intertwined, interfere with each other and form a repertoire of conflict regulation that actors can resort to and manoeuvre in-between in order to settle their disputes.
- Such contexts also show the interpenetration of different logics and aims of discursive strategies. Mediation may be shaped by the prospect that, if it fails, the other components of our general research theme (retaliation, mediation and punishment) come in. Mediation may seek to avert reversion to violence (retaliation) or to avoid formal adjudication and punishment. Negative consequences of failed negotiation can be regarded as threats, used against mediators or by mediators.

- Conflict may arise between different aims like 'peace' and 'justice' or 'truth' and 'overcoming the past'. Mediators may choose to ignore or under-communicate conflictual issues for political convenience or short-term pacification at the expense of more sustainable solutions.
- Mediation and other forms of conflict regulation are closely intertwined with the legal and judicial systems of states. They still constitute alternative modes of dispute settlement, which, however, not only take place outside state institutions, but are also applied and used within public judicial systems. Hence, 'alternative' conflict regulation can hardly be equated with 'extrajudicial' only, but belongs to the public judicial sphere as well and constitutes a transitional zone that might be characterized as 'infrajudicial'. As a result, future research should study mediation as a form of interaction between the state, the justice system, private parties and various mediators.
- The actors of mediation and other forms of conflict regulation can hardly be separated along the dichotomies of 'non-state', 'public' or 'private parties' only. Depending on the settings and the procedures, the roles and functions of actors of conflict regulation can vary and shift.
- Mediation and other forms of conflict regulation take place on different scales. They are not only practised at the community level but are interrelated with 'national' and 'international' levels and thus can acquire a 'global dimension'. Although some contributions demonstrate an imbalance of power ('imported mediation'), this can hardly be characterized as a 'top-down-model' only, since local actors to some extent could also influence or use central institutions.
- The interdependences, flexibility and blurred boundaries between various 'alternative', 'non-state', 'infrajudicial', 'judicial' and 'public' modes of conflict regulation demonstrated in this volume might challenge narrow theoretical concepts of 'mediation'. However, the lack of clear-cut categories and attributes of mediation and related other modes of conflict regulation seem to be their main advantages as they often not only solve the individual disputes at hand but also strive to facilitate the establishment of social order and longer-term peace.

Karl Härter is Professor, Research Group Leader and Senior Research Scientist at the Max Planck Institute for European Legal History in Frankfurt/Main. He is a member of the International Max Planck Research School on Retaliation, Mediation and Punishment, the Association for Constitutional History, the Commission for Hessian History and other academic and historical institutions.

Carolin Hillemanns is scientific coordinator at the Max Planck Institute for the Study of Crime, Security and Law (formerly Max Planck Institute for Foreign and International Criminal Law). She is a trained mediator. She has given presentations and conducted research in the fields of corporate social responsibility, international criminal law and policy, transitional justice, international human and victims' rights law, institutional law of the European Communities, democracy and federalism, globalization, and German constitutional law.

Günther Schlee is one of the Founding Directors of the Max Planck Institute for Social Anthropology in Halle, Germany. His main publications include *Identities on the Move: Clanship and Pastoralism in Northern Kenya* (Manchester University Press, 1989) and *How Enemies Are Made: Towards a Theory of Ethnic and Religious Conflict* (Berghahn Books, 2008).

Index

www.ingramcontent.com/pod-product-compliance
Ingram Content Group UK Ltd.
Pitfield, Milton Keynes, MK11 3LW, UK
UKHW021837100926
8556IPUK00004B/401

9 781789 208696